The Ride of Their Lives: The Untold Story of the Legendary Timely Writer and the Martin Family

Michael Bergeron and John F. Martin

Published by Timely Writer Publishing, 2024.

Table of Contents

TW
TIMELY WRITER
TyV
PUBLISHING

Introduction

Years ago, when I was writing about the movies for *The Boston Globe*, I thought a handful of films were perfectly cast from top to bottom. "*Casablanca,*" "*The Maltese Falcon*" and "*Chinatown*" come immediately to mind. And so it is with Michael Bergeron and John Martin's "*The Ride of their Lives: The Untold Story of the Legendary Timely Writer and the Martin Family.*" It is a ride not merely aboard the courageous, brilliant Timely Writer, but a journey through a twilight zone of time and place that seemed lost. Thanks to Bergeron and Martin, the era lives again. Fueled by a family connection and a personal touch, the authors relive the days when a horse gave new life to a dying New England sport as they restore a brilliant racehorse to his proper place in the history of a sport that deserves more like him.

First, the star. Timely Writer. Purchased for $13,500 by Francis and Peter Martin, two Dorchester brothers who had the *Racing Form* delivered daily to their butcher shop and kept the phones hopping with meat orders and gambling bets with various New England-based bookies. While the brothers owned Thoroughbreds before, they spent more time running at the Brockton and Marshfield Fairs than at Saratoga Race Course. And Timely Writer, as the book title suggests, took them, along with trainer Dominic Imprescia, jockey Jeffrey Fell, and every racing fan in New England on the ride of their lives. From the clam flats of Dorchester to the top of the mountain at Churchill Downs in Louisville, Kentucky, as the favorite leading up to the 1982 Kentucky Derby and Triple Crown races.

I'll leave the compelling details to the authors, but first, I'd like to thank them for the supporting cast and the set design. I lived through part of the story. In fact, I'm the unidentified *Boston Globe* reporter in Chapter 9 who sent Mr. Writer a get-well card when he was recovering from surgery. Through interviews with dedicated and thoughtful racing fans such as Kay Coyte and Elizabeth Tobey and dogged research into articles written by my late pal and racing mentor, Sam McCracken, Bergeron and Martin elevate Timely Writer into his rightful place aside alongside the stories of Seabiscuit and Phar Lap.

Personally, I think their recollections of the Massachusetts Fair Circuit and colorful trainers, such as Carlos Figueroa, also brought back the aromatic mixture of cotton candy, popcorn, and fried clams unique to the Marshfield Fair. And, in recording the magnificent story of a brilliant winner, they didn't forget the losers or the bygone era where Zippy Chippy and hundreds of other Thoroughbreds tried one last time to visit the winner's circle. It was another time and another place. After falling in love with these mysterious and lovely animals, it set me on a personal trail that changed my life over 20 years ago. And, at least for me, for the better.

When it was announced that Belmont Park horse track in New York was being re-constructed, as the Founder and President of Old Friends Thoroughbred Retirement Farm in Georgetown, Kentucky, and unbeknownst to Michael and John as they were writing their book, I called Lorita Lindemann my trainer and daughter (she wanted a father, and I needed a daughter) to inquire about the relocation of the remains of Timely Writer since he and Ruffian were the only Thoroughbreds ever given the prestigious honor of being buried in the grass infield at Belmont. Lorita worked out all the details, and within a few weeks, the remains of Timely Writer and his headstone were relocated to the Nikki Bacharach Memorial Garden at Old Friends in November 2023. We buried Timely Writer next to Skip Away, Alphabet Soup, and Noor, just across from Charismatic, War Emblem, and Medina Spirit, and we are honored to present his story every day. All of us are proud to support Michael and John and the magnificent story of Timely Writer, who was the horse of a lifetime...not just for his owners and family but for an entire generation.

- Michael Blowen, Founder and Past President of Old Friends
  Thoroughbred Farm

Prologue

"Year after year, Boston seems to be the focus of some of the world's top sports stories – some sweet and some bittersweet. Usually, it's one of our teams that gives us our most memorable moments – the ecstasies and the agonies. But this year . . . the top story of '82 was provided by three men and a horse. They did this without winning the big one. They did it by accepting misfortune with grace . . . and looking ahead to tomorrow.

The horse I speak about is Timely Writer, and the men are Francis and Peter Martin, who live in Boston, and their trainer, Dominic Imprescia, whose career has flourished in our city.

Together they captured the imagination of every sports fan across the country, and they did this by sharing a dream .... and not giving up on that dream when things went wrong. The good times for the Martins came last spring. Here they were, two Boston men who worked themselves up the hard way in the meat packing business, now heading with Timely Writer to the Kentucky Derby, which is to horse racing what the World Series is to baseball and the Super Bowl to football.

Here were two of the one-time "little guys" of the world on the brink of one of the world's most famous pots of gold, a winning "run for the roses" in the Derby. And no one ever thought they could lose, because their horse was the fastest and best young thoroughbred in the universe.

The Kentucky Derby favorites are commonly reserved for horses from Kentucky and owners who are well-to-do corporation executives, not for horses out of the East Boston stables and city fellows from Boston. The Martins brought Boston into the Derby picture.

Francis and Peter found that once-in-a -lifetime horse in Timely Writer. . . . But just as everything appeared "all roses," Timely Writer was stricken with a very untimely case of colic three weeks before the Derby. The ailment was so severe that it not only scratched Timely Writer out of the Derby, but surgery had to be performed to save his life.

The dream was shattered. The number one rated horse in the country was beaten not on the race course, but by sickness. It was a difficult and disheartening moment for the men. And although they never got their chance to win the big one, they remain winners none the less. They portrayed championship class and made us proud to have them represent our city at the most prestigious horse racing event in the world, even though their horse couldn't run. Those waiting to see Timely Writer circle the race tracks again probably won't be disappointed, I understand the Martins vow he will be back this summer – healthy, strong and ready.

Timely Writer is more than just a horse trying to win the Kentucky Derby. He is a symbol of three men who followed a dream, worked hard, and despite setbacks, they never said quit. That's the Martins' way. I like to think that the Martins' way is Boston's way."

Kevin H. White, Mayor of Boston, Massachusetts (1968-1984), summer of 1982

Notes from the Authors

I first met Frannie & Mary Martin in the spring of 1995. In January, I had started dating their youngest daughter, Janice - and my future wife. I was in the middle of attending law school during the evenings in Boston while working two jobs six days a week and with little money. I had already met Janice's older brother, John, and sister, Maryellen, so the last hurdle was to meet the parents. Frannie and Mary were returning home to the Boston area after riding out the winter in Fort Lauderdale. As their condo in Florida was less than thirty minutes from Gulfstream Race Track, the weather and the horse races suited the couple just fine.

I had already visited the Martin home once while they were in Florida, so for a kid raised in the woods of Connecticut, the four-bedroom home with a pool on a one-acre lot 20 minutes from Boston was a place I found a bit intimidating to "meet the parents" for the first time. The house included a door knocker in the shape of a horseshoe on the front door, an ornamental jockey statute on the front lawn, and a beautiful painting of some thoroughbred who raced in the early 1980s. Other than these items, it was not a home decorated with trophies, photographs of winner's circles, or horse racing memorabilia covering the walls.

The couple I would come to call my in-laws was gracious, kind, funny, and enjoyable to speak with during our first get-together. Though Peter Martin passed before I married into the family, Frannie was always so complimentary and proud of his older brother when speaking about him. I would finish law school and become a practicing lawyer in 1996. Over the next five years, Janice and I would get married and start raising a family – three daughters in four years beginning in December of 2000 – one of which was given the middle name of "Frances" in honor of her grandfather. Frannie and Mary loved being grandparents, with six in total between the three siblings, and they often spent their weekends entertaining their children and grandchildren at the pool during the summer.

It had been just over a dozen years since Timely Writer had finished his last race when I met Frannie, and whether he liked it or not, Mary was ensuring Frannie that he was retiring and winding down ownership of his remaining horses. The couple were not braggadocio people, and never once did I hear either one of them tell the whole story about their lives with a colt by the name of Timely Writer, the notoriety they had achieved with him, or their journey that brought them to the steps of immortality in horse racing. For sure, they would laugh and tell stories of the fun times they had at the horse tracks over forty years, but there were never significant details about the lives they led in the early 1980s.

Over the years, I have taken note of the many people who stopped and talked with Frannie or Mary about the glory days of Timely Writer. People approaching the couple thanked them for the success and memories Timely Writer had brought to their lives. Friends and acquaintances of Janice and her siblings would talk to me about the incredible story of the Martin family, their horse and what it meant to everyone. Many of these people would speak about how their story needed to be a book and/or a movie. As Janice and I spent twenty years raising kids while working full-time, myself as a trial attorney, I never had time to give the story much consideration.

Frannie passed from cancer in 2009 after fighting it for more than 25 years. Mary, independent to the end, would outlive Frannie by over a decade, passing away in November 2021 at 93. Though neither one of the two ever put pen to paper about their experiences, a treasure trove of memorabilia was located in Mary's basement upon her passing. Mary left multiple scrapbooks of Timely Writer, which contained every race program, race result, countless newspaper articles, and photographs of winner's circles. Additional storage boxes contained original magazines, trophies from elite horse races, and cassette tapes of every race, including news interviews of the cast of characters surrounding Timely Writer.

Opening the boxes and albums brought history to life. As the pages turned, the story was intoxicating - and unbelievable if it were not true. People approaching my in-laws over the years were correct – the tale of Timely Writer and the Martins needed to be told. The story was about more than just two brothers running a meat distribution center while grinding it out on the inferior horse racing tracks for over twenty-five years as a second job. It was more than just two guys catching lightning in a bottle with the purchase of Timely Writer in 1980, finding themselves with the overwhelming favorite to win the Kentucky Derby in 1982 and to sweep the remainder of the two Triple Crown races. Their story is about all of this and more. Their story is about life – through the good times and bad – and how a family and their horse showed a country how to handle life's events with grace and humility.

Upon Mary's passing, I had been grinding it out as a trial attorney for 25 years. I had been organizing, writing, and telling stories to countless courts and juries throughout Massachusetts for a generation. Under the guidance of my brother-in-law John, who lived through the events as a 19 and 20-year-old, writing this book seemed a natural fit for one of the few skillsets I possessed. John and I agreed to partner up to tell the story of his parents, his uncle, and Timely Writer. As we put the story together for two and one-half years, it was unlike any other I had encountered. I suspected the story would be good when we began the project – never envisioning the depths of its greatness and meaning. As we put together chapter after chapter, I found myself riding the emotional roller coaster my in-laws had gone through – fascinated at times, laughing at times, and shedding tears of joy and sorrow along the way.

John and I hope you share the same experiences as you saddle up for the untold story of the legendary Timely Writer, the Martin family, and *The Ride of Their Lives*.

Michael A. Bergeron

Acknowledgments

We thank everyone who spoke with us while writing *The Ride of Their Lives*. Whether it be family, friends, or supporters, this book could not have been written without the help of all involved. In particular, a few individuals were extraordinary in sharing their time and memories:

Tony Everard, the ageless legend of Ocala, Florida, is a central part of *The Ride of Their Lives* and the most critical person in writing this book. Tony first met with us regarding the creation of this book in October of 2022 when we traveled to Ocala, Florida. I had never met Tony, and John had not seen him in almost 40 years. From the first moment we met with Tony, it was as if we had been friends forever. Over two years, we met with Tony in Ocala, discussing events from decades past, such as horse racing and his fascinating life. We talked about Timely Writer, horses, and life over breakfast and lunch at *Darrell's Diner* and steaks for dinner at his home. Tony was unselfish with his time, whether in Ocala or with the countless follow-up telephone calls, as we worked towards completing the book. Without Tony, Timely Writer and the Martins would never have been brought together; without Tony, our book and their story could not have been written.

Michael Blowen, a former writer for the *Boston Globe* and the founder and past president of Old Friends Thoroughbred farm, crossed our paths while we were about halfway through writing the book. Having never met Michael, he was already part of the story as he had been written into one of the early chapters before he transported Timely Writer's remains from Belmont Park to his final resting place in Georgetown, Kentucky. In the final fateful act in a decades-long story of Timely Writer and the Martins, the former Bostonian journalist brought the champion colt home. The address of Timely Writer's reinterment may say Georgetown, Kentucky, but it feels a bit like home as Michael watches over the colt's gravestone from the grounds he created. Michael's selfless act and support throughout the writing of this book are forever appreciated.

Kay Coyte is a journalist, professional photographer, editor, a central figure in chronicling the final race of Timely Writer, and, most importantly, a selfless mentor in offering advice and suggestions in creating and publishing *The Ride of Their Lives*. We could not have brought this story to print without Kay's guiding hand. Thank you, Kay!

Elizabeth Tobey's relationship with the Martins over the years, as chronicled in *The Ride of Their Lives,* is the heart-warming subplot of the entire book. John Martin accidentally discovered Liz's connection to his parents as we were writing the book. After tracking down Liz for this story, her help in re-creating events and her relationship with the Martins more than 40 years prior cannot be emphasized enough. Liz provided original handwritten notes, cards, and photographs exchanged between her and the Martins from the 1980s, bringing their remarkable relationship to life. Their relationship epitomized the quiet generosity and kindness of Frannie, Mary, and Peter Martin – a central part of their characters, as reflected in the story.

Susan Lawlor Tamasi has been a family friend of the Martin family since she began her college years at Suffolk University in the 1980s. Sue is also originally from Dorchester (OFD) and was central in bringing the city and its surroundings to life in chapter 2 of *The Ride of Their Lives.* Sue's time sharing her memories, the history of Dorchester, and draft submissions for portions of the chapter were critical as we brought Frannie and Peter back to their Dorchester roots. Although Sue does not appear in chapter two, she finds herself immersed in the final scene of the book's ending, as her private conversations with Mary Martin over the years serve as the foundation for the conclusion to *The Ride of Their Lives.*

Lastly, I would like to thank my mother, Suzanne Bergeron, who was unselfish and tireless with her time providing additional tutoring in our home. She provided countless hours of support during the elementary school years, with extra attention devoted to grammar, vocabulary, and writing skills. The extra attention from my mother served as the foundation for surviving law school, my professional career as an attorney, and in writing this book. For this, I have been forever grateful. Thank you, Mom!

Chapter 1
Triumph: Timely Writer & Boston Take Over Miami

Many believe the legend of Timely Writer and his owners first began in the warm sunshine of Miami during the spring of 1982. Though Timely Writer swept through the Florida horse racing circuit that March and April, the truth is the foundation of what became the centerpiece of their rags-to-riches story began decades earlier when the colt's blue-collar owners leaped from the grandstand to the owner's box.

As the Martins, Peter, Frannie, his devoted wife Mary, and their high school-aged children made their way to Hialeah Race Track for the running of the $250,000 Flamingo Stakes on the morning of March 6, 1982, the richest horse race in Florida history at the time, their improbable road to glory in an industry dominated by generational wealth was never more apparent as their once in a lifetime horse from Boston was about to pronounce himself as the best thoroughbred in the country – and the prohibitive favorite for the 1982 Kentucky Derby - the most famous horse race in North America. The Martin brothers, Peter and Francis ("Frannie"), raised in the neighborhoods of Dorchester, Massachusetts, were a long way from their Boston roots as they stood on the doorstep of immortality in the "sport of kings."

The road to success for Timely Writer began one year prior with first-place finishes at prestigious racetracks sitting at opposite ends of New York - Saratoga Race Course and Belmont Park Race Track. Before the wins in New York, the Martin brothers had never owned an elite thoroughbred racehorse during their 30 years in the business. Wins at the New York tracks confirmed Timely Writer's talent level while giving birth to a national fandom and infatuation with the colt, his owners, and their fairy-tale story. As horse racing fans noted during the early '80s, "Timely Writer had an 'everyman' quality that reminded folks of Seabiscuit. In addition to his talent, the two-year-old was distinguished by his humble existence."[1]

Timely Writer was purchased at the Kentucky Thoroughbred yearling sales in Keeneland in September 1980 for $13,500—a purchase price many considered pocket money in the horse racing business. The low-cost colt would be racing in the spring of 1982 at the Flamingo Stakes in Miami and then the Florida Derby in Hallandale three weeks later, challenging horses purchased for more than ten times his value. Timely Writer would be pitted against the likes of D'Accord, son of Triple Crown winner Secretariat, owned by Bertram Firestone and his wife, Diana Johnson Firestone. Mrs. Johnson Firestone's grandfather founded health products manufacturer *Johnson & Johnson*, while her husband was one of the major players in Thoroughbred racing and the horse breeding businesses. The Firestones married in 1973, buying a 1,400-acre horse farm in Virginia. They had teamed up with legendary trainer LeRoy Jolley, making history in 1980 with a filly named Genuine Risk, as she became only the second female ever to defeat an entire field of colts on her way to winning the Kentucky Derby.

Another challenger scheduled to run in the Flamingo and Florida Derby was Star Gallant from the Buckram Oak Farm in Lexington, Kentucky. Star Gallant's owner was Saudi Arabian businessman Mahmoud Fustak, who also happened to be the brother-in-law of Saudi Arabian ruler King Abdullah. Fustak was the first Saudi Arabian to make his way into horse racing in the United States, having bought a 500-acre farm in 1978. The farm would sell for 17.5 million dollars in 2005 to Jess Jackson – of the Kendall Jackson Winery. Timely Writer and his team, undeterred by the wealth they were pitted against, were a testament to the courage of the underdog – having raced the previous season against the likes of Herschelwalker, owned by an heir of the Whitney family dynasty.

Herschelwalker was affectionately named after the top college football player in the country, who was the star running back for the 1980 National Champions Georgia Bulldogs. Walker, the horse, was owned by Sandra Payson. Payson's mother, Joan Whitney Payson, was one of the founders of the New York Mets baseball team in 1962 – getting involved after she and her husband were disappointed their New York Giants baseball team moved to San Francisco in 1957. The Whitney family traces its history back to the 1600s in London, England. After they arrived in what would become known as the United States of America, the family became a staple in New York for centuries, establishing themselves in business, philanthropy, and the social circles of New York. Their family members were some of the original leaders of the country's thoroughbred breeding and racing businesses – their experience going back more than 100 years before Timely Writer and the Martins challenged one of their horses in 1981.

The absurdity of where the Martins found themselves in 1982 was not lost on them as they made their way from their rooms at the Best Western Motel to one of the grandest horse racing tracks in the country just outside of Miami. These blue-collar workers and owners of a meat business in Boston had made Florida their temporary home at the low-cost motel during March and April with friends, family, and what seemed like half of Boston. Family, friends, and followers reveled in watching their prized colt take on the racing establishment while soaking in the sunshine and glory as their fairy tale story played out before the country.

As out of their elements as they may have been, there was no fear of the moment for the Martins as they set their sights on an improbable road to glory. Decades of grinding it out at the much inferior horse tracks in Massachusetts had schooled the Timely Writer crew well. The brothers knew early on that their bargain basement purchase had the type of talent many had never witnessed before. Frannie, the larger-than-life personality with the white butcher's coat as a work jacket and an office desk littered with horse racing programs scattered on top of meat orders, went on the record predicting wins at the Florida horse races to award-winning columnist Michael Madden of the *Boston Globe* in the weeks leading up to the Florida stakes races. Exuding an infectious confidence, Frannie told the journalist, "We're going to win it all. Believe me ... we are going to win it all."[2]

Madden, or "mad dog" as he was known within the print media, prepared his readers for what may lay ahead in 1982 prior to the Martin family heading south: "if Timely Writer, Fran and Peter Martin and [trainer] Dom Imprescia head down to Florida and take the Flamingo and the Florida Derby and if they head up to Louisville next May and enter the Derby, well . . . just go along for the ride with them because this will be fun. Not just because they're from Boston and Timely Writer nibbled his oats all summer at Suffolk [Downs], but because the Firestones, the Phippses, the Vanderbilts spend millions looking for precisely this experience . . . and seldom get it." [3] As the Mayor of Boston would pen in an open article to the citizens of Massachusetts in the coming summer months, these men, their dream, and their horse had captured the imagination of an entire country.

The Florida racing circuit in March of 1982 served as the barometer for determining which top three-year-old horse would be the favorite for the Kentucky Derby at Churchill Downs in Louisville - held annually on the first Saturday in May for over 100 years. Nine previous winners of the Flamingo Stakes had gone on to be crowned the Kentucky Derby winner, including three in the last seven years. With former winners the likes of Northern Dancer (1968), Foolish Pleasure (1975), Seattle Slew (1977), and Spectacular Bid (1979), it was a legendary crowd Timely Writer would be joining and inevitably leading to comparisons by both track observers and fans for the remainder of his career and after.

The Martins, in their first appearance at the Flamingo as owners, were guests at a track unmatched in beauty. Hialeah Race Track, built just outside of Miami in 1922, was honored three years before the Martins's arrival by its inclusion in the National Register of Historic Places. In 1982, with the beauty of its Mediterranean-style architecture highlighted by the Florida sunshine, the track was considered one of the grandest in the country—earning the nickname "The Grand Dame." Contributing to its beauty and singularity, the track's grass infield had been registered with the National Audubon Bird Sanctuary. The track's famous pink flamingos, who arrived via a special transport in 1935 from the island of Cuba, were year-round residents of the track's grass infield area, with their habitat forever protected.

With palm trees dominating the skyline, the track boasted average temperatures of 80 degrees in March. Each "winter" season, patrons of the track were treated to luxury, beauty, and warm weather. The track, however, had a flaw that came with all its beauty. Due to its natural geographic setting, as it sat only 25 feet above the ocean level, patrons were often welcomed by puddles of water upon making their way to the gates of the Hialeah. Predicting the weather in Miami is a meteorological challenge on any given day, as it is not easy to forecast when rain will arrive in Florida. When it does come, there is no accurate estimate of the amount of rain or its duration.

Rain started in the early morning of March 6th, with heavy rain lasting until just before noon. Water was clogging storm drains and flooding the streets as patrons made their way to the racetrack for the opening of the front gates at 11:00 a.m., with the first race scheduled for 1:00 p.m. As luck would have it, Hialeah was running a rain jacket giveaway for its customers as they entered through the gates. Due to attendance at Hialeah Park averaging smaller numbers than usual, officials ordered only 24,000 jackets - never contemplating the number of people making their way to the track that morning to watch the horse from Boston.

As a result of the heavy rain, people were forced to change their usual walking routes from the outer parking lots to the entry gates of the horse track. Alternative side roads were clogged with patrons searching for their way to the main gates of Hialeah, with water as high as the top of their ankles before passing through the admissions booths while grabbing a free raincoat. Many parking lots were so flooded that the attendants were forced to shut lots down. Inexplicably, patrons were passing through the entry gates in record numbers. Much of the early crowd was jockeying for spots at the wooden picnic tables lining the grounds in the general admission area, with others setting up folding lawn chairs by the horse path leading from the barns to the saddling area of the horse paddock.

Hialeah's attendance record of 37,182, which had stood without a challenge for 27 years, would be shattered as the Martins and nearly 41,000 people stuffed themselves into the venue on the first Saturday of March 1982. The number of people was so unexpected that bars around the track ran out of beer as early as the fifth race. Parking attendant Sterling Anifantis, who had been working at the track since 1954, was in awe at the crowd, telling reporters, "I've never seen anything like it. They just kept coming."[4] Even the high-priced Mercedes and Cadillacs, which transported the horse owners and wealthier guests for their reserved tables trackside, were turned away by attendants at the valet parking.

The inclement weather cleared the Miami area thirty minutes before the start of the Flamingo Stakes, allowing patrons to venture outside to enjoy the bright sunshine and fresh air. As more and more people found their way to the outside rail of the horse track, competition increased for prime spots along the metal fencing lining the homestretch before the finish line. Before the parade of horses for the Flamingo Stakes, which showcases jockeys mounted in their saddles atop the well-chiseled one-thousand-pound athletes making their way to the starting gate, people along the metal fencing were more than 25 people deep as post-time inched closer.

The Martin family had squeezed into their owners' box of seats long before the start of the 10th race, waiting nervously throughout the afternoon for the most important race of their lives. As the family sat in their owner's box, it was a given that others from wealthier social circles would look them over, with some giving them a side-eyes glance. One media member observed the contrast between the other owners sitting around the Martin family, concluding, "The Martins fit right in." The brothers sat "dressed in conservative suits, the butchers look[ed] as genuine as any of the millionaires eying their lesser steeds. As active players in the sport of kings, neither brother tried to pose as royalty, but both *do* come across as gentlemen rather than bumpkins."[5]

Timely Writer, with the talented and young Canadian Jockey Jeffrey Fell on board the mount for the Martins' Nitram Stables, had no luck with his starting gate position. As a result of a random drawing of entry gate positions earlier in the week, gate number 16 of the record 16 entries for the Flamingo Stakes seemed to seal the fate of Timely Writer's hopes. These concerns were shared during the Saturday afternoon national television broadcast by sports commentators and horse racing experts working the race for *Wide World of Sports*. In the days before streaming and cable television, audiences of millions tuned in regularly to watch the main sporting event every Saturday afternoon. American Broadcasting Company (ABC) was one of three national television channels at the time and the first to develop and broadcast sports as a national television show. Sports on television had become the electronic fireplace for the family gathering spot every Saturday afternoon so they could "watch the thrill of victory and the agony of defeat." *Wide World of Sports,* the precursor to *ESPN*, assigned Hall of Fame sports journalist and television announcer Jim McKay for the national broadcast.

Hall of Fame thoroughbred trainer John Veitch from the historic Calumet Farms was at McKay's side. Calumet was the leading farm in the thoroughbred racing business – having existed since 1924. Veitch was a Hall of Fame trainer, the son of a Hall of Fame trainer, and brought up in the industry since his birth in Lexington, Kentucky. There was no finer person or trainer. Veitch was the trainer of the legendary thoroughbred Alydar, who, together with Affirmed running by his side four years earlier, made their own history in front of a national television audience. The pair dueled one another in epic battles during each of the three Triple Crown races – the Kentucky Derby, the Preakness, and the Belmont Stakes. Together, Alydar and Affirmed brought the country to its feet during the spring and summer of 1978 - battling neck and neck to the finish line in each of the three historic races.

As the rain cleared and the sun shone brightly before the Flamingo, Veitch and McKay positioned themselves in front of the radiating flower beds for their pre-race television commentary. Showing off their matching golden suit jackets, the signature stamp of *Wide World of Sports* announcers since its inception in 1961, Veitch was not optimistic about Timely Writer's chances of winning. Veitch shared his comments with the millions watching television, explaining he did not see what he was looking for in the colt's prep race at Hialeah a few weeks prior. Timely Writer finished 5th in his first race back after taking four months off from racing during the winter of 1981 into 1982. As Timely Writer appeared not fit enough for the Flamingo, Veitch thought he would come up short in his attempt to be crowned champion – a race Alydar won with Veitch at his side. Veitch predicted a great race, but due to the crowded field and rain-soaked track, which had left puddled water in certain areas on the dirt surface, the race set up well for one of the long shots.

Timely Writer, if he were to be considered in the same company as Alydar and Affirmed, would first need to overcome his post position at the far gate to compete for the race of 1 and 1/8th mile. The placement of the outside gate was so close to the race track rail that patrons lining the front row of the metal fencing were within 10 feet of Timely Writer as he was brought into the small confines of the metal waiting area. As jockey Jeffrey Fell was inching the colt into the starting gate, he could see the rusty metal fencing on the outside dirt of the track. The fence was no more than 4 feet high and served as a barrier to keep patrons away from the dirt track. Hialeah workers had placed cement curbs, taken from the parking lot spaces, along the base of the inside of the fence to keep the crowd away from the shorter rusty fence. A television camera at the start of the race captured the packed crowd along the dirt track already pushing up and against the fencing, with many yelling words of support into the pinned ears of Timely Writer.

Starting gate 16 added extra ground to cover from the outside spot, which was a significant disadvantage and needed to be overcome quickly. Timely Writer needed to burst through the crowd of 16 horses, sprinting for that first left-handed turn on the track. If not, Timely Writer would be buried at the back of the pack – having to make up too much ground while fending off horses and danger at every turn.

1982 Flamingo Stakes Winner's Circle

With the starting bell releasing the sixteen gates in unison, the opening moments of the race were chaotic. Due to their strategy, designed beforehand by trainer Dominic Imprescia and jockey Jeffrey Fell, the early moments of the race went according to the script. As the gate opened, Fell pushed Timely Writer out quickly, rushing to the middle of the track with urgency. Timely Writer's initial quickness allowed him to overcome half the field before the first turn, settling in nicely at the 9th spot outside the pack of horses after the turn, where he could relax over the next ½ mile. This move out of the starting gate was crucial to the success of the rest of their plan, with Fell eyeballing the leaders in the front of the pack from a distance while keeping Writer in a stalking position. Jockey Jeffrey Fell may have been atop Timely Writer for only his 3rd mount, but the talented jockey knew enough to keep his colt out of trouble and within striking distance of the leaders until just over 1/4 of a mile was left to the race. Fell patiently waited for the right moment to turn Timely Writer loose on his unsuspecting opponents.

Settling in at the 9th spot for the first part of the race, though, was not enough to calm Frannie's nerves.

Timely Writer's running style played havoc with the forever energetic owner. Frannie was watching impatiently from the owner's box, sweating from the Miami heat, chain-smoking cigarettes, constantly moving, often shouting, swearing at times, and occasionally hitting his leg with a rolled-up racing program. Frannie's brother and business partner was a study in contrast. As the rain and clouds had cleared from the Miami sky, Peter was enjoying the sun's warmth while calmly watching the brilliance of the best thoroughbred he had ever witnessed. The accountant with a degree from Bentley College, one of the best business schools in New England, sat stoically as he watched along with the record-breaking crowd and millions more glued to the television tubes in the parlors of their homes. Peter's eyes were focused on the pack of horses going into the last left-handed turn of the Flamingo Stakes, waiting for the moment only a few knew was coming. While Mary sat as the buffer between her husband and brother-in-law, with her three children sitting behind them, she led the cheering of the family's horse as Timely Writer made his way around the far turn.

For the patrons at the track and those watching at home who never had the opportunity to watch Timely Writer as a 2-year-old in 1981, his performance over the last 3/8ths of a mile is where he transformed himself from a raw two-year-old champion, forever the topic of conversations about unlimited potential, into an established three-year-old champion and the best thoroughbred in the country. A winter of rest from competitive racing for the colt, which allowed his trainers to focus on a program that allowed him to add muscle and strength, transformed Timely Writer into an imposing gladiator-like three-year-old who was about to burst onto the national scene as the heir apparent to the golden age of racing.

As Timely Writer made his way to the beginning of the far turn, he increased his speed significantly. With patrons positioning themselves leftward, a vision of the orange and black silks of Nitram Stables covering jockey Jeffrey Fell could be seen surging past every horse – the jockey without any need to use the riding crop in hand to urge on his colt. The orange and black flume seen from the stands was Timely Writer making his patented move, picking off the best three-year-old horses in the country one by one, with power and ease in each stride. Timely Writer was coming through the far turn like a slingshot around the pack of horses.

Timely Writer hit the top of the homestretch on his way toward the first section of the grandstand, where patrons had been lining the metal fencing along the dirt track and where enthusiastic fans had been climbing atop the curbs at the base of the interior of the fence. As the record crowd at Hialeah cheered on this improbable fairy tale horse from Boston, Timely Writer gave the crowd a show. The first row of the crowd along the fence looked as if the fans stood seven feet tall - most supporting themselves by the palms of their hands pinned to the top of the horizontal rail. Many of these fans leaned their upper torsos into the track area, yelling words of encouragement at Timely Writer as he passed them toward the finish line.

Once Timely Writer opened a significant distance between himself and the next horse in the homestretch, the colt looked to his right. It was a look and a pause to the right as if he was acknowledging the delirious crowd for a second. Timely Writer then looked behind him – as if he was looking for where his competitors had gone. Jockey Jeffrey Fell knew he needed to remind his ride that they were not in Miami to play in the sand of the track, so he used the crop on his backside to focus the colt back to the target at hand. A slap to the rump of Timely Writer by Fell served as a reminder of what was needed, producing the extra energy for the colt to surge past the finish line for a 4-length victory.

As the television cameras were trained squarely on the champion after crossing the finish line first, Timely Writer could be seen running on the now wide-open dirt track with his competitors long left behind. With an endurance first shown as a one-year-old at the training farm of Tony Everard, Timely Writer would not stop running. As the colt cut through the fresh air of Florida at speeds up to 40 miles per hour, his whiskers and ears pinned backward by the force of the energy he was creating, it seemed Timely Writer wanted to run for miles. Moments such as these were Timely Writer's nirvana - and it was up to Jeffrey Fell to bring the champion back to reality. Fell was struggling for some distance to slow the colt down - constantly tugging back on the reins he held in his hands and tethered to the front of Timey Writer's bridle and bit. Eventually, after more than one-half mile past the finish line, Fell was able to rein in the champion, with the pair making their way over to the winner's circle for the required photographs, presentation of trophies, and a flower bed of orchids for Mary Martin.

So impressive was Timely Writer's performance just witnessed that television commentator Veitch dismounted off his earlier criticism, gushing with high praise, proclaiming Timely Writer as the horse to beat for the Kentucky

Derby – before Writer had even run the Florida Derby scheduled for the first Saturday in April. Veitch, with a resume in hand few ever held, knew greatness in plain sight and let the television audience know that the race they just watched was one of the more tremendous races he had ever seen. As Timely Writer finished his move through the far turn, a move nicknamed "one Fell swoop" by jockey Jeffrey Fell, Veitch believed Timely Writer would tire approaching the stretch heading towards the finish line. Coming out of the last turn in the manner Timely Writer did, and due to the amount of energy and speed needed for such a prolonged move on the outside of the pack, Veitch believed the colt would naturally fade back to the other horses he had just blown past as he went through the homestretch towards the finish line. Most horses cannot sustain a run from the 3/8 pole on the outside of the pack, battling multiple horses at the top of the homestretch while maintaining the energy needed to sprint through the finish line for the win. Only a once-in-a-generation horse can perform this type of move. Veitch had a front-row seat to this type of talent just four years earlier. In 1978, Veitch witnessed the legendary performances of Hall of Fame horses Alydar and Affirmed during their epic battles in the three Triple Crown races. Veitch had just watched greatness again - this time at the Flamingo Stakes as a television commentator.

The trainer's compliments did not end there, though, as he went on to say Jeffrey Fell was perfect in handling Timely Writer during the race, running Writer properly. It appeared as if Fell fit like a glove in the saddle, navigating the picturesque Timely Writer through and around the pack of opponents while dealing continuously with mud kicking up into his racing goggles from the inclement weather. Veitch stated that if Timely Writer and Fell had been pressed by his competitors, there was no telling how fast of a winning time he would have put up at the finish line. Perhaps the best trainer in the country, Veitch's comments and compliments drew upon legends from the past. Veitch signed off from the television broadcast, declaring the Martins had much to look forward to on the first Saturday in May. With these words coming from the likes of Veitch, it was as if the audience was watching the coronation of the next great thoroughbred.

As Timely Writer made his way towards the winner's circle for the presentation of the trophy and wreath, jockey Jeffrey Fell noticed an unusually large crowd gathering. Winner's circles are sectioned off areas near the track and reserved for family and members directly associated with the horse, with track officials and dignitaries also finding their way to the circle for the presentations and photographs. The 1982 winner's circle for the Flamingo Stakes differed significantly from those in years past - especially for a track known for its conservative decorum. Official photographer Jimmy Raftery attempted to chronicle the ceremony as Timely Writer arrived but found himself boxed out from his usual space by the large crowd. The number of people in the winner's circle had been growing to numbers that were not permitted, forcing Raftery to try and gain control of the chaotic circle. Raftery, whether he knew it or not, as he was barking out directions for an official photograph of the Flamingo Stakes champion and his owners, shared much of the same blue-collar background as the Martin brothers standing in the center of his camera lens.

Timely Writer's assistant trainer, Dominic Imprescia, Jr., was responsible for keeping the champion colt calm at the designated spot within the circle while holding the reins of Timely Writer for the picture-perfect photograph. With the masses of people growing, including 100 approved photographers, Imprescia could no longer keep Timely Writer's head still for the cameras and believed his horse was getting anxious. Pandemonia was in full bloom at the winner's circle. Imprescia was so concerned about the safety risk to Timely Writer and everyone gathered around the nearly 1,100-pound Thoroughbred, he yelled to Fell to dismount from the champion so he could get the colt away from the crowd. Raftery, who had been getting crushed earlier by the crowd as if he were at a Gloria Estefan concert in Miami, began yelling at Imprescia to get the jockey back on Timely Writer. Imprescia shot back at Raftery that Writer had already taken enough photographs for the ceremony. The yelling match continued with Raftery shouting, "those aren't the right photographers!"

As Imprescia left the circle in a hurry with Timely Writer in one direction and Raftery angrily left in the other direction, the backdrop to the chaotic festivities was complemented by the quiet beauty of the pink flamingos scattered around the lake of the grass infield just a short distance away. A look around the winner's circle by track officials saw more than fifty people joining the Martin entourage. As Raftery left the scene, he shouted, "I've never seen such a zoo in 30 years." Track executives voiced their displeasure about the number of people joining the family in the winner's circle to the Martin brothers, some of whom were sporting the pink rain jackets handed out by Hialeah employees earlier in the day. Peter Martin, the quieter and more practical of the two brothers, snapped back at the officials, "They're not our friends; they're friends of the horse."

Trainer Dominic Imprescia, Sr., came to the track on the morning of the race as if he knew he would be center stage in the winner's circle. The World War II veteran and former used-car salesman turned horse trainer was dressed for success. Anticipating the win, Dominic put on his best Flamingo outfit – a plaid pink sport coat, a pink carnation tucked into the chest pocket, a pink tie, and pink slacks. As to where the outfit came from, Dominic winked and told reporters he had it for "a while… just waiting til now to wear it." As to the crowd who stormed into the winner's circle, in an observation laced with sarcasm, the charming Italian from Fitchburg, Massachusetts, stated he thought they were all newsmen. Dominic was unable to say where all the people came from, but did notice "there was an army out there for the 'people's horse.'" Peter, Frannie, Mary, their three adult children, trainer Dominic Imprescia, his son Dominic Jr., friends, and the entire Timely Writer army all seemed like they would stay for the remainder of the afternoon in the winner's circle – if not for the last race of the day needing to be run at Hialeah.

Once the scene at the winner's circle cleared, interviews with journalists and television stations were in full force. Dominic could be seen at the winner's circle being interviewed on national television by broadcaster Jim McKay, while the Martin brothers, arms around one another and smiles across their faces, were entertaining the print media. As Dominic finished his praise of jockey Jeffrey Fell, McKay tried to coax the Martin brothers away from the photographers and reporters some distance away. As he unsuccessfully attempted to persuade the brothers to join him on national television, McKay told the millions watching television about the story of Timely Writer and his owners. McKay spoke about an improbable tale that began with a horse bought at a bargain price two years prior by two brothers in the meat distribution business who made their start decades prior racing horses on a fair circuit sprinkled throughout horse tracks in Massachusetts. Brothers who, as McKay pointed out, had the gall to take their last name and spell it backward, creating the made-up word of "Nitram," which would serve as the stable name for their horse racing business. The backward-named stable was now considered the prohibitive favorite to win the 1982 Kentucky Derby.

The interview with Dominic on live television had not gone unnoticed, with John Martin, the son of Fran and Mary, doing his best to join the broadcast. Twenty-year-old John had become a local celebrity of sorts amongst his crowd of friends from the Boston area during Timely Writer's two-year-old racing season in 1981. The year culminated with John's television appearance during the local news station's three-minute segment about the success of Timely Writer and the Martin family. The new racing year brought with it a new television appearance for John. This time, John found a way to make his national television appearance for his friends back home in the Quincy and Boston areas. A smirking John could be seen moving in and out of the live interview behind the unknowing Jim McKay as the announcer spoke about the family's story with trainer Dominic Imprescia. After giving head nods to his friends back home watching the race, and with the coaxing from his two sisters off camera, John left well enough alone, walking away from his unscripted television appearance and thirty seconds of fame.

For sure, some of the crowd who cheered on Timely Writer and the Martin family at Hialeah were transplanted New Englanders vacationing south during the cold winter in the north. The great majority of the crowd, though, including those who jumped the short metal fence from the parking curbs, running over the soggy dirt track towards the winner's circle, were blue-collar people from parts unknown. People who were celebrating the self-proclaimed "little guys" victory with their once-in-a-lifetime horse. In the days after the race, Peter reflected on the crowd supporting his family. "All those people were little people. They weren't a Fitch [family] or a Galbraith, or a Firestone... we are not either – we are Dorchester people. That's all. It's not supposed to happen, but it has. A Boston horse is not supposed to be a big horse; they demonstrated that when they all flocked out when he won the Flamingo."[6]

In the immediate aftermath of the winner's circle, the support team for Nitram Stables and trainer Dominic Imprescia returned Timely Writer to Barn Q, stall 56, for a well-earned celebration party. There was no partying in a fancy owner's suite for the guys at the barn. The party at the stall was small but vocal and celebratory. No signs or banners proclaiming themselves champions. Perhaps because the money came to the brothers later in life or due to how they were raised in the neighborhoods of Dorchester, Peter and Frannie talked and walked with commoners without the need to display banners or feel accepted by the higher social circles. Joy was found and shared with others by sitting on the benches lining the inside of the barn and horse stall with Timely Writer, their racing team, and friends from other stables. Men, boys, and ladies shared stories of the day and the thrill of the race as they drank from cans of beer and bottles of champagne with the $6.95 price tag still on them. The second half of the celebration was scheduled for later in the evening, with family and close friends dining at the famous Christine Lee's restaurant along Miami Beach.

The day after the Flamingo win, Peter and Frannie returned to their meat business in Boston. Timely Writer remained behind in Florida for training for his next race – the Florida Derby. Before the next race at Gulfstream Park in Hallandale, Florida, though, the brothers announced an additional partner would be joining their ownership team. Success at the highest level of the thoroughbred racing business leads to fame and fortune. After the outstanding accomplishments from the 1981 racing season, the Martins' telephone began ringing about the sale of Timely Writer. During the winter of 1981, one potential buyer dialed up Frannie and offered $200,000.00. Thinking the offer was a prank, Frannie laughingly inquired about which 1/8th of the horse the buyer would like to purchase. Upon realizing the buyer was serious, Frannie quickly ended the conversation, letting the inquiring buyer know he was uninterested. The calls about selling Timely Writer continued from the winter of 1981 into the Florida racing season of 1982. The Martins were listening but had their list of conditions for any potential sale. The brothers insisted that any potential sale required them to retain at least 50% of Timely Writer's ownership and keep all decision-making and management duties.

Potential buyers were offering three million dollars and above for 50% ownership of Timely Writer. Nearly all potential buyers, though, had their own set of conditions. One such offer came in from Kentucky breeder Brownell Combs II. Combs was the owner of Spendthrift Farms. Standing at stud at Spendthrift Farms were Seattle Slew and Affirmed, both of whom were purchased as part of multi-million-dollar syndication breeding agreements. Before 1973, there had been only nine triple crown winners in Thoroughbred racing history, with the great Citation in 1948 as the last thoroughbred with consecutive wins in the Kentucky Derby, the Preakness, and Belmont Stakes. Secretariat put the nearly 30-year drought to an end in 1973 with a Frenchman in his saddle by the name of Ron Turcotte. Seattle Slew and Affirmed matched the feat in 1977 and 1978 - the only time in horse racing history that the Triple Crown had been won in consecutive years. With the race on to find the next Triple Crown winner, Timely Writer would share the horse barn with his two legends if Combs had his way.

Combs wanted Timely Writer for horse racing and breeding purposes, with a source close to him said to have leaked a story to the newspapers that a partnership between Combs and the Martins would be announced soon, resulting in the purchase of the colt by Spendthrift Farms and a multi-million-dollar syndication agreement for breeding rights to follow. Behind the scenes, though, Combs was looking to replace Jeffrey Fell as the jockey for Timely Writer once the deal was signed. Combs wanted his people involved, marginalizing the involvement of the Martin brothers while getting rid of the jockey and, in all probability, their trainer. If Combs thought the leaked story would pressure the Martins to close the deal, he was wrong. The Martins ceased all negotiations after the publication of the story.

Another potential buyer looking to pry Timely Writer away from the Martins was an individual by the name of Louis Wolfson. Wolfson, born in 1912, spent his 95 years as a businessman, financier, thoroughbred owner, breeder, and philanthropist. The son of Jewish immigrants from Lithuania, he was an outstanding athlete and attended the University of Georgia to play football. Wolfson dropped out of college after two years, raising ten thousand dollars to start Florida Pipe and Supply Company. Wolfson became a millionaire in 1930 at the age of 28 – during the Great Economic Depression. The 1940s and '50s saw Wolfson purchasing various corporations, making hundreds of millions of dollars for himself while creating what came to be known as the modern hostile corporate takeover.

Wolfson established Harbor View Farm in 1960 in Fellowship, Florida, breeding and racing 1978 Triple Crown winner Affirmed. Wolfson led all horse race owners in money earned in '78, making it a three-peat with the same accomplishments in 1979 and 1980. Harbor View Farm was also honored in 1978 as the top breeder. Just three years before offering millions for Timely Writer's purchase and breeding rights, Wolfson's farm held the dual honors of owning the best horses and having the best breeding barn in the country. Harbor View Farm seemingly had it all. For Wolfson, he sought another asset for his business ventures - the purchase of Timely Writer as the potential Triple Crown winner for 1982. Wolfson was a person whose business centered upon the art of hostile corporate takeovers – and many assumed there was no chance the Martins would turn down the money and opportunity offered at Harborview Farm.

As reported by the Boston newspapers, Wolfson phoned Frannie to discuss purchasing Timely Writer, offering hundreds of thousands of dollars above the three-million-dollar price tag others had presented to the Martins for 50% of Timely Writer. Wolfson would also bring in his trainer to take over the direction of Timely Writer. The negotiations seemed one-sided, with a significant advantage going to the billionaire Wolfson as he dealt from a position of power and wealth. Without question, the corporate raider could take advantage of the unrefined Martins – or so he thought. As Wolfson negotiated from the office at his opulent horse farm, with Frannie listening from his corner desk in the family's three-bedroom ranch house in Quincy, Massachusetts, Wolfson laid out how and why the sale price was more than reasonable. The sale, however, was conditioned upon the use of Wolfson's trainer replacing Dominic. Frannie's reply was simple and to the point, "No deal. Dominic could train a Billie goat, and I mean it…. I started with Dominic, and I'll finish with him."[7]

Thoroughbred owner Peter Brant also presented the same monetary offer Wolfson had made. With the purchase of Timely Writer, Brant would swap out trainers, bringing in Leroy Jolley to take over management of the champion colt. Brant was 20 years younger than Frannie but was also dealing from a position of great wealth. Brant was the beneficiary of his father's great success. Brant's father co-founded the paper converter company *Brant-Allen Industries*. In the early 1970s, Peter brought his father's company to the next level. Brant transitioned the business to manufacturing by creating paper mill companies. Brant's estimated worth was over one billion dollars at one point in his career. Brant would become one of the world's leading art collectors, an admired philanthropist, an accomplished polo player, and owner and breeder of two Kentucky Derby winners. However, all the successes and accomplishments of the billionaire buyer did not change Frannie's response to the multi-million dollar offer for 50% of Writer – the answer was still no deal.

Offers from Wolfson, Combs, and Brandt all came with explanations as to why the Martins should accept their generous proposals. Reasons expressed for justifying the sale of Timely Writer was that "it was better than running a little meat store in Boston,"[8] which Frannie found insulting. "Peter and I don't give a damn about the money . . .. the important thing is we know there is a long way to go, and anything can happen, but how many opportunities like this come around in a lifetime?"[9]

The two blue-collar brothers from Dorchester had a horse that billionaires and multi-millionaires in the thoroughbred racing industry wished to pry out of their hands. It seemed inevitable that Timely Writer would be added as another trophy to a stable not named Nitram. The Martins, however, had different ideas about who they would partner with for the remainder of their journey.

Dr. and Mrs. William Reed of Kentucky would make them an offer they could not refuse. The Reeds were owners of Mare Haven Farm in Lexington, Kentucky. Dr. Reed's veterinarian background was impeccable, and he was regarded internationally as one of the finest equine doctors of his time. Shortly after earning his veterinary degree from Ohio State in 1944, Dr. Reed's breakthrough in the equine business came when he diagnosed and treated a thoroughbred named Stymie. Stymie was near the end of a Hall of Fame racing career, which included finishing in the top three 98 times during his 131-lifetime starts. Stymie fractured his sesamoid in the right forefoot following a fourth-place finish in the Monmouth Handicap in New Jersey in 1948. Reed's successful diagnosis and treatment of the legendary thoroughbred prevented future injury to Stymie and put Dr. Reed at the forefront of the equine veterinarian industry.

In March of 1971, Dr. Reed went on to save the life of Kentucky Derby favorite Hoist the Flag. Hoist the Flag was the two-year-old horse of the year in 1970 and was preparing for races in the months leading up to the Triple Crown. On March 12, 1971, Hoist the Flag won the Bay Shore Stakes race at Aqueduct Race Course in Queens, New York. He set the track record and became the first racehorse to run 7 furlongs in under one minute and twenty-one seconds. The jockey aboard Hoist the Flag was Jean Cruguet, who went on to ride Triple Crown winner Seattle Slew six years later. Nine days after the race at Aqueduct, Hoist the Flag was breezing along in a 5-furlong workout before running the Gotham Stakes when he misstepped and broke his right hind leg in two places. The injury put the life of the horse of the year in jeopardy. Veterinary surgeons, led by Dr. Reed, performed a bone graft, using screws and metal plates to secure the breaks while creating the first-ever fiberglass cast for a horse. Though he would never race again, the life of Hoist the Flag was saved, and he went on to a successful career as a stallion, siring 257 foals and becoming the leading stallion of 1987. Jockey Jean Cruget, of Seattle Slew fame, gave an interview in 2001 stating Hoist the Flag was by far the best horse he rode.

Knowing the Reeds' background, the brothers had a significant level of respect and comfort with the doctor and his wife, Audrey. The families had developed a lasting friendship at the racetracks over the previous year. It was a perfect partnership between the Martins and Reeds as each couple could surround themselves with trusted business partners and, at the same time, come to an agreement that allowed the Martin brothers control of their champion.

As a veterinarian working in the business of thoroughbred racing, Dr. Reed was prohibited from thoroughbred ownership rights while the horse raced competitively. Dr. Reed and his wife offered three million dollars for 50% of Timely Writer's future breeding rights. The Martin/Reed agreement dictated that Timely Writer would retire at the end of the 1982 racing season; the Martins would control Timely Writer's racing schedule for 1982 while receiving 100% of the race earnings; the Martins would hand-pick all of the mares (female partners) of Writer when he retired to stud; Jeffrey Fell would remain as the jockey; and Dominic would stay as the trainer. They all agreed that if, for some reason, the colt was thrown off his form, then he would be retired. Upon retirement, Dr. Reed had ten of the best mares in the country, as approved by the Martins, waiting to send Timely Writer's way. With each subsequent victory by Timely Writer in 1982, Reed estimated that Timely Writer's value would increase for breeding, with his stud fee in the area of $75,000.00 to $100,000.00 per mare.

If there was any hint that Dr. Reed thought Dominic wasn't up to the task as a trainer for the remainder of the 1982 racing season, Reed publicly backed him, stating, "you have to remember that the colt had only one win since last October... [t]he man deserves the highest level of flattery. There are very few trainers who could have had this colt as fit and sharp as Dominic had him." [10]

With Timely Writer's impressive win at the Flamingo, potential entries for the Florida Derby were reluctant to take on the champion. This resulted in the field of entries chopped in half to 8 competitors. The one and 1/8-mile race, billed as the "Run for the Orchids," would be held at Gulfstream Park in

Hallandale, Florida. It was thought to be a two-horse battle between Timely Writer and undefeated Star Gallant, who had yet to challenge the champion of the Flamingo Stakes.

Frannie and Peter, the Irish in them from growing up in the neighborhoods of Dorchester, reached out to their colleagues and friends Tony and Joanne Everard, asking the fun-loving couple to sit with them at the Florida Derby in their owner's box for some "luck of the Irish." Born and raised in Ireland, Tony left his birthplace in 1958 at eighteen years old aboard a boat from Liverpool, England, for promises of greener pastures in the United States of America. Joining Tony on the voyage were two horses, a dog, and his brother Joe. From their days together in Boston, Tony and his wife Joanne were trusted friends and a vital part of Martin's extended family. Everard's brilliance was the singular reason the family owned the champion colt. The purchase of a lifetime for the brothers after Everard set his eyes on the one-year-old Timely Writer at a non-descript horse farm during the summer of 1980 in Ocala, Florida.

Also returning with Frannie and Mary for the Florida Derby were their three children, including their youngest daughter, Janice, who attended a catholic high school just outside of the Boston area named Archbishop Williams ("Archie's"). With parents who owned a horse with God-given talents, the teachers at Archie's were intent on supporting the family. Janice's return trip to Florida included an envelope from the teachers with money and instructions for wagers on the Florida Derby. Instructions were given to Janice that the money was to be used to place bets on Timely Writer to win. The teacher organizing the money and bets amongst her colleagues was Sister Catherine. Sister Catherine and her fellow nuns and teachers at Archie's spent the week leading up to the Derby praying for the Martins and Timely Writer to win.

In the days leading up to the Derby, the favorite of the so-called experts was the speed horse Star Gallant. Star Gallant, whose owner was the brother-in-law of Saudi Arabian King Abdullah's family, was undefeated in four races with dazzling workouts in the weeks leading up to the Florida Derby. The lightning-fast colt's trainer compared him to Triple Crown winner Seattle Slew as they prepared to take on Timely Writer. The Martin racing crew welcomed the challenge – the crew from Boston focusing on a showdown against a horse and an owner with ties to a royal family. Timely Writer's handlers began stoking the flames the week before the race. The Miami newspapers were marketing the event like a marquee boxing match with full-page ads resembling those previously reserved for Muhammad Ali fights. *Boston Globe* sports journalist Sam McCracken observed in his column in the days beforehand, "the race had all the theatrics leading up to it like the 1972 Muhammad Ali-Joe Frazier boxing match in the Philippines," known as "the Thrilla-in-Manila."[11]

The Martin crew was hearing and reading everything about the talented and undefeated frontrunner Star Gallant and an undefeated speed horse from Canada named Distinctive Pro. During his workouts at Gulfstream Park, the exercise riders for Timely Writer had their orders from Trainer Dominic Imprescia and his son – be like Ali! In no uncertain terms, they were told to stare down the other side, trying to intimidate and psyche them out. They were to let the opposition know that Timely Writer had already beaten the undefeated two-year-old filly of the year Before Dawn, and undefeated champion colts Deputy Minister and Out of Hock during a showdown at the Champagne Stakes at Belmont Park in New York. The boys from Boston had proven to be a team that did not shy away from competition.

Tensions arose during a 6:45 a.m. workout session two days before the Florida Derby. In full view of a television crew and visitors, Timely Writer's exercise rider Ambrose Pascucci, wearing his best pair of rolled-up Jordache jeans for the media, was sharing workout time with one of the favorites, Distinctive Pro and rider Constantine Hernandez. As the riders began to gallop out their horses on the track two times around, Pascucci was relentlessly calling out Hernandez in front of the crowd, "How about head-to-head right now, jock. Let's see whose got it." Hernandez ignored the yelling from Pascucci, eventually turning down the challenge and responding the horses could wait for race day. So it was; the jockeys and their horses would settle things on Saturday.

On the morning of the Derby, the racing entries were reduced to a seven-horse field, with the unexpected scratch of Distinctive Pro five hours before post-time due to an injured shin splint. Without strong enough competition for Timely Writer, bettors were confident about how the race would conclude, pouring money on the Flamingo champion to win the Florida Derby. Post time listed Timely Writer as the favorite for the first time in his career at odds of 4-5 (a $2.80 return for every $2 bet to win). As Timely Writer was brought out onto the track in the pre-race parade of entries, the three-year-old colt looked the part of a champion. "[H]is mane freshly clipped, he looked lean and muscular, his burnished coat gleaming in the sunshine and his ears pricked in eagerness to run."[12]

The bell went off as soon as the starting gates were filled with the entries, signaling the race's start. With the front of the gates quickly opening, Timely Writer was first out of the gate, but the quicker Star Gallant was first to the turn. This initial move by Timely Writer showed he was talented enough to run on the lead when needed and, more importantly, allowed him to get outside the pack for his early shadowing of the front runner - which did not bode well for Star Gallant. With a speedy ½ mile time of 47 and 1/5 seconds, Star Gallant was right where his racing team wanted him, but like the strategy used at the Flamingo, Timely Writer was stalking Star Gallant in the shadows, not far behind.

Jockey Jeffrey Fell kept his eyes focused on Star Gallant, sizing up the race as it developed before him. Fell saw the front runner begin to tire from his passenger's seat atop Timely Writer. Fell also knew that his horse under him had a lot of energy left. Timely Writer was striding so easily that Fell never needed to use the riding crop on him. Fell challenged Star Gallant earlier than expected, as the Florida Derby was 1/8 of a mile longer than the Flamingo Stakes. Star Gallant may have been leading the Florida Derby, but Timely Writer and Fell had the front runner right where they wanted, with 3/8 of a mile left to the finish line. Fell gave Timely Writer a firm tug on his reins, a click of each of his heels, letting his ride know it was time to shift into another gear. The jock and the colt, wearing their matching orange and black colors once again, were on their way to tracking down another undefeated horse in a championship race. As Timely Writer pulled even with Star Gallant at the top of the homestretch, he paused and looked at his competitor as if to simultaneously say hello and goodbye. When Fell saw Writer do this, he raised the horse crop just high enough for Timely Writer to see it from his blinkered cover hood. Timely Writer got the message, pulling away from Star Gallant, surging down the stretch, and opening up a two-length lead for the victory.

The television cameras trained on Timely Writer once again after the finish line. As the cameras followed Timely Writer, the colt still looked fresh, without any sweat on his coat or any flaw in each of his strides. Star Gallant was now the 5th unbeaten horse Timely Writer had taken down in six months. Fell would later tell reporters it was the "easiest race I ever had him on. [A] classic horse, a natural distance runner."[13] As the triumphant Martin team made their way to the winner's circle with hugs and high-fives for all, Trainer Dominic Imprescia was once again dressed for the occasion.

Dominic's girlfriend Ann had spent the weeks before the Florida Derby combing through clothes racks of men's suit jackets at retail stores throughout Broward County, ultimately finding the perfect coat for the occasion. Imprescia broke out his lavender jacket early Saturday morning as the ideal complement to the horseshoe of orchid flowers displayed in the winner's circle. The Martins celebrated the win by posing for photographs in front of the giant orchid horseshoe carrying the name of their champion.

Appearing in the winner's circle at the Florida Derby is a once-in-a-lifetime experience. To appreciate the moment's beauty, one must understand its unique history. One of the world's largest florists, Exotic Gardens, is annually chosen to create the giant horseshoe displayed at the winner's circle, which carries approximately 200 orchids on the Styrofoam frame. James Donn, the founder of Exotic Gardens and former Chairman of the Board for Gulfstream Park, developed a strain of Orchid flower that he called the "Nellie Donn" in honor of his wife after she passed away. The stem of each orchid is placed in a vial with water in the days before the Derby. The stem is sealed at the vile and put on the Styrofoam frame. The orchids completely cover the frame and last for a week or more, thanks to the sealed vials. The horseshoe with the winner's name is immediately hoisted and placed behind the winner's circle. Palm trees dotting the landscape further back are the perfect setting for photographing each champion and his circle of family and friends. It is a moment and setting which reflects the crowning of the three-year-old champion Thoroughbred for the Sunshine State.

The sheer joy and chaos after Timely Writer finished first in the Florida Derby was like none other. Finding superlatives to describe an in-person account of one of Timely Writer's performances began to seem more inadequate as each race passed. Steve Hummer, the long-time sports editor for *The Palm Beach Post*, did his best to tell the tale of Timely Writer at the Florida Derby on the first Saturday in April of 1982. Hummer's story was given the most sought-after space in the newspaper - the front page of the Sunday sports section. With a photograph of jockey Jeffrey Fell aboard Timely Writer covering the top half of the front page - the picture running from one side of the newspaper to the other - Hummer's headline for the two-page article read, *"Derby Winners' Tale Could Pass for Fiction."* The title of the lengthy article drew on the improbable real-life fairy-tale story of the champion and his owners. As Hummer attempted to explain the unexplainable, his awe of witnessing Timely Writer in person was apparent to all as he penned the battle of Star Gallant and Timely Writer.

As the journalist stood watching the race develop, he focused his sights on the top left corner of the race track as the racing entries took the last turn towards the home stretch. With the sun setting west of the turn, a blur of orange and black silks could be seen passing the far more defined colors of every other racing entry. As Hummer and the nearly thirty thousand patrons at Gulfstream Park witnessed, reading about Timely Writer was one thing, but viewing him in person was another. As Hummer told his readers, Timely Writer's challenge match with Star Gallant over the last 3/8 of a mile ended with the colt from Boston "blowing past the unblemished Derby challenger in a stretch run that may become legend."[14]

On everybody's mind, as Timely Writer surged through the final furlong of the Florida Derby, was that the colt and his band of overachievers were now the overwhelming favorite to win the Kentucky Derby. In less than twelve months, the Martin crew went from racing Timely Writer in front of 10,000 people at their home track in Boston to the starting gates at historic Churchill Downs in Louisville, Kentucky. Awaiting the Martin family for the Kentucky Derby on the first Saturday in May of 1982 would be more than 140,000 people, the great majority of them cheering on their horse, whom the media had affectionately labeled "the people's champion."

Dominic with his matching lavender jacket in the winner's circle of the Florida Derby on the far left

Before they left the Sunshine State for home, the Martins hosted a celebration party for over 100 of their closest family, friends, and colleagues. Peter, Frannie, and Mary were spending some of the money they picked up courtesy of the two stakes wins in Florida for a night of celebration. Frannie knew precisely where they would hold the celebratory party as he had a score to settle with the racing establishment from a few months prior. The brothers brought their party to Miami Beach, treating their guests to food, libations, and music throughout the night. A banquet room was reserved at the famous Fontainebleau Hotel on Miami Beach. The historic hotel was opened in 1954 by hotelier Ben Novack on the property formerly owned by Harvey Firestone. The hotel is located in the heart of what is known as "millionaire's row" in Miami Beach. It was one of the most recognized hotels in the country – later added to the National Register of Historic Places in December 2008.

Fontainebleau had become the place to be seen, making numerous appearances in movies and television shows. One of the first movies to use the scenic backdrop was "A Hole in the Head," showcased in movie cinemas in 1959. Frank Sinatra, the country's best crooner and a favorite of the Martins, was cast in the lead role. The year 1964 saw the James Bond film, "Goldfinger," open with a panoramic aerial shot of the hotel with the credits rolling in unison to the music soundtrack. A year before the Martins hosted their celebration, Al Pacino and the movie *Scarface* filmed beach scenes at the hotel. The hotel even hosted live sporting matches, with legendary boxer Roberto Duran retaining his world light heavyweight title in a 13-round knockout in January 1977.

As Frannie and Mary danced and sang throughout the evening at the Fontainebleau, celebrating with family and friends late into the night, and as they reflected on their family's journey together since the beautiful bay-colored colt came into their lives as a one-year-old, Frank Sinatra songs dominated the evening. Frannie's special request, "My Way," found he and Mary singing Sinatra's words in harmony, and as if the lyrics told their story:

> "I've loved, I've laughed and cried. I've had my fill, my share of losing. And now, as tears subside, I find it all so amusing to think I did all that. And may I say, not in a shy way, Oh, no, oh, no, not me, I did it my way."

With the songs of Sinatra continuing, one particular song brought everyone together in the center of the dance floor. Arms in the air, swinging them side to side, the celebratory crowd from Boston was singing "New York, New York," shouting out the lyrics, "I want to wake up in a city that never sleeps, to find I'm "A" number one, head of the list, cream of the crop, at the top of the heap, king of the hill." Sinatra's words proved poetic, as for that one night in Miami, Timely Writer and the Martin family were on top of the thoroughbred racing world.

One of the many benefits of owning the favorite for the Kentucky Derby is the recognition that comes with it within the world of radio, television, and print media. In the decade of the '70s and '80s, the most important sports magazine in the country was *Sports Illustrated*. It was the largest sports subscriber magazine, becoming the first to have over one million subscribers. The magazine reached millions of homes and people every week. In the decades before the advent of the internet and access to instant news, it was a time when magazines mattered.

Sports Illustrated was delivered to its subscribers' mailboxes once a week, with millions more sold over store counters. Every week, the magazine contained articles from the best sports writers in the country. Readers devoted time during their day to reading the stories in the magazine. First, reading the articles on the sports they enjoyed the most, then moving on to the remaining stories, learning about sports they did not follow. To be depicted on the cover of "SI," or part of a featured multi-page story was a badge of honor for any athlete - confirmation that the athlete's story was worthy of national recognition.

Every student-aged athlete or sports fan knew the day of the week the SI magazine would be delivered by the postal carrier - typically Thursdays. Upon returning home from school, one would head straight for the mailbox to retrieve the much sought-after weekly magazine. In the days before electronics and iPhones, from which any news story could be retrieved immediately, it was a race within the family to recover the magazine from the mailbox before another sibling or parent got to it first. If you were not the first to read it, there was no telling when the magazine would be available for reading if it fell into the hands of others. A *Sports Illustrated* magazine in hand, for many, was a must-read before starting school homework or eating dinner.

Timely Writer on the far-left swoops around the final turn at the Florida Derby and onto the pages of Sports Illustrated in April 1982

One week after the Martins returned home to the Boston area, confirmation that they had made it was sitting in their mailbox with the weekly publication of *Sports Illustrated* on April 12, 1982. In a multi-page article with colored photographs chronicling their success in Florida, an entire country was now reading about these "little guys" living out their real-life fairy tale story. With their two back-to-back wins in Florida, an entire nation was "embrace[ing] the image of a modestly bred, stretch-running colt owned by two Boston meat suppliers, trained by a former used car salesman who wore pink and lavender jackets to match the flowers draped over his horse's withers. Timely Writer had become the people's horse, and he was the one to beat in the Kentucky Derby."[15]

Timely Writer would be delivered via an airplane shuttle to Churchill Downs during the second week of April as the prohibitive favorite for the Kentucky Derby. Kentucky newspapers sent photographers to Lexington to photograph the arrival of the presumptive favorite - the daily journals in Kentucky filling their newspapers with stories about the champion and his family from Boston. As Timely Writer settled into his stall in Kentucky, with time for others to reflect on what the bay colt had accomplished in Florida and how he did it, the experts considered the colt without a peer and the favorite to sweep the Triple Crown races. One horse racing critic opined Timely Writer is "capable of doing whatever is necessary to win, and it will take a whale of a horse to prevent him from winning the Triple Crown." [16] Racing enthusiasts were set to place Timely Writer on the same mantle as other legends of the past, though recognizing his popularity was second to none. "Seattle Slew, Secretariat, Citation, Spectacular Bid, Affirmed, and perhaps a few others ha[d] brought a more impressive record to the Kentucky Derby, but, except for Citation, none had a more substantial claim of favoritism for the Churchill Downs classic at this stage than Timely Writer does."[17]

Joe Hirsch of the prestigious *Daily Racing Form* spoke for novices and experts alike, astutely observing, "Timely Writer had the respect of the American racing community as the best of his generation going into the classic campaign. Without exception, horsemen from all parts of the country with whom we've spoken over the past few weeks singled him out as the dominant force in the Kentucky Derby, the one they all had to beat. Such unanimity of opinion is rare and speaks volumes for a colt whose consistency and strength of acceleration stamped him as one of the ones."[18]

In the weeks following their return from Miami, the Martin family brought their stories of celebration from Florida to Massachusetts. They returned to their homes, sharing the thrills of their victories with friends stopping by each day. Peter and Frannie tried to get back to the normalcy of their meat packing business in Boston, only to find even more fanfare, in the form of congratulations cards and telephone messages, than those greeting them at home. Janice returned to her high school classroom at Archbishop Williams, where she promptly returned the white envelope entrusted to her by Sister Catherine - with its contents an unspoken vow of silence between the two.

As the first Saturday of May inched closer, a captivated public awaited the crowning of their champion in Kentucky. Timely Writer had gone from a horse nobody wanted to a horse everyone adored in just two years.

Throughout the remainder of 1982 and beyond, people across the country would embrace the Martin family while joining their roller coaster ride with Timely Writer.

42

Chapter 2

Shipping Up TO Boston: The Martin Brothers & Dorchester for Life

Originally from Dorchester (OFD) was a concept born in the early 1980s - the result of ole fashion community pride. The building blocks of the organization, though, can be traced back hundreds of years earlier. The birth of the town goes back to the early 17th century when English Puritans, due to the religious persecutions inflicted upon them by the British monarchy, fled their country to seek new opportunities, land, and religious freedom. The first ship of Puritans set sail in 1620 aboard the famous *Mayflower*, settling and establishing in Plymouth, Massachusetts. The next wave of Puritans came in the years after this first landing, with additional ships named the *Mary* and *John* transporting significant numbers of their followers from Europe to Massachusetts, with many settling 40 miles north of Plymouth. These people spent years developing the land into what became known as Dorchester - eventually incorporating the area into a town in 1679. It was the first settlement in Massachusetts to organize as a town government. The first formal structure included selectmen as town representatives, who then created public schools using taxpayer money.

Subsequent generations of Puritans became the town's foundation for hundreds of years. Their homes and taverns served as meeting places for the "Sons of Liberty" – an organization of members who spawned an American Revolution. A generation of revolutionaries whose families traced their lineage back to their ancestors who fled the same British oppressors. It was from Dorchester Heights, the highest neighborhood in the town, with unencumbered views to the city and Boston Harbor, where the Continental Army led by General George Washington forced the British to flee Boston on March 17, 1776 – a date later declared "Evacuation Day" by the politicians of Boston in 1901. A declaration that left more than one resident forever suspicious about the politics involved in securing a permanent day off from work for a city that had already been parading and partying on St. Patrick's Day, March 17th, for over twenty-five years.

Less than a century removed from the American Revolution, families in Dorchester found themselves "losing" their town through annexation to the City of Boston in 1865, thereby creating a little "neighborhood" for the big city. Town residents did not join the city of Boston quietly - taking two years before a majority of voters agreed with the offer from the city. Before annexation, Dorchester had been a farming town with some industries scattered along Dorchester Bay and the Neponset River. Not content to be known as a neighborhood to Boston, as it was an area with life experiences different from "city folks," the residents grew to create a separate sense of identity - one personal to their families, friends, and community. Social circles and associations would develop within the town over the years ahead, eventually leading to an acronym (OFD), symbolizing community pride. Potential members for acceptance into the group must be originally from Dorchester or current residents. Upon acceptance into the association, plenty of OFD clothing and paraphernalia are available for the residents to show off their college-like pride.

OFD symbols can be seen throughout neighborhoods, cities, the state, and, at times, across the country. For those non-OFD individuals, one only needs to make their way through the city and neighborhoods of Boston to find its members. Look for motor vehicles with the black and white oval "OFD" emblem attached to the rear bumper; look for people wearing t-shirts, hats, and sweatshirts with the OFD embroidered symbol . . . and listen. Listen to the conversations of people as they speak with one another in their Boston accents, boasting with pride that they are OFD, boasting with pride about the neighborhood or parish they call home, and bragging about how they know the same families from Dorchester as they stand face to face talking, rather loudly at times, and in a language which does not seem to contain the letter "r" within their alphabet.

For many, the trappings of the town forever impact the remainder of their lives. Whether Dorchester residents move to other towns, travel throughout the country, or leave town for the winter, they seem to find a way to manifest their pride wherever they may live. Even in death, OFD survives. As any good family from Dorchester knows, the foremost priority when one of their own passes away is to draft an obituary as soon as possible. The first line of the obit typically reads as follows: name of the decedent, date of birth, date of death, and a marking in bold: OFD.

The town of Dorchester was forever a part of the Martin brothers as they grew from boys to men at their parents' home located at 87 Centre Street. The brothers later grinding it out on the racetracks in Massachusetts for a generation, barnstorming the country's east coast at the elite horse tracks while taking on a racing industry and its wealthiest participants without fear or shame. As an article in *Boston Magazine* described in the spring of 1982, the oddity of these blue-collar brothers finding success at the elite level did not appear that different from either a visual or observational perspective. The brothers' "business is the foundation; the horse is the glamour . . . forced to classify the Martins, you'd have to call them nice guys, who are bucking the odds to finish first these days. They believe in the Golden Rule, the Puritan Work Ethic, and the American Dream."[20] To understand Peter and Frannie's journey to the 1982 Kentucky Derby and beyond and how they survived the emotional roller-coaster playing out before a country, one must understand how their upbringing impacted and prepared them for the ride to come.

The turn of the 20th century was an exciting time in Dorchester as its infrastructure expansion helped create a vibrant area. The influx of families across the country and the ocean saw many people migrating to Dorchester. Three-story apartment buildings ("triple decka's" as they would say) developed across the town's landscape, further expanding its middle-class base's footprints. The cost-efficient triple-deckers served the needs of the incoming working middle-class families, allowing extended families to live together in the same building over three separate floors. The construction of the Old Colony Railroad and trolleys running along the streets made it easy for people to travel around Dorchester and into the adjoining city of Boston. With gorgeous panoramic views of the Boston harbor and the Atlantic Ocean and charming landscapes spread throughout its hills and valleys, the offerings popularized the neighborhoods of Dorchester and became a sought-after community.

The town seemingly had a church in every neighborhood, including St. Mark's, where the brothers found themselves every Sunday morning. The church sat less than ½ mile from the Martins' home and made it easy for the parents and brothers to rush down the sidewalk every Sunday for mass at 11:00 a.m. The brothers, from their Centre Street home, spent their years walking past the church they attended for an education at the Catholic school bearing the same name. It was a tight community, built on faith, family, friends, neighbors, and loyalty - and where the Martin brothers learned to be hardworking and honest.

The streets, neighborhoods, parishes, and schools of Dorchester were where the four Martin brothers grew from kids to young adults during the 1930s and '40s. Like most Dorchester kids short on grass lawns at home, the brothers flocked to the streets to play any outdoor activity, such as stickball, dodgeball, street hockey, and basketball. Hoop games were played on the black pavement of the public streets, with a basketball rim nailed 10 feet up on a wooden telephone pole. Kids proved their athletic ability on the roads and fields of their town. The nature of the times forced kids and teenagers to interact daily with one another - leading to the early development of social and networking skills while creating a tight-knit community as they grew older together.

Weekends in Dorchester often found parents sitting on the front stoops of their porches or in chairs set up in their yard or driveway, sharing a smoke, gossiping, or whispering about a loved one who had passed away, and occasionally keeping an eye on the kids and teenagers who were nearby. Sometimes, parents made their way down the streets to break up fistfights between youthful competitors during neighborhood games - often forcing the offenders to shake hands. Games between friends and rivals did not resume until the awkward demands from parents were completed, though any handshake was typically half-hearted.

Frannie was the youngest of the four brothers, born on September 12, 1926. Peter was the brother closest in age to Frannie, though some eleven years older, with brother John twelve years older than Frannie, and brother Harold thirteen years older. As the fourth child schooled behind his older brothers, Frannie was wise beyond his years. Peter was the closest to Frannie as the older brothers soon left the family home upon graduating high school. If Frannie could be described as the extrovert of the family, Peter was the introvert. A reserved person, Peter was known as the intellect of the family. After graduating from St. Mark's, Peter entered college, becoming the first and only sibling in the family to attend and graduate. Peter earned multiple degrees, with a bachelor's degree from Northeastern University and a Master's degree from Bentley College in accounting, later attending a graduate business program during the evenings at Harvard University. Although more reserved than Frannie, Peter shared his brother's kind, compassionate heart. Asked to describe Peter, those who knew him observed, "[h]e was a generous man, a philanthropic man, a man who gave because he wanted to, not because he thought he had to."[21]

Soon after Frannie started high school in 1940, he began waking before the sun rose. Frannie was up earlier than most his age to help his older, adult-aged brother John deliver milk from the local dairy farm via a horse and milk cart (buggy). John would navigate the buggy delivering milk products to the neighborhoods in and around Adams Street in Dorchester. During these years, Frannie developed his lifelong passion for horses, though the breed pulling the milk buggy was a bit different than the thoroughbreds he would come to love. The 1,500-pound horses, typically a Belgian breed, were thick and robust, with enormous hooves to support their weight, moving ever so slowly through the neighborhoods. The horse's reins led back to the horse-drawn vehicle carrying multiple trays of one-quart milk bottles sealed with waxed foil caps for pasteurization. Local dairy farms sent out horse-drawn vehicles every morning as it was the most cost-effective way to get the product out to the consumers due to milk not being refrigerated in grocery stores. Like a young boy's newspaper delivery route, Frannie helped John deliver the morning milk. With John's guidance, Frannie was schooled in the equipment of the horse, including the horse's reins and the proper care of such a magnificent animal. Eventually, Frannie could steer the horse and his buggy through the use of the reins, stopping the horse at each home for the milk deliveries. Frannie quickly grabbed the milk racks, jogging up the stairs of the customer's house to check the insulated boxes near the front door. Bottles of empty glass quarts were removed from the milk storage boxes, replacing each with fresh milk. Customers looked forward to seeing Frannie each morning– the young lad consistently delivering on time with a big smile and a friendly hello.

Growing up in Dorchester through the 1940s, found the Martin brother's two-story home at 87 Centre Street blanketed by landmarks such as Codman Square, Dorchester Center, Wainright Park, and Dorchester Avenue. On any given weekend night throughout the decades, the brothers and their friends frequented the Neponset Drive-In on Morrissey Boulevard for movie night. The brothers often sneaking friends or family members through the payment gate by hiding them in the trunk of their car. Nobody was allowed out of the vehicle's trunk until it parked parallel to the carefully staggered metal poles with the attached outdoor audio speakers. Once parked, the speakers were hung onto the rolled-down driver's side window, with everyone from the trunk jumping out to watch and listen to the movies projected onto the large outdoor screen some fifty yards or more away.

Other nights included heading down to the neighborhood movie theatre at Fields Corner on Adams Street. An admission fee of 25 cents allowed the boys to catch up with what was going on in the world through the weekly newsreels shown on the screen before the start of featured movies – including sports reels about a great racehorse named Seabiscuit who was capturing the affection of an entire country. After the movies, the boys often went down to Hendries Ice Cream Parlor for sodas and chatting with girls.

Weekend days would occasionally find one of the brothers and his friends at the most southern-end neighborhood of Dorchester – known as Lower Mills. Bringing the Martins to the Lower Mills neighborhoods were the lingering scents of chocolate. The Baker Chocolate Company was founded along the banks of the Neponset River in 1780 – the first company to produce chocolate in the country – and the source that satisfied the brothers' sweet tooth.

Weekend nights provided additional entertainment with visits to roller-skating rinks and dance halls sprinkled throughout Dorchester. The 1930s through the 1950s were the heyday for indoor roller-skating rinks, with Chez Vous on Gallivan Boulevard leading the way. Chez Vous brought energy to the crowd as loud musical soundtracks played over the dimly lit oval floor, with patrons swaying to the musical tunes atop their rollerblades. Small businesses similar to The Baker Chocolate Company, Hendrie's Ice Cream, and Chez Vous were scattered among the bustling town of Dorchester. Many other family businesses, such as hardware stores, diners, pharmacies, and cobblers, became part of the lexicon for the city as it made its way into the second half of the century.

Although it would be years until Dorchester saw a much greater diversity of people within its borders, the 1950s brought controversial conversations about the civil rights movement to its town, with discussions spreading across the country in the following decade. One of the great leaders of the 1960s civil rights movement was a graduate student named Martin Luther King, Jr., a Dorchester resident beginning in 1951 while attending the School of Divinity for his doctorate at Boston University. The student impressed many during his time in the Boston area, including a member of the Board of Trustees at Boston University named Peter Fuller. Fuller was the son of a former governor in Massachusetts – and an owner of thoroughbreds. Fuller and Dr. Martin Luther King, Jr., would remain friends through the civil rights movement of the '60s - a movement which would cost Dr. King his life on April 4, 1968, in Memphis, Tennessee. It was a movement and a relationship that began originally in Dorchester. Many believed it was also a friendship that cost Fuller the first-place finish at the 1968 Kentucky Derby.

St. Mark's 1944 varsity baseball team, with Frannie kneeling in the front row on the left

Frannie's high school days were occupied by playing ice hockey and varsity baseball for St. Mark's High School. He was a star second baseman, making Newman's Prep baseball team during the summer months, with his talents later securing a roster spot with the prestigious Boston Hobos of the Cape Cod summer league. Upon graduating from high school in the spring of 1944, as with most 18-year-old men at the time, Frannie left St. Mark's and his gas attendant job on Dorchester Avenue to enlist in the United States Navy for service in World War II. Frannie would be joining his brother Peter in the Navy, who, at the age of 26, nearly six months after Pearl Harbor was bombed in Hawaii by Japan, voluntarily enlisted for military service in World War II. Peter would serve three and a half years for his country, eventually discharged on December 5, 1945 - four months after victory over Japan was declared.

Shortly after enlisting in the military, Frannie's athletic ability was noticed during boot camp. Navy officials had ideas other than combat duty for the youngest Martin brother. Frannie was approached and asked to play baseball for the Navy team. Never contemplating that his military service would center on playing sports, Frannie was overwhelmed with the invite and saw it as a tremendous honor to play baseball for his country and the American troops. The Navy baseball team barnstormed military bases throughout the country, providing welcome distractions and entertainment for the American forces. Christmas holidays were especially difficult for military members as the troops often struggled with separation from their families. Holidays for Frannie and the Navy baseball team involved playing games at the military bases with other forms of entertainment mixed in afterward for the soldiers. One of Frannie's biggest thrills was after the games were concluded, as he worked as a chauffeur for celebrities such as Bob Hope, Lucille Ball, and Raquel Welch, transporting famous entertainers around the military bases. The entertainers brought laughter, hope, and beautiful ladies, all a welcome distraction for the troops.

Shortly after his military service, Frannie started working at his aunt and uncle's business - Kyes Supply Company (pronounced as Kise). The small meat business was initially located in Boston's historic Faneuil Hall. While Frannie was learning the business, Peter, with multiple college degrees in hand, went to work for an accounting firm in Boston. Peter eventually soured on the city lifestyle and confines of an office setting. Four years after Frannie began at Kyes, Peter joined him, managing the accounting and financial affairs of the business. Frannie and Peter were a tenacious pair at the company and never gave up on their childhood dreams of horse racing, working together on the local fair horse racing circuit during their spare time. Anyone entering the business storefront always found Frannie with a warm welcome, and if you stayed long enough, you would hear a story and laughter filling the building halls. Peter was always nearby, the quiet brother, reserved, kind-hearted, and a deep thinker – a person of wisdom. Both were hardworking, strong, and open-minded.

In the company's early years at Faneuil Hall in Boston, sawdust could always be found on the floor, soaking up the meat fat lying about after a full day of cutting up carcasses. Employees could be seen smoking cigarettes during work –a work zone practice that would challenge the regulatory agencies of modern times. Early mornings and late nights were the recipe for the business's success. Hard work produced success for the company, eventually outgrowing their work area and moving to the meat district at Foodmart Road in Boston.

The new location for the business stood in a no-frills cinderblock building, which housed nearly 20 other similar meat and poultry businesses. Also on sight at the new building was "Rocky the Bookie." Though Massachusetts had no difficulties legalizing gambling on horses and dogs, it refused to legalize sports gambling. This political stance allowed illegal sports betting to grow amongst organized crime associations, with characters such as Rocky flourishing at the business establishments at Foodmart Road. Rocky was the local "book" accepting sports wagers and off-track horse and dog racing bets from his client base for his bosses. Kyes Supply welcomed Rocky with open arms and wallets as they settled into their new storefront.

The new location included a 2,000-square-foot office, workstations for cutting meat, and two meat freezers totaling 1,800 square feet, always set at 30 degrees or lower. Work typically started in the early morning hours at 6:00 a.m. The long work day was non-stop movement – with the required ability to dodge employees moving in and out of the freezer doors with products in their hands. Watching the men moving hundreds of pounds of meat with their two-wheel dollies from the ramps of the delivery trucks to the freezers in the morning, later hanging three-hundred-pound racks of ribs for transport in the afternoon, reminded visiting family members what a day of hard work involved. The core of the "team" grew from the early years in Boston Fanuel Hall, consisting of Peter, Frannie, older brother John, two office managers, five butchers, all wearing their required white coats, two selectors, two drivers, four support personnel, and three salesmen – including Frannie as the lead.

Kyes Supply had a cast of lovable workers and nicknames aplenty for their employees. Some of these "Good Fellas" at Foodmart Road included Joey Batson; John Marchie, a chubby truck driver named "Porky;" and a young Irish lad named John Bly, who came with the thickest Irish brogue and lived above his friends' Irish pub at the Blarney Stone on "Dot Ave." The biggest comedian of the crew was known as "Honka." Though many never knew Honka's birth name, it was Billy Mann. Billy's gift at birth was the largeness of his nose, which earned him the nickname he proudly gave everyone when asked his name.

Strong leadership and work ethic turned Kyes Supply into a successful and fun meat business with prominent personalities and a passion for horse racing. A typical day saw large stacks of meat orders ready for delivery, with a bigger pile of horse racing programs nearby for studying the day's races. One stack was never seen without the other. Grinding out meat orders, running a small horse stable, and placing horse bets, Frannie and Peter worked at the office and Suffolk Downs Racetrack in Boston seven days a week. It was two businesses blended with passion.

Practical jokes amongst the cast of characters at Kyes Supply occurred weekly. Each employee worked with his head on a swivel, never knowing when a baseball of hamburger fat would sizzle by one's head, and always on the look-out for co-workers inflicting "wedgies," "noogies," and "wet-willies." Each new hire was also the subject of the "meat freezer prank" within the first week of employment. The sub-zero meet freezers housed expensive products that moved in and out of the storage freezer throughout the day. Strict orders were in place to keep the freezer doors closed at all times. The Martins good-natured humor was the catalyst for ritual pranks. New employees would be sent to various businesses, which were all in on the joke, with the assignment of purchasing screen doors for the freezer doors. Inevitably, the new employee would be gone for hours before returning to work without the requested screen doors in hand - and to the belly-laughing of fellow employees at the thought of someone purchasing screen doors for sub-zero freezers.

Kyes Supply never let any part of its meat go to waste. Bones from the carcasses of the beef were saved and re-sold to other companies to be used for cooking stock or bone broth. The fat of the meat cut and discarded to the floor during the workday was gathered and shoveled up into large bins at the end of the day - later re-sold to companies to produce household products such as candles and soap. These menial tasks during the workday were also subject to daily pranks. One late day, six-foot-five-inch Tom Darcy was scraping the fat from the meat off the floor. Darcy's routine was to squeeze the fat into a pile, then scoop it up and throw it into a nearby bin. As Darcy continued throwing the piles of fat towards the large bin, and without a need to look at the bin as he flung the fat, he heard the noise of over 20 pounds of fat hitting the floor – a noise much different than that of fat landing into a tub of discarded meat. Quickly looking to see what happened, he noticed Frannie's brother John and others hysterically laughing. John had moved the bin five feet past Darcy's throwing range. The relatively tall Darcy, however, was not in the mood for joking, immediately raising his shovel overhead and chasing the quick five-foot-seven-inch John Martin throughout the work area – to the roar of laughter echoing down the hall. The disagreement was only neutralized after the company mediator, brother Peter Martin, came from the office area to negotiate a truce.

The foundation for the continued success at Kyes Supply was Frannie Martin - a true-blue salesman. Frannie always wore a genuine, big smile and a personality to match, leading him to seal many a meat order. Frannie often repeated a phrase to customers when asked what meat they sold: "we sell beef, pork, lamb, veal, turkey, we have it all. If we don't have it, then you don't need it."[22] His gregarious natural personality was the perfect fit for a successful salesman and friend to all. Frannie's sales trips saw him traveling throughout New England, including Salisbury Beach, Hampton Beach, the University of New Hampshire, Waterville Valley, and several youth camps that catered to underprivileged children around Massachusetts and New Hampshire. As witnessed by fellow employees and clients, Frannie would stop by these precious camps, greeted by a gaggle of campers and counselors running out to greet the nice guy who could tell a good joke. Frannie's kind soul connected with the campers, shining through by talking about sports, school, families, and horses. These visits often ended with Frannie's encouragement to "keep up the good work, kid! See you next time!" There was never a "goodbye" with Frannie Martin in town.

In 1959, Frannie and Mary Connolly married in Brighton, with three kids joining them in the first five years of marriage. Before returning to the Boston area to help with her ailing father, Mary moved from the Boston area to Washington D.C. She found work with the Central Intelligence Agency (CIA), relocating agents abroad with new names, backgrounds, and living arrangements. If Frannie was the personality and vision of Nitram Stables, Mary was the voice of reason, supplying the needed discipline and wisdom. The family settled into a three-bedroom home in Quincy, with the two girls, Maryellen and Janice, sharing one bedroom and a bed, while older brother John had the third bedroom. From his Quincy home, Frannie lived 10-15 minutes from work by car – and another five minutes to the Suffolk Downs horse track. Peter, a lifelong bachelor, and uncle to many, lived his entire life where he began – Dorchester.

Whatever town the Martin brothers found themselves in throughout adulthood, they were incredibly proud to have grown up in Dorchester. They were "little guys" with big hearts. To their core, they believed in faith, family, and friends. They valued living a simple life where they worked hard, played fair, never lost hope, and always led with kindness. Perseverance, optimism, and good common sense guided their personal and business lives. You always walked away feeling better if you ran into the brothers at the meat shop, the racetrack, Quincy, or Dorchester.

Adulthood found the brothers catching up at various watering holes in Dorchester, notably the Eire Pub at 795 Adams Street. Opened in 1962, it was a classic Irish Pub, promoted initially as a "Men's Bar," the establishment later came to its senses with the inclusion of women. The bar was forever frequented by the regulars of Dorchester, which also hosted Presidents of the United States, governors, mayors, athletes, and actors, all making their way through the door to share pints of beer. By the decade's end, the Pub had a neighbor at 793 Adams Street. Frannie and Peter's oldest brother Harold and his wife Katherine were raising a family in Milton but could not resist the temptations of Dorchester and opportunity. Harold, with a guiding hand from Peter and his accounting acumen, opened "Adams Fish Market," running it with his wife and children in the center of Dorchester for over a decade. Most Friday afternoons saw local politicians and sports celebrities stopping by the Market to purchase fresh fish for the weekend. Friday afternoons also brought younger brother Frannie into the Market on his way home from Kyes Supply. Though Frannie intended to catch up with his brother, he was also armed with pounds of meat as he bartered his product in exchange for Harold's fresh fish for family dinners Mary would cook during the week ahead.

Saturday mornings for Frannie, for nearly 50 years, brought him back to the Adams Village section of Dorchester. The center of the village, Adams Corner, was named after the father and son who became Presidents of the United States. It was where Greenhills Irish Bakery was located – and where Frannie could often be found. Knowing of the limited on-street parking in the area, Frannie always parked behind the building, making his way through the back entrance and down the narrow hallway. Once at the front counter, Frannie had his pick of choices from breakfast or lunch, including an Irish breakfast sandwich, scones, Irish tea, and sweet raisin soda bread. Frannie often stayed for breakfast, sitting with friends or speaking with friendly faces nearby. On his way out, Frannie frequently brought scones home for the family, the famous Irish broiled dinner, or shepherd's pie.

In 1969, a company named Frank Bertolino Beef joined the businesses operating at Foodmart Road. Frank Bertolino and his parents came to the United States from Sicily, Italy, in 1956, making their home in Everett, Massachusetts. Frank could neither speak nor write English at the time. He worked with his cousin as a carpenter, building caskets for funeral homes. Within five years of immigrating to the country, and after saving enough money from the casket business, Frank created his meat business at age twenty-five. With a business that had outgrown its original building, the company's namesake moved it out of the Italian section of Boston known as the North End.

As the Italian from Sicily set up his business at Foodmart Road, one of the first individuals welcoming him was an Irishman from Dorchester - Frannie Martin – located just eight storefronts down from one another. The two began a life-long friendship with similar business interests and a love for horse racing. Bertolino Beef processed "hanging cattle" as their meat business was a "breaking house." With supermarkets as accounts, Bertolino Beef broke down the large hindquarters of the animals, cutting them down to the specifications of their customers. On the other hand, Kyes Supply was an institutional purveyor, a food line customer business shipping meats to their customers, such as chicken, pork, veal, lamb, and steak. Their product was shipped to hotels, universities, schools, and camps. With Bertolino Beef in the same building, Kyes Supply had access to a manual racking system attached to the ceiling, some 3oo yards long, with five different rails transporting the large hindquarters into the various meat businesses. Employees at Bertolino Beef would load 350-pound hindquarters, ten at a time, onto the rail located at their business. Employees from Kyes Supply had the task of pushing the racked meat from Bertolino Beef on the rail towards their business, eventually turning the rail switch, thereby directing the hindquarters from the main rail into the Martins business for storage in the freezers. These racks of meat were later broken down and distributed to clients throughout New England. During the 1970s, every week, one hundred orders of 350-pound hindquarters, ten per order, made their way down the rail from Bertolino Beef to Kyes Supply.

The latter part of the 1960s brought Frannie back to his parent's home on Centre Street on most Saturday mornings. Frannie took his young kids, John, Maryellen, and Janice, to visit with their grandparents before walking to the local stores on "Dot" Ave for whatever suited their tastebuds. The decade's end also reunited Frannie with the hockey scene in Boston as his son, John, went through the youth hockey leagues. Frannie's early years in Dorchester were spent playing the winter sport as his baseball games were done for the season. His time in the Dorchester Youth Hockey Leagues coincided with the first phase of the sport's explosion in New England, as countless French-Canadian kids brought their pastime with them as they made their way across the border, many settling into the schools and programs in

Massachusetts in the early to mid-20th century. During these years, ice hockey games on lakes and ponds throughout New England sprung up like tulips on grass lawns during the spring season. As soon as the outdoor ice thawed for the winter, the spring season brought street hockey games to the suburbs of Boston. The sport of street hockey in the city often required an extra task from its participants during the games - moving the nets to the side as parents navigated the streets while returning home from work.

Little did Frannie and his son know in the late 1960s, or anyone for that matter, that the city and region were about to be captivated by a professional hockey team with larger-than-life personalities, skills to match, and whose hold on the area still lives on more than fifty years later. For Dorchester, it meant a rabid hockey town that existed before the 1970s would find itself in the middle of the sport's second explosion - with neighborhood kids like Chris McCarron papering their walls with Bobby Orr posters.

The Boston Bruins of the late 1960s and 1970s were rock stars in the region – they were the Beatles. The team played in five Stanley Cup finals from 1970 to 1978, winning twice in 1970 and 1972. They transcended the sport of hockey, becoming cultural icons along the way as the New England region fell in love with them. Many prominent personalities were on the team, including Derek Sanderson, Johnny Bucyk, and Wayne Cashman. The core of the Bruins, without question though, were three players who arrived in the city within a year of one another – all later elected to the National Hockey League (NHL) Hall of Fame.

The Boston Bruins, in a six-team league, had missed the playoffs eight years in a row until a teenager by the name of Bobby Orr arrived. The 18-year-old kid from Canada, after playing four years in the Bruins minor league system, landed in Boston in 1966 and quickly became the savior of the franchise – and the league. With talents never before witnessed, Bobby Orr transformed the Bruins and the NHL. Orr won Rookie of the Year honors in his first season, followed by eight consecutive years as the league's best defenseman, three straight years as the league's most valuable player, and also led the league in scoring twice - as a defenseman. He revolutionized the position and the game of hockey, becoming the youngest player elected to the Hall of Fame at 31.

The talented Italian-Canadian Phil Esposito joined Orr on the Bruins in 1967 via a trade with the Chicago Blackhawks. In the 1968-1969 season, "Espo" became the first player in the league's history to score 100 points, tallying an unheard-of 126 points (goals plus assists). Esposito would exceed the 100-point season another four times, including a record 76 goals in the 1970-71 season, which lasted until Wayne Gretzky broke the mark in 1982 with 92.

Orr and Esposito formed a trifecta with a goalie from Canada named Gerry Cheevers, who had been drafted by Boston in 1965. After honing his craft in the minor leagues, Cheevers became the full-time goalie in 1967. Cheevers' flopping goalie style revolutionized the position. His personally designed goalie mask, a pattern of stitches across the entire face, became the most recognizable goalie mask in the game - one that served as the inspiration for modern-day goalie helmets.

Cheevers began his professional hockey career in the Ontario Hockey Association at the age of sixteen. Before finding greatness in hockey, Cheevers spent his youth working during the off-season at local horse tracks in Ontario. The young Cheevers earned $50 per week working at the tracks. Various jobs included hot-walking horses on the back stretch at Fort Erie, selling mutuel tickets to gamblers, and working in the publicity department at the Ontario Jockey Club. These early years taught the future Hall of Fame goalie to better understand horses and the business.

With his success in professional sports and the resulting monetary rewards, it seemed a natural fit for Cheevers to invest money in Thoroughbred racing while playing goalie for the Boston Bruins. Starting in 1972, after the Bruins's second Stanley Cup championship in three years, Cheevers began purchasing horses - slowly creating his stable of horses. During the 1975 fall season, Cheevers employed a stable agent for purchasing Thoroughbreds and a hired a trainer. With names of colts such as "Score for Orr," and "Bobby Orr," Cheevers called one of his racing stables "Four and Thirty." A stable name that Cheevers created by combining the jersey number (4) of the best hockey player in the world, Bobby Orr, and the jersey number (30) of a two-time Stanley Cup-winning goaltender.

Cheevers various non-hockey interests served as an example of the Renaissance men who dotted the Bruins roster. The Boston Bruins took over the town with their style while making themselves a fabric of the community. Players could be seen eating at the same restaurants, drinking at the same bars - and gambling at the same horse track. The team was part of the community's lexicon, both on and off the ice hockey rink, always a topic of discussion amongst people every day. Cheevers and the Bruins had a cross-over appeal that brought non-hockey fans into the team's fandom, with the public and media following the players' off-ice interests at every turn.

Though Cheevers was born in Canada, Boston saw him as one of their own. Cheevers toughness, grittiness, and blue-collar work ethic personified the people of Boston. Cheevers was an exuberant character of sorts while entertaining the media *before* hockey games. On the day of games, the goalie could often be found smoking large cigars after playing gin rummy card games with teammates in the locker room before he took the ice. It was not unusual for Cheevers to be seen in the Bruins locker room smoking cigarettes, drinking beers, and pouring through the Daily Racing Form – the daily horse racing newspaper Cheevers had delivered to the locker room.

After a critical stake's win by one of Cheevers' two-year-old colts in November 1976, which was broadcast in the Bruins locker room before one of their hockey games, left-winger Wayne Cashman could be heard bellowing, with strategic pauses between the last names, that "horse racing has the Vanderbilts, the Whitneys, and the Cheeverses."[23] The comedy of the goalie's name inserted into the same sentence as America's aristocracy produced the intended response, as the team with the best record in the National Hockey League spent their time belly-laughing as they dressed for the evening's game. As Suffolk Downs was just a quick car ride from their hockey rink at the Boston Garden, it was only natural for Cheevers and his teammates to find their way over to the horse track.

Cheevers found success early in thoroughbred racing. After pouring through the bloodlines of the one-year-old horses for sale in 1975, Cheevers purchased a colt for $20,500, which he would name Royal Ski. The chosen silks for Royal Ski were an odd-looking color combination of purple and gold. A color pattern Cheevers brought with him from his one season with the Cleveland Crusaders of the defunct World Hockey Association. Cheevers stable of horses had grown to 20 by 1976, with some, including the talented Royal Ski, stalled at Suffolk Downs. The Stanley Cup-winning goaltender turned horse owner often crossed the paths of brothers Frannie and Peter Martin in and around Suffolk Downs.

Frequenting the horse barns at Suffolk Downs during the 1970s was another set of brothers born and raised in Dorchester. Brothers Chris and Greg McCarron were two of nine siblings from an Irish family raised on Shenandoah Street. While the Martin brothers from Dorchester were toiling away running Nitram Stables at Suffolk Downs during the 1960s and 70s, Chris and Greg were racking up wins as jockeys. At Suffolk Downs in 1964, older brother Greg began perfecting his craft. Seven years younger and dreaming of playing professional hockey like Bobby Orr, Chris spent his early years on ice skates in the youth hockey leagues.

It wasn't until the summer of his junior year at Dorchester High School in 1971 that Chris put his hockey dreams to the side, hot walking horses and working as a groom for a trainer at Suffolk Downs and Rockingham Park in New Hampshire. Chris was still under the legal age of 18 years to enter the track, but due to his newfound employment, he no longer had to sneak into the track to watch his older brother. With a freckled face to match, the curly-haired redhead learned well by watching his brother throughout his early teenage years at Suffolk Downs. Chris became a rags-to-riches story himself. Less than two years removed from Dorchester High School and three years from brushing horses, he burst onto the national scene by setting a record for wins by a jockey in a season. The total wins record earned Chris an Eclipse Award as an Outstanding Apprentice Jockey in 1974. McCarron broke the record with win number 516 of the year by outracing his brother Greg at Laurel Race Course in Maryland, with their father Herb watching on in the stands, having flown in from Logan Airport in Boston that morning to watch his sons compete against each other.

Both sets of brothers from Dorchester, one cast as jockeys and the other as owners, awaited uncertain futures at racetracks across the country in the years ahead. What could never be predicted is that the collection of brothers, along with the hockey goalie from Canada doubling as a horse owner with stalls in Boston, would find their lives intersecting at racing's most significant events, with the owners and their horses considered a favorite for the Kentucky Derby.

Chapter 3
The New England Horse Racing Circuit: Only in Massachusetts

"Fair horses are cheap horses that are either too old, too weak or too tired to win on the regular circuit."[24]

During their barnstorming days at the elite racing tracks in 1981 and 1982, the Martin brothers were known for telling anyone who would listen that the last great horse to come out of Boston was a colt owned by the great Paul Revere. The colt, a favorite horse of one of the original patriots, transported Revere to towns north of Boston more than 100 years prior as he shouted to his fellow rebels, "The British are coming." The warning from Revere was that the occupying military forces of England were on the move in an attempt to quell a revolution they had on their hands. The tongue-in-cheek banter by the Martins as to the state of horse racing in New England, however, was not entirely inaccurate.

Though Timely Writer never made the historic ride from Lexington to Concord, he spent his years with the brothers, traveling from Boston, Massachusetts, to Miami, Florida, and many stops in between. Throughout the adventure, the colt left an imprint upon the places he and his owners visited, letting people know he and his entourage from Boston had arrived on the racing scene. As Timely Writer was a once-in-a-lifetime horse owned by a couple of "little guys" from Boston, the odd pairing inevitably brought many questions about the background of the colt and his owners. The answers to the inquiring minds would cement an even more profound affection for their loveable rag-to-riches story.

The horse racing careers of Frannie and his brothers first began during the early 1950s at what was known as the fair racing circuit in Massachusetts. Horse racing licenses in Massachusetts included weekly meets at various town fairgrounds from one end of the state to the other. At its zenith, the fair horse racing circuit consisted of 8 towns, each allotted an annual two-week license for thoroughbred racing. In addition to the Brockton Fair Grounds in the middle of the state, other horse racing fairground venues included Berkshire Downs, Great Barrington Fair, Marshfield Fair, Middleborough Fair, Northampton Fair, Topsfield Fair, and the Weymouth Fair. During its heyday, the circuit would run from spring to autumn as owners and trainers made their way to each of the eight towns. The midways of the fair traveled along with the horse racing circuit. Various food vendor trucks sold everything from fried dough to French fries, popcorn, and cotton candy, satisfying the patron's appetites as they gambled during the horse races. Despite suffering from a lack of quality horses and jockeys, the fair circuit drew significant crowds. The racing purses were small, and the horses were slow, but with Ferris wheels, tractor pulls, racing pigs, and lady mud wrestling, the gamblers and fair patrons were entertained.

Unlike the tracks found in Kentucky and New York a century prior, Massachusetts' fair horse racing circuit was not supported by men of significant wealth. It was a blue-collar crowd of owners and trainers with other full-time jobs who brought a ragtag approach to the "Sport of Kings." Some of the owners often doubling as the trainer and groom. At times, owners were gambling on horses that were competing against their own. Although the fair horses were not nearly the talent level of thoroughbreds found at the elite race tracks on the East Coast, the grin on the faces of the owners as they stood in the winner's circle with their prized possessions was nearly equal to the scene found in the winner's circle after the running of the Kentucky Derby.

Frannie's second full-time job, though the first love of his life, began in the early 1950s as he worked by the side of his older brothers on the fair racing circuit– less than 20 years after the sport of thoroughbred racing was declared lawful in his home state. Horse racing would become Frannie's second job for more than forty years. Like many of their contemporaries, the brothers learned the business and craft of thoroughbred racing at the various fairgrounds spread throughout the state. It was at the Brockton Fairgrounds where Frannie first started in the industry. The Brockton Fair, built in the city's center, had existed since October 6, 1880, with the first thoroughbred race run at the ½ mile oval track in September of 1941.

Frannie, similar to his rendition of the "Paul Revere" story, loved to tell people and journalists during his years at the prestigious tracks of New York, Florida, and Kentucky about the success he had as an owner on the fair racing circuit in Massachusetts. Unlike other wealthy Kentucky and New York tracks, the Brockton Fair horse racing track ran on a much smaller surface, affectionately called the "bull ring." The tracks more than lived up to the nickname, as they were known for their hairpin turns, short sprints to the finish line, jockeys swiping at one another with their riding crops to gain an advantage, and some somewhat questionable finishes.

One of Frannie and Peter's horses, Red Holly, who they purchased for $750.00, won an important 1- and 1/16-mile race at the Brockton Fairgrounds in September 1958 – setting a track record at the distance which stood until the fairgrounds discontinued thoroughbred racing in 2020. Frannie would sheepishly grin when telling the winning story of Red Holly, often laughing as he made his way through the story of the race and its aftermath. As Frannie recounted, it was a bittersweet victory for Red Holly the day he blazed across the finish line in first place. After finishing first, the jockey for Red Holly began slowing the horse down by pulling up on his reins. Red Holly, though, with the hard tug of the reins from the jockey, immediately collapsed onto the dirt track. Luckily, the jockey dismounted from Red Holly and escaped injury. However, Red Holly was flat on the ground and not moving much.

As the jockey stood beside the horse, looking down in disbelief, Frannie and his brother John ran to his aid. First observations by the brothers saw the colt's eyes darting around within his sockets. Frannie spent time soothing the horse, including closing his eyelids. After a short time, Red Holly looked better, with the colt's eyes re-focusing. The brothers raised and steadied the horse, accompanying Red Holly to the winner's circle. Frannie never knew the medical reason as to why Red Holly fell shortly after crossing the finish line. To his attentive audience, though, he chalked it up to a severe case of dizziness. After all, Frannie figured his prized horse had to circle the small oval track and its tight corners far too many times over the one and 1/16-mile distance. The short track, its tight turns, and the speed of Red Holly circling the oval track led Frannie to diagnose his prized colt with a short-term case of vertigo.

The Martin brothers' time and success on the fair racing circuit coincided with the change of ownership at the Brockton Fairgrounds in 1957. Brockton businessman and entrepreneur George Carney purchased the Fairgrounds, the 43-acre site in the middle of the city, and its horse racing dates. Nicknamed "The City of Champions," boxing gyms dotted many of Brockton's Street corners, with retired undefeated heavyweight champion Rocky Marciano one of its own – the champ growing up a short distance from the fair and forever calling the city his home.

Carney was born and schooled in the ways of business in the city of Brockton. He dropped out of high school in 9th grade to learn at the side of his saloon keeper father. A rugged, charismatic, and larger-than-life personality, Carney earned respect from owners, trainers, and patrons in the horse and dog racing industries, creating countless jobs while navigating in and around the minefields laid out by the politicians of Massachusetts.

Upon purchasing the Brockton Fairgrounds, Carney improved every facet of the experience. He marketed the Fair as the total family experience for everyone, with a dash of patriotism mixed in, as depicted during the 1959 Brockton Fair when Army military helicopters performed while simulating an air rescue operation under battle conditions. Carney brought in musicians and celebrities to entertain the crowds, paying members of the popular Howdy Doody television show and later dispatching them to Brockton Hospital children's ward for a private performance. The Fair included auto thrill shows, demolition derbies, horse pulling and performances, arts and crafts, and thoroughbred horse racing. Carney was a businessman who knew how to entertain. Opening day on September 13, 1959, saw more than 40,000 people enter the gates.

The 1960s and 70s saw Carney tinkering with his product, improving it for the patrons, including changing Fair Week to July 4th, with more patriotic events and firework shows added. He also cared for the horsemen, increasing purse money for the owners beyond the standard first four horses to cross the finish line. Carney looked out for the "little guys" in the racing business, as he also increased trainer and groom fees. For blue-collar guys like Frannie Martin and his brothers from Dorchester, who were looking to make a start in a sport they loved, Carney provided opportunities that would not have otherwise existed.

Carney had a larger vision regarding the business end of the fair and thought big. Suffolk Downs prided itself for more than fifty years as the Boston venue where the Beatles played their music to an audience of 25,000 people. It was the last stop on their United States tour in 1966. In reality, the idea of bringing the Beatles to Boston came from Carney. In March of 1964, as reported by the *Boston Globe* in a headline reading "Brockton Fair Invites Beatles,"[25] Carney sent a telegram to manager Harry Epstein offering to pay the band $100,000 to play at the Brockton Fair during the July 4th week. Though arrangements could not be made for George, Ringo, Paul, and John to play on the grass infield of the thoroughbred track, Carney showed people and his hometown he was a serious businessman and would be around for a while.

The king of fair racing venues in Massachusetts, though, was located in Berkshire County - in the rural town of Great Barrington. As the town borders the eastern part of New York, Berkshire County is the furthest western county in the state. It finds itself closer to New York's capital in Albany than its capital in Boston. The fair racing venues throughout the state could not compare to that found in the Great Barrington, as the town and its fair were nestled next to the Berkshire Mountains. It was the most popular stop on the circuit due to its amenities and the sheer beauty of its surroundings.

Horse racing at the Great Barrington Fair ran every year from 1940 through 1983, serving as the last stop on the fair racing circuit as summer turned to autumn in New England. As bettors stood before the rail of the track, the hint of the coming fall season could be seen in the hills behind the venue. Looking past the weeping willow trees dotting the back side of the ½ mile track, the leaves from the trees were beginning to change color.

People making their way to the fair grandstand at Great Barrington were treated with unusual comfort. With seatbacks attached to fold-up seats spaced out every eighteen inches for the bettors, the discomfort of metal benching did not exist for its customers in the grandstand seating area. People could even sit at a table in a separate clubhouse area of the fairgrounds for a little extra money. However, the races and finishes at Great Barrington found similar difficulties as the other venues. Andy Beyer, a Harvard student in the early 1960s, spent much time watching and analyzing horses at nearby Suffolk Downs. Assembling data from different tracks, Beyer spent his post-Harvard years calculating variables such as speed figures and track conditions to determine the better horse in any given race. In 1978, while the turf writer for the *Washington Post*, Beyer spent an entire year at various tracks throughout the country, putting his formula to work while chronicling it for a future book. Beyer's book, *My Fifty Thousand Dollar Year*, included the story of the only track he left early.

Colleagues warned Beyer about putting his formula to work at the Great Barrington Fair. Stories relayed about long-shot horses bet down to odds of 1-9 due to significant amounts of money placed on inferior horses. As one particular race began at Great Barrington, the horses considered the favorites were steered by their jockeys to the outside rail. The jockeys using the tactic to slow down their horses to clear the way for the long shot made the favorite. Another story around the fair track centered on a jockey who could not get his horse to slow down as he led the race. The jockey's answer to the problem was to "fall" from his saddle, disqualifying the horse under the rules and ensuring his horse lost.

Undaunted by the cautionary tales, Beyer put his mathematical formulas to work at the unspoiled turf nestled amongst the mountains in the Berkshires. Beyer, however, would never finish his day at the Great Barrington races, leaving earlier than expected after losses climbed to one thousand five hundred dollars. It was apparent the formula Beyer created to ensure gambling success would not work on the fair racing circuit. The flaw in the system Beyer created was that it could not calculate human intervention as a variable within the mathematical formula. Despite the challenges of picking winners at the Great Barrington Fair, the track's beauty and benefits were forever appreciated by its patrons as they watched the horse races throughout the day.

Due to its location in the city's center, Brockton Fair's horse racing was the polar opposite of that found in Berkshire County. It had energy and action daily. It was horse racing in the town of Marshfield, though, which personified the fair racing circuit. Marshfield had neither the largeness of Brockton's footprint in the center of a city nor the space of the countryside fair set in Great Barrington. With space as a commodity, Marshfield Fair parked cars in the infield of its ½ mile track during days of horse racing. The nearby dusty stalls included horse-chewed wooden doors marking the years since they had been replaced, with the summer dust and dirt from the barn area covering the clothes of the nearby patrons.

Marshfield Fair was where families could overlook the inherent daily discomforts while spending quality time connecting through the trappings of carnival rides, horse racing, and countless other festivities. It was where dads and moms could bring the kids during the weekdays while school was off for the summer. Experienced dads knew to park the car in the track's infield before the races began, bringing the kids to the midway at the fairgrounds where the rides were located. After purchasing several fair-ride tickets and giving the kids money for games and the dunking booth, many dads took the short walk to the horse track for some time alone. There was enough time during the afternoon for a beer, the best batch of fair fries, and gambling on a couple of horse races. With no cellular telephones saddled to their sides, dads could take in the innocence of an afternoon at the horse races with the pre-determined final meeting place for him and the kids at the dunking booth once the last race finished.

Large crowds gathered at the dunking booth to watch dads attempt to impress kids by throwing their best pitch at the bullseye a distance away.

Dunking the clown sitting on the wooden bench into the water with a fastball to the center of the target was no small feat. The pressure of constant jokes and insults from the wise-cracking clown, with kids and the crowd laughing along, made many a man less than courageous as they launched a fastball wide of the intended target.

It was at the racetrack of the Marshfield Fair where additional entertainment could always be found – leaving many fans shaking their heads and laughing about the questionable finishes. Stories of horse racing shenanigans and events from the day, never seen at elite racing tracks, occurred regularly at the fair. On one particular day, Marshfield Fair had scheduled a special trotters race as part of the program. Trotter races are unlike anything seen at the typical thoroughbred racetrack. In a trotter race, the jockeys are directing the horse, though not from the saddle atop the horse, but in a two-wheeled cart with reins connected to the horse. The jockey sits on the small cart, directing his colt or filly from the reins running from his hands to the horse's sides. The ½-mile oval track at the Marshfield Fair was much tighter than the typical one-mile thoroughbred track. As the events of the day have been repeated over the years, one particular horse and his driver were being pressed by another competitor along the inside rail - with his competitor's two-wheeled cart running parallel to the right-handed side of the horse. The horse became nervous and anxious early in the race as his competitor was still running alongside. Along the back stretch of the track, an opening on the inner rail appeared as an entry to the infield – which was used as a gate for parking cars before the start of races. As the horse neared the vacant space of the inner rail, and in the blink of his driver's eyes, the horse and his carriage took a quick left into the infield of the horse track. Patrons watching from the top of the grandstand saw the horse, his driver, and the cart racing through an aisle of cars parked on both sides. As the racehorse frantically sought his safe place free from competitors, the horse cart and its driver bounced off the rear of the parked motor vehicles. The runaway horse came to a screeching halt after losing his balance due to the horse-cart careening off cars behind him. Fortunately, the horse and jockey landed unscathed on the infield. The horse was declared medically fit, though he needed a new cart for the next race.

Daily activities at the Marshfield Fair also allowed the teenagers to explore the boundaries of summer fun at the race track. Across the horse track, located under the grandstands at Marshfield, young teenage boys could be found near the betting windows searching out an older brother or friend, or even a sympathetic adult, to place their gambling dollars. Once the horse races finished in the late afternoon, many of the same boys headed to the carnival rides, seeking out girls they had last seen when school ended in June.

On the last day of the fair, when the final horse race had finished, owners organized horse transport vans to prepare for the next town races. The owner's horses, who frequently lost and would not be entering future races, were given away on sight to various organizations, farms, or families. As these owners left one town for another over the summer, they brought their colorful, charismatic, and passionate personalities to each destination—owners who were in it for the love and excitement of horse racing. Trainer Carlos Figueroa, with his pencil-thin mustache, signature Panama hat, bright Hawaiian shirts, overly starched white linen paints, and Ferrari sunglasses, epitomized the larger-than-life characters found on the fair racing circuit. A native of San Juan, Puerto Rico, Carlos first traveled to New York in 1949 to work at horse tracks. Once established, he brought his business and family to New England in the 1950s. Carlos quickly made his presence known on the fair racing circuit while stabling horses at Rockingham Park in New Hampshire and Suffolk Downs in Boston. It was the fair circuit, though, where Carlos' personality flourished.

After much success on the fair circuit, Carlos designed a large wooden sign that traveled with him from one town to the next. One of his first tasks after settling into the horse barn that his not-so-talented equines were assigned was hanging the sign proclaiming "King of the Fairs" outside the horse barn. During the races, Carlos could often be seen in the grass infield, standing atop farm tractors, arms flailing away, urging on his horses in his heavily accented second language of English.

As one story goes with Carlos, during the spring of 1963, he purchased a horse for $70 called Shannon's Hope. Carlos immediately put the horse to work on the fair circuit. Shannon's Hope won his first four races – one each day for four straight days. On Day five, Shannon's Hope was scheduled for a day off, though word got out about his record-setting accomplishments. Day 5 brought a representative from the American Society for the Prevention of Cruelty to Animals (ASPCA) to his horse barn for a visit. The representative met Carlos in the early morning at the barn to check on the fitness of Shannon's Hope, also informing Carlos that such a race schedule was cruel to the horse. Carlos respectfully disagreed, telling the representative, "the horse is bred to run. He likes to run. It's in his blood. One hour after the race, he's ready to jump over cars."[26]

Like Frannie, Carlos also had his own Paul Revere story, explaining to the representative that Massachusetts made a hero from a jockey named Paul Revere. Unlike Paul Revere, though, Carlos said he was running Shannon's Hope on an even dirt strip, not through the woods of Lexington and Concord, and using a light jockey on Shannon's Hope, not one the size of Paul Revere. After listening to Carlos and examining Shannon's Hope, the representative indicated the colt was fit to race and left without taking any action against Carlos. Day six brought another race for Shannon's Hope - and another win - 5 wins in 6 days for a $70 horse who somehow brought about historical comparisons to the "Ride of Paul Revere."

Boston Globe journalist Michael Blowen, during his years visiting horse tracks, got to know Carlos professionally and personally. Michael's shared stories of Carlos, some of which made their way into his newspaper articles, involve Carlos telephoning the press box at Suffolk Downs to speak with journalists about news stories they should write – most of which centered upon his success as a trainer. Blowen described Carlos this way: "he was one of the brightest, funniest people I've ever met, and under other circumstances, he might have been in the [Racing] Hall of Fame. But those circumstances never showed themselves."[27]

The circuit was many things to many people, including the ground floor for opportunity. Similar to the story of the Martins' ascension from the minor leagues of horse racing is the early resume of Jim Raftery – the photographer who found the brothers from Dorchester in the center of his camera lens at the winner's circle of Hialeah Park in Miami during March of 1982. Raftery grew up on Commonwealth Avenue in Boston, taking various jobs as a teenager and young adult at race tracks around New England. Such jobs included exercising polo horses, galloping thoroughbreds, schooling jumpers, and selling frankfurters at hot dog stands. Raftery would lead the first set of horse entries onto the track at Rockingham Park in New Hampshire on opening day in 1933. Raftery also gave the jockey business a chance, winning his first horse race at age twenty in 1935 at the Marshfield Fair - preceding the Martins' appearance by nearly twenty years.

Not pleased with his jockey career, Raftery eventually changed professions, but only after picking up a camera abandoned near his hot dog stand at a Tampa Bay, Florida, horse track. Raftery took the camera home, finding a passion and profession he pursued for the remainder of his life - taking countless photographs for racetracks from Massachusetts to Florida. A career first started at a hot dog stand led Raftery down a path "photographing some of the most prominent guests to visit racetracks, including Winston Churchill, Bob Hope, Grace Kelly, Harry Truman, and the Duke and Duchess of Windsor. Raftery would become one of the best professional photographers in American horse racing history for over a half-century." [28]

Years after his passing, the National Museum of Racing and Hall of Fame in Saratoga Springs, New York, with the help of photographer Barbara Livingston, recognized Jim Raftery's work in the summer of 2022 by presenting his finest works. Raftery's photographs at the museum captured people's everyday lives without regard to economic status. From patrons to track workers to celebrities and sports stars, all those photographed displayed the enjoyment found at the various gathering spots tucked into the corners throughout each horse track. Photographs in Raftery's portfolio also included the legends of racing - a historical time capsule of elite horses, jockeys, and trainers - and the famous flamingos residing at Hialeah Park. If one were to pause and observe the walls supporting Jim Raftery's work at the museum in Saratoga Springs in July of 2022, a not-so-hidden homage was paid to Jim and the pink flamingos' years at Hialeah. The palette of choice decorating the walls behind the Raftery collection was a light pink pastel.

As Jim Raftery accomplished a generation before them, Frannie and Peter's success on the fair circuit launched them onto the horse racing circuits at more accomplished tracks in New England. Hard-earned money from their meat business allowed them to develop a stable of better-quality horses. Nitram Stables focused on Suffolk Downs in Boston and Rockingham Park in Salem, New Hampshire—which sat just one hour north of Suffolk Downs.

At Rockingham Park in Salem, New Hampshire, thoroughbred horse racing first became legal in New England. The "Rock," as it was affectionately called, was built in 1906 and hosted motorized racing and gambling on weekends in the early years. Lou Smith, who would become the leading figure in horse racing in New England over the next sixty years, opened the Rock for horse racing on July 1, 1931 - though without state-authorized approval. Racing lasted for six days before the Attorney General shut the racetrack down. Lou spent the next eighteen months getting the politicians in line, with the appropriate legislation filed and approved, before re-opening on June 21, 1933. Three-year-old Seabiscuit began racing at Rockingham as just another horse in 1935 and 1936 - not winning a race in his six attempts.

With New Hampshire legalizing horse racing on the northern border of Massachusetts, Rhode Island legalized it the following year on the state's southern border – and Rhode Island was having a grand time at it and making buckets of money. Narragansett Track, affectionately known as "Gansett," opened its doors in 1934 in Pawtucket, Rhode Island, the smallest state in the union, ending its ban on horse racing, first enacted in 1777. Conveniently located about one hour south of Boston, it offered a state-of-the-art one-mile oval dirt surface and a new highway constructed nearby, sporting an off-ramp leading directly to the track's parking lots. Trains nicknamed the "Narragansett Special" brought customers directly to the train station from the north in Boston and from the south in New Haven, Connecticut. Twenty-two horse barns with over 1,000 stalls were immediately available for racing on Labor Day in 1934, housing the best horses from the likes of the wealthy Vanderbilt family and Calumet Farm. A crowd of 37,281 customers showed up on opening day- the largest sporting event in the history of Rhode Island to this day. The track reported a net profit of just over two million dollars for the first two years.

Gansett was strategically placed approximately 45 minutes from the summer resort of Newport and its high society clientele. Attendees on opening day included former heavyweight boxing champion Jack Dempsey, Alfred Vanderbilt, Jr., the great-grandson of the wealthiest man in the world, and the founder of the family fortune Cornelious Vanderbilt. Also attending was Cornelius Vanderbilt Whitney, whose parents' marriage merged two of the noblest and wealthiest families in the country. New York Yankees teammates Babe Ruth and Lou Gehrig also frequented the track in the first few years. The track served as the venue for the maiden race for an unknown colt at the time called Seabiscuit. The colt raced another six times throughout his career at Gansett. War Admiral, the 1937 Triple Crown Winner, visited the smallest state in the country in 1938. After winning the MassCap earlier in the year at Suffolk Downs, War Admiral raced and won the lucrative Gansett stakes race. 1942 Triple Crown winner Whirlaway duplicated the same feet, taking the MassCap and Gansett in 1943.

Other states outside New England, though, were more than a half-century ahead of the region in the business and sport of Thoroughbred horse racing. Kentucky hosted its first official horse race in 1828, with New York following suit in 1863. Due to the conservative religious influence of the Puritans in Massachusetts, who were motivated by their desire to leave organized sport behind them, politics prevented legalized gambling on horse racing in the state until 1935. In all likelihood, Massachusetts would not have changed its ways for some time but for the economic depression crushing the country and its state. Massachusetts was desperate for additional revenues for its government-sponsored programs. Legalizing gambling with a horse track in Boston was their financial cure – and a trough for politicians and their friends to feed upon for the remainder of the century.

Suffolk Downs was one of the country's most interesting tracks ever built. It was constructed in just two months in 1935. Within its geographic footprint lay a horse track on the east side of the City of Boston and horse barns in neighboring Revere. Neighborhoods in Revere were situated across from the horse barn area. A wooden fence erected by Suffolk Downs served as a barrier separating the neighborhoods in Revere from the horse barns and racing track – though nothing could be done about the odor coming from the thirty tons of horse manure produced per day lingering through the nearby homes.

Once the horse owners, trainers, and jockeys passed the wooden fence and horse barns to the track, a line of Evergreen trees greeted them along the track's backstretch with a kidney-shaped pond in the grass infield. Kids from the neighborhoods of East Boston, Revere, and Dorchester were known for sneaking into the track from this area. A belly slide under the wooden fence across the streets from the neighborhoods of Revere, followed by a quick dart to the Evergreens along the backstretch, allowed the under-age, non-paying patrons to watch the races for free. This same entry point also permitted people of all ages access during the winter months — the sizeable frozen pond served as the surface for ice skating and hockey games.

Adults, young and old alike, too proudful or just too weighty to sneak under the fence by the stables during the racing season, drove up to the top of the hill in Revere overlooking the racetrack. Many a dad brought his kids to watch high-quality horse racing on Saturday afternoons from the streets of Orient Heights. Whether the location was from the top of a hill, under the evergreen trees, or from the grandstand of the race track, patrons saw Seabiscuit and other legends run in Boston regularly. Large audiences at the racetracks during its early years proved the public was willing to part with their money for a sport that provided a welcome distraction during difficult times. An underdog horse named Seabiscuit came along at the right time for the country. At Suffolk Downs, Seabiscuit would begin his legend, captivating a country well into the next decade. Seabiscuit ran eight times at Suffolk Downs, including five days after Suffolk opened its doors – finishing 4th in the Mayflower Stakes as a two-year-old colt. Less than a year later, on June 29, 1936, trainer Tom Smith first eyeballed three-year-old Seabiscuit. Smith was at Suffolk Downs at the direction of horse owner and businessman Charles Howard. Smith stood at the rail, staring at one particular horse. Smith recalled:

"he looked down his nose at me, like he was saying 'Who the devil are you?' I stared right back at him, I liked his looks. He was on his way to the post in a three-quarter race. No, I didn't know his name. Checked on my program for that – Seabiscuit, three-year-old, good breeding. Mr. Howard and I were looking for that kind, if they could show us anything. He showed me quite a lot. Acted up a bit at the gate, broke slowly, began to move up on the far turn and coming home he ran over horses. Won going away in 1:11 4/5. When he came back to the stands, I nodded at him. Dammed if the little rascal didn't nod back at me kinda like he was paying me an honor to notice me."[29]

Charle Howard bought Seabiscuit at Saratoga Race Course at Smith's urging in August. Under Smith's direction, with jockey Red Pollard now in the saddle, the legend of Seabiscuit was off and running, including a win at the Massachusetts Handicap in 1937. Over the decades to come, other Hall-of-Fame Thoroughbreds made their mark at Suffolk Downs. The future hall of famer Stymie and future patient of Dr. William Reed was at the height of his racing career when he entered the MassCap in 1947. Previous race winners included Seabiscuit in 1939 and Triple Crown winner Whirlaway in 1942. As the field of entries turned for the homestretch after the last far turn, Stymie was far back as he waited to make his stretch run. Suddenly, Stymie went to another level of speed unlike that seen by patrons at Suffolk Downs. Stymie caught the field of entries in front of the grandstand, surging ahead through the finish line, becoming the first horse to earn over $700,000 in career earnings.

Though Suffolk Downs hosted elite horses over the decades, the track and its city never had the "big horse" to call their own. It would take over forty years from the opening of Suffolk Downs until such a horse took up full-time residence in the city on a hill. Timely Writer's future owners' rise from the fledgling fair racing circuit to a full-time stable at Suffolk Downs overlapped with the change of ownership at the track in East Boston. A publicly owned company called Reality Equities purchased Suffolk Downs in 1969, bringing in an experienced sports director and former owner of major league baseball teams by the name of William Veeck, Jr. Veeck's resume included owning the St. Louis Browns, Cleveland Indians, and Chicago White Sox - though he knew next to nothing about horse racing.

Veeck was born in Chicago in 1914, working part-time jobs as a kid for the Chicago Cubs at Wrigley Field. The young Veeck was a popcorn vendor for the Cubs during the day and a concession salesman for the cross-town rival Chicago White Sox at Comiskey Park during the night. His father was a local sportswriter who also worked for Chicago Cubs owner William Wrigley, Jr., who died suddenly in 1933 when the younger Veeck was 19. The young and well-educated Veeck gained notoriety while working for the Cubs in 1937, creating an idea of planting ivy on the outfield walls at Wrigley.

The dawn of World War II in the 1940s found Veeck enlisting in the United States Marine Corps, serving in the artillery unit for three years before a piece of artillery seriously injured his right leg. The injury led to the amputation of Veeck's right leg from the knee down, resulting in Veeck using a series of wooden legs over the years. Shortly after Veeck's return from the war, he sold a financial interest he had with the Triple-A Milwaukee Brewers, parlaying it into the purchase of the Cleveland Indians in 1947. The following season, Veeck was at the helm when the Cleveland Indians won the baseball World Series. Veeck brought sound business practices and entertainment to every sports business. In 1951, Veeck signed the 3' 7" Eddie Gaedel to a baseball contract. Gaedel wore the number 1/8 on his jersey, making his only appearance in the major leagues by drawing a four-pitch walk. Veeck also hired Max Patkin, the "clown prince of baseball." Veeck installed Patkin as the first base coach, with his new coach wearing a baseball uniform and his clown face.

Veeck eventually sold the Cleveland team, using the money to purchase the Chicago White Sox in 1959. The White Sox appeared in their first World Series in 40 years and broke attendance records. Veeck's time as owner of the White Sox included implementing the first exploding scoreboard. Due to failing health, Veeck sold his percentage of the White Sox in 1961 for $2.5 million. After regaining his health and unable to close on the purchase of what would have been his 4th major league baseball team, Veek drew interest from Realty Equities. They brought in the maverick and businessman Bill Veeck as the director for Suffolk Downs. The Boston politicians and media, awaiting Veeck's appearance, looked forward to educating the Chicago businessman about business in their city.

Veeck went to work immediately at Suffolk, implementing creative promotions and rehabbing the facility. A complete makeover of the facility was begun, including plenty of new paint to cover the original coats from 1936, new railings, upholstered seats, and demolition of the draconian bathrooms, which had 10-cent coin slots for toilet use. On Veeck's watch, everyone could use the bathroom for free.

Regarding horse racing, Veeck sped up the time between races, reducing it from 30 to 27 minutes, slashed entrance fees in half for senior citizens, and welcomed children into the park. Veeck was determined to create a welcoming environment, including a family atmosphere. On Mother's Day, free petunias were given out to all moms. In a business dominated by men since its inception, and in an era when female jockeys had to go to court to ride as jockeys, Veeck created the "Lady Godiva Race," which was the first ever horse race limited to only female jockeys. It was delightful irony for Veeck when Penny Ann Early was the jockey who won the inaugural Lady Godiva Race. Anna won her lawsuit the previous year against the state of Kentucky after Churchill Downs refused to give the more than qualified female jockey her license.

Veeck also showed his tough-minded business side during his term at Suffolk Downs, not backing down to entrenched Massachusetts politicians or racing competitors in Rhode Island, New Hampshire, and even within Massachusetts. Veeck brought a lawsuit against the State Racing Commission, forcing it to allow minors into the track in the company of their parents. Veeck maneuvered to obtain additional racing dates for Suffolk Downs by purchasing the defunct Berkshire Downs in the western part of Massachusetts, promptly transferring the racing dates to Suffolk Downs after the sale. When the politicians and its racing commission members refused to give Veeck the extra racing dates he lawfully purchased, he brought them to court – and won. Veeck also refused to play along with the political shake-downs awaiting his arrival.

In Veeck's first year in Boston, Suffolk Downs received a real estate tax bill for $613,000. Rather than pay it in full, Veeck delegated an assignment for his lawyers and accountant, having them obtain an independent assessment for the valuation of the property. Once received, Veeck filed for an abatement on the tax assessment, winning again and receiving a reduction in the tax bill of $58,500. Undeterred, the City of Boston reassessed the property the following year, sending a tax bill for $859,339.47. Once again, convinced inflation from one year to the next did not justify a nearly $250,000 tax increase, Veeck challenged the city. A few weeks later, after sending in his independent property valuation, the city issued Veeck a check for $623,823.63. Veeck offered this observation about running a business in Boston: "[w]hen you're operating a racetrack you find the politicians coming around, eyes agleam. They don't want their pictures taken, and they expect you to sign every tab. It's a different ballgame. You're looked upon as a little bank to shake something out of."[30] "The one thing the politicians have succeeded in doing has been to create an atmosphere in which it is felt that nothing can be done without paying somebody off."[31]

Veeck was a man of many cities, businesses, and experiences over his lifetime. Boston, though, was a city unlike any he had experienced. In his book, *"Thirty Tons a Day,"* which was self-titled based upon the amount of horse manure removed from the racetrack per day, Veeck described his experience navigating the business of horse racing with the politicians of Boston as his "partners":

> "It is impossible to get involved in something as closely tied to politics as horseracing without coming out with the distinct impression that politics is the principal industry of Boston and, quite probably, the whole of the Great Commonwealth. The politicians come at you like a swarm of locusts."[32]

One of Veeck's more interesting alliances and lasting friendships in Boston was with Brockton businessman George Carney. By the end of the 1960s, Carney's racing empire included thoroughbred racing dates at the Brockton, Weymouth, and Middleboro Fairgrounds, with a dog racing track in Raynham. Also in Carney's sights at the time was a dog track in New Hampshire and obtaining controlling interest at Rockingham Park. Veeck, the outsider from Chicago, found a man cut from his own cloth in Carney. "George Carney, a slim dark-haired Irishman, has a little of the empire builder in him too. The first time I saw him, which was during the commission hearing on the dates, he assaulted the commissioners in blunt, exuberant language out of nothing more than high spirits and the sheer joy of harassing the Establishment. He was young and restless and bursting with ambition – the boy had style."[33] The thirty-five-year-old Carney became a natural ally of Veeck, with the two of them taking on racing and its antiquated political system.

Over his two years at Suffolk Downs, Bill Veeck produced two of the track's better financial years while increasing attendance from the previous years. Realty Equities, the publicly owned company that owned Suffolk Downs, however, was in financial hardship. The company decided to sell Suffolk Downs for $11.5 million, forever ending the stewardship of Bill Veeck. The politics and the business of horse racing in Boston soured Veeck as he left Suffolk Downs and longed for a return to the sport and business of major league baseball.

In 1975, Veeck repurchased the Chicago White Sox, bringing his ideas and entertainment to the world of sports. Veeck was the one who coaxed White Sox announcer Harry Caray to sing "Take Me Out to the Ballgame" during the seventh-inning stretch of every home game – a song and practice that endured the test of time. Upon leaving Boston, the one friendship Veeck kept throughout the decade and beyond was George Carney. Veeck from Chicago kept an eye on Carney in Boston as he continually battled politicians sitting atop the state house on Beacon Hill. "The more I got to know him, and I got to know him quite well, the more of that abiding deep-seated reservation I came to see in him. He played the game as well as it could be played, and yet he played it with the overbalancing bravado of a man who was laughing to maintain some core of personal honor -pure and intact – and inside himself." [34]

After Veek departed from Suffolk Downs, the slow, steady decline of the racetrack began and continued throughout the decade, earning it the nickname of "Suffering Downs" from its regulars. At one point, 17 horse tracks were conducting horse racing in five New England States. The good ole days, however, were gone forever with the closure of Narragansett Race Track in Rhode Island in 1978.

Fortunately, the chaos of Suffolk Downs and the politics of Massachusetts didn't much affect the daily routine of the Martin brothers throughout the 1970s. They were winning some races, had plenty of fun, and made plenty of friends. During these years, the most talented horseman the Martins ever met was a transplant from Ireland named Tony Everard. After coming to the country in 1958, Everard made his way to Rhode Island the following year, settling in at Narragansett Park through a connection from an employer back home in Ireland. Everard, who tamed his first horse at the age of eleven, began training at the horse stable of Jim Beaty at Narragansett Park. Everard found himself, just a couple of years removed from his home back in Ireland, moving in and around horse barns at Narragansett adjacent to streets named War Admiral Place, Whirlaway Place and Seabiscuit Place.

Once the racing calendar concluded at Narragansett, Everard followed the racing circuit north to Suffolk Downs and Rockingham Park as the racing dates in New England rotated venues. Upon settling in at Suffolk Downs, Tony quickly found common interests and friendships with the Martin brothers, Dominic Imprescia and Frankie Bertolini. Asked to describe Everard's personality, Frannie spoke of a kindred spirit, "he likes to have a good time like me, a real character."[35] After spending just under a decade at the horse tracks throughout New England, the Everards relocated to the Miami area after horse owner Jim Beaty decided to ship his racing stable to the Sunshine State. With Tony relocated to Florida, the Martin brothers continued their slow and steady improvement at Suffolk Downs throughout the 1970s while purchasing useful horses through their now-relocated buyer's agent, Tony Everard, in Ocala.

Their friend and colleague Frank Bertolino joined the fun with the brothers at Suffolk Downs. Frank's entrance into the horse racing business was a bit unique, finding his first thoroughbred by way of his meat business. One particular customer owed the Italian American some money for several past-due meat orders. The unpaid debt continued for months as the man fell on hard times. Feeling bad about his client's situation, Frank was unsure what to do with the longstanding customer. Upon seeing the beautiful thoroughbred the customer owned, he made his client an offer he couldn't refuse. Frank proposed that he would cancel the debt in exchange for the horse. With the shake of a hand and the cancellation of the debt, Frank started his one-horse racing stable under the name San Fran Stables.

In 1975, Frank found a colt he adored named Country Monarch, leading to a stable name change to Monarch Stables. Frank believed so much in the colt's talent that he entered him into the prestigious Masscap the following year. Bertolino looked to match the success of a recent winner of the Masscap, the 1973 Kentucky Derby and Belmont Stakes winner Riva Ridge. The 1976 MassCap saw a fine effort from Country Monarch, with the colt finishing fourth place behind a Dorchester jockey named Chris McCarron. Though Bertollino came up a bit short in the MassCap, the year and the remainder of the decade saw him standing in several winners' circles - and finding his way into some of Frannie's circles for photo-ops with his dear friend.

Frannie Martin (second from right) & Frankie Bertolino (3rd from left) at Suffolk Downs in May of 1976.

As the decade of the 1970s was nearing an end, it brought the birth of a non-descript foal at an unremarkable breeding farm on April 21, 1979, in Ocala, Florida. The foal, a colt bred from two unremarkable and unraced thoroughbreds, spent the remainder of the year grazing in a pasture about a twenty-minute drive from Tony Everard's horse training center. The beautiful bay-colored colt continued to grow for the remainder of the year as his mother, Timely Roman, nursed him along into the new decade some eight months later.

In early 1980, Nitram Stables saw a sizable profit through the success of a colt they owned named Gavin's Turn – an "earner" for the Martin brothers at various tracks throughout the East Coast. The Martin brothers had purchased Gavin's Turn years earlier below their annual budget of ten thousand dollars. They were lucky to triple their investment in just one race when Gavni's Turn finished in second place at the Pennsylvania Futurity - the brothers pocketing $30,000.00 from the purse. With the winnings, the brothers put aside $10,000.00 for Tony Everard to purchase a "useful" horse for them later in the year. Unbeknownst to the brothers, the winnings from Gavin's Turn second place finish would forever change their lives over the next three calendar years.

Chapter 4
Birth of a Champion: Tony Everard & Finding Greatness

It was 1:30 a.m. on September 5, 1980, in a hotel room in Lexington, Kentucky, when Tony Everard telephoned his trusted friend and colleague Frannie Martin. The middle of the night phone call was to let Frannie know he had purchased a yearling at the Fasig-Tipton Preferred Yearling Sales on behalf of Nitram Stables – and needed to explain why he exceeded the Martins' budget of $10,000 by 35%. Much of the time on the phone, knowing Frannie routinely woke at 4:30 a.m. for work, Tony apologized for the late-night call, but it was imperative Frannie know about his purchase as the buyer's agent for Nitram Stables. With excitement in his thick Irish brogue, Everard explained the reasons.

Everard was no stranger to the yearling purchased on behalf of the Martins. Going into the sale, Everard intended to get a second look at one colt he had previously seen in Ocala, Florida. Everard first saw the colt at a breeding farm owned by Dorothy Davis. Tony's adopted hometown of Ocala is approximately halfway between Disney World in Orlando and Busch Gardens in Tampa Bay. As a result of its climate and geography, Ocala provides the perfect mix of weather for the business of horse breeding and training. Its location allows horse farms to work year-round, avoiding the colder winters of every state northward and the extreme heat of southern Florida.

Everard was well aware of the history and lineage of the colt he had just purchased for the Martins, explaining the colt's background to Frannie during the middle of the night conversation. Throughout 1978 and into 1979, a pregnant mare named Timely Roman was at Dorothy Davis' barn. Timely Roman's partner was a stallion named Staff Writer. Timely Roman would deliver the foal at the end of her eleven-month pregnancy in April

1979. The 90-pound colt stood within the hour of his birth. Like all the other weanlings, the colt would spend the next six months of his life nursing his mother while living alongside other colts, fillies, and their mares at the Davis farm. The first few months for a newborn foal focus on diet, nutrition, and growing. A typical colt weighs in the area of 500+ pounds after the first six months. Like every other Thoroughbred, the colt would never have a relationship with his father (sire) and be taken from his mother (mare) in October to prepare for competitive horse racing.

As the colt was born a Thoroughbred, per rules within the horse racing industry, he and all the other foals born in 1979 were turning the age of one year on January 1, 1980. Upon turning one, the son of Timely Roman looked more than a year older compared with all the yearlings who were sharing the wide-open grass fields with him. He would continue to grow and strengthen through the summer months of 1980. Dorothy Davis scheduled a private showing in August for interested buyers for the yearlings at her farm, telephoning local trainer and buyer Tony Everard as one of the invites.

Everard followed up on the invite from Davis, taking the 20-minute drive from his training farm, Another Episode Farm, located on the other side of Ocala. Tony looked at more than 20 horses at the farm that morning, with none leaving any impression upon him - until he locked eyes on one particular colt. Everard turned to a colt whose physical appearance caused him to pause before looking towards the eyes. Everard's assessment of any young thoroughbred begins at the head of the horse - as he is looking for big, attentive eyes. Eyes that are curious in the surroundings. As Everard watched the unnamed colt turn his way, he saw the most prominent brown eyes staring back at him – never blinking or turning away. Tony was now interested, turning his attention to the body of the bay-colored colt. Everard noticed the horse was big for his age, had a beautiful shine to his coat, and was so gorgeous that even an experienced horseman was captivated. Tony's attention then turned downward, focusing on the four legs holding the colt upright. Four legs perfectly balanced beneath the bay colt, a future champion standing upright and firm, not one hoof out of step, with short cannon bones from below the knee to the hooves. As Tony's eyes danced around the physical makeup of the horse, assessing each area with experience and talent few possessed, he finished by turning back to the head of the colt. The big, brown eyes still looking back at Everard. Tony was in awe, staring at greatness, and greatness was staring back at him.

Davis, impressed as well, was looking to sell the colt for more than the standard fee coming from the sales of Staff Writer's offspring. The foals of Staff Writer were not receiving much attention as none had yet to finish first in any competitive races during their two and three-year-old campaigns. In an industry hyper-focused on the performances of offspring, Staff Writer had yet to produce as a stallion. Critical to the valuation of the one-year-old colt standing before Everard was the fact that Staff Writer had never raced competitively due to suffering a career-ending injury by stepping on a drain pipe before the start of his two-year-old racing season. The lack of racing history was another negative factor impacting the potential sale prices of his offspring. Davis, though, saw what Everard was looking at and was looking to get $10,000 for the colt, setting a minimum purchase price of $4,500.00 for interested buyers at her farm. Everard, though, knew the one-year-old sales of Staff Writer were going for no more than three to four thousand dollars, so he was intent on waiting out Davis for a better price. With no offer from Everard or any other buyers that morning, Davis pulled the colt back from any future private sales as no buyers were willing to spend a minimum of $4,500. In an industry laser-focused on genetics and bloodlines, it appeared as if it was going to be difficult for Davis to find a buyer for a colt who was bred by unraced parents.

As Davis could not sell the colt on her terms, she decided to transport the colt to the biggest thoroughbred auction in North America - the Fasig-Tipton Preferred Yearling Sales in Lexington, Kentucky. Fasig-Tipton Company, Inc. was founded in 1898 by William B. Fasig and Edward A. Tipton as the first equine auction house in the country, with main offices at Madison Square Garden in New York City. The auction house moved its headquarters to Lexington, Kentucky, in 1972, with subsequent satellite offices in Ocala, Florida; Saratoga Springs, New York; Elkton, Maryland; and Grand Prairie, Texas. Though Davis did not expect her colt and his lineage issues to sell for six figures, a more realistic sales price may have been that of 1977 Triple Crown winner Seattle Slew in 1975 when he sold for $17,500. Davis believed a buyer would come up with the $10,000 asking price in the worst-case scenario.

Before the yearling sale, Davis consigned the colt to Horse Haven for the sale. Horse Haven would take care of the grooming for the auction, as the colt would need to look his best while being paraded in front of prospective buyers. Like the manicure of a person's toenails, the hooves were spruced up and painted black. A currycomb brush was used to prepare his coat, bringing any embedded dirt from his coat to the surface. A stiff brush was used to remove the loosened dirt and hair. Softer brushes were used to brush the coat two more times. An even softer brush was used to buff the coat. Finally, a cloth was used to remove any remaining dirt from the top of the shined coat. A similar process was used to comb out the mane and tale. The result is a brushed-out tail and mane to match, combined with a glimmering, shining coat. Various rubbing oils were added at the end of the process. Davis' colt was showing up at Fasig-Tipton looking like a polished Ford Mustang - and every bit the stud his future owners were looking for.

As the colt was paraded in front of potential buyers on the second day of the two-day sale, with Everard watching from a short distance away, the son of Staff Writer was bigger than the other yearlings coming before him. In addition to his increased size and strength, Everard also noticed the air of confidence the colt projected in front of the crowd. The colt demanded the room's attention with a head held high and legs perfectly positioned under him. Projecting self-assurance at such a young age, combined with the physical attributes the colt was born with, was enough to convince Everard that the colt had the potential to be a grand champion.

With near-encyclopedic knowledge of thoroughbreds and their bloodlines, Everard would not let the colt's unraced parents bother his continuing interest as he looked at the yearling before him. The "encyclopedia" serving as Everard's resource was *The American Stud Book*. As Tony continued to stare, memories of the colt's grandfather, Northern Dancer, raced through his thoughts. Although others may have missed the lineage of the colt before him or not looked past his unraced parents, the colt's forefathers confirmed the horse's potential for Everard.

The magnificence of the colt standing before Everard, as with all thoroughbreds foaled in North America, traced his beauty and bloodlines to one of three Oriental stallions imported to England between 1680 and 1730. English aristocrats in the local horse business imported stallions from the Middle East to mate with their native mares. Pairing these horses from two countries produced a breed forever known as the Thoroughbred. Selective breeding between the three foundation sires and English mares over fifty years resulted in hundreds of foals. These foals serving as the groundwork for a breed unlike any other seen before or after. As observed by a 19th-century English gentleman and journalist, Charles Apperley, who published his writings in *The Sporting Magazine* under the pseudonym Nimrod, the union was a breeding process which resulted in "the noblest animal in creation."[36]

Unlike other buyers at the equine sale, with the young colt's lineage staring up from the pages in his hand, Everard was not overly concerned about the unraced sire and dam. The bloodline of the grandparents and beyond led Everard to believe greatness was hiding in plain sight. Staff Writer was the son of Northern Dancer - a legendary racer and one of the most outstanding stallions. The career of Northern Dancer totaled 18 races, with the colt crossing the finish line 14 times ahead of all others, coming in second place twice and third place twice. First-place wins included the 1964 Kentucky Derby and the 1964 Preakness Stakes, and third place at the Belmont Stakes - just missing the Triple Crown. Northern Dancer was the three-year-old colt of the year in 1964 and was inducted into the Canadian and United States Racing Hall of Fame. Upon Northern Dancer's retirement to stud as a four-year-old in 1965, he spent his next 22 years living as a stallion. Of his 645 named foals, he sired 411 winners and 147 stakes winners. He was the leading sire in North America, Great Britain, and Ireland six times.

Looking back a bit further at the lineage of Staff Writer, the name of Native Dancer appeared. Native Dancer was the sire to a filly named Natalma - the mother of Northern Dancer. Native Dancer, the great-great-grandfather to the colt who had Everard's undivided attention, was one of the most accomplished thoroughbreds in American racing history. Owned by Alfred G. Vanderbilt II, a member of the Vanderbilt family dynasty, Native Dancer was the thoroughbred champion of the year from the ages of two through four. He was the first thoroughbred the newly invented television made famous. Three of Native Dancer's nine wins during his undefeated two-year-old campaign of 1952 came at the prestigious Saratoga Special, Hopeful and Champagne Stakes. As a three-year-old, after losing the Kentucky Derby by a head, Native Dancer would never lose again, including wins at the Preakness, Belmont, and Travers in the same year. After an unprecedented racing career during which he won 21 out of 22 races, Native Dancer would become a successful stallion, including the grandfather of Ruffian, considered to be the most incredible filly in the history of American Thoroughbred racing. The object of Everard's interest at the Kentucky sale showed up as the grandson of Northern Dancer, the great-great-grandson of Native Dancer, and shared bloodlines with the greatest filly to ever race. With royal bloodlines and racing legends in his lineage, the colt should have attracted significantly more attention as he was put up for sale.

As Timely Writer raced before overflowing crowds in 1981 and 1982, his sheer beauty and athleticism were apparent. From thoroughbred specialists to the average person and children alike, people were awed by his grace and strength. It was reflected in a face that appeared as if it had been chiseled by a sculptor, legs that were long and dancer-like, the white marking on his forehead resembling a soaring meteor, his commanding brown eyes, and a stride that demanded attention as he walked before you. It took the keen eye, intelligence, and vision from a sage such as Tony Everard, though, to recognize greatness at the yearling sales of 1979. The 1970s saw nearly 40,000 thoroughbreds born annually. Of these thousands of horses foaled yearly, less than six would be considered serious contenders for the Triple Crown of racing during their three-year-old season. Though it would be some time before Timely Writer displayed the heart of a champion, Everard knew nearly three years before the Kentucky Derby of 1982 that he had the 'look of eagles,' which came around once in a lifetime.

Everard opened up the bidding after his soon-to-be colt was paraded before interested buyers on the second evening of the two-day sale. Most buyers' agents and horse farms had either left before the second evening of the two-day event or had gone through their budgets. Hence, the pool of potential buyers was smaller than usual as Everard looked to secure the purchase of a useful horse for the Martins. After Everard's opening offer, the bidding increased in increments of $250 faster than he expected. Everard knew it would take more than the $10,000 budgeted by the brothers for the purchase. The trainer thought so much of the colt that he put the budget aside while raising his bid each time, offering an extra $250 over his competitors. After 14 increases above the Martins' budgeted amount, the auctioneer slammed the wooden gavel to the podium, indicating the sale was final. Everard had the final bid and delivered a "useful" horse to the Martin brothers for $13,500.00.

As Frannie ended the early morning phone call from Everard, breaking his budget was of no concern as he trusted his friend's keen eye, knowledge, and experience. Frannie knew they may have caught lightning in a bottle for the price they paid. Now that he had an owner, the yearling of Staff Writer and Timely Roman needed a name. The brothers and Tony Everard left that task to Mary. Always well-read and a literary talent, Mary was more than capable of giving the colt a name. Days after the purchase, Mary would combine the first name of the colt's mother, Timely Roman, with the last name of his father, Staff Writer, creating a combination that rolled off the lips of everyone – including journalists.

Timely Writer, a big, beautiful, but unproven horse, now belonged to the Martins. It was Tony Everard's job to make him a champion at his training facility in Ocala, Florida. Everard's work with Timely Writer drew upon an expertise he developed going back to his childhood in Ireland. The Irishman's early years with horses began at eleven when he tamed his first on a farm in Ireland. Everard spent his youth outside of Dublin learning his craft, riding horses on the rolling farm hills of Ireland and later racing competitively in steeplechases. He would leave his homeland for the promise of better pastures, always intending to return home wealthier and wiser, running his own horse farm.

Tony Everard training Thoroughbreds in New England during his early years.

With the assistance and connections from his boss in Ireland, Everard came to the United States as a 19-year-old in 1958 on the S.S. Midda from Liverpool, England, with his brother Joe by his side, not much money in their pockets, two horses, and a Shepherd dog in tow. His boss in Ireland worked out a deal where he would pay for the brothers' tickets for the journey if they took care of the horses throughout the six-day trip, delivering them to their destination in the United States. As the S.S. Midda was concluding its journey and passing the Statute of Liberty before pulling into the immigration port at Ellis Island in New York Harbor, excitement spread across the ship. Tony and Joe were on the ship's deck eating ice cream when Tony calmly leaned over, telling his younger brother to sit tight and finish eating - "We may never get to taste anything this good for a long time."[37]

The two brothers were hoping to open a butcher shop while working at a local racetrack in Virginia shortly after settling into the new country. As the butcher shop did not come to fruition, Everard shipped to Rhode Island to stay with some friends and begin work as a horse trainer. Tony gained much experience at the horse tracks in and around New England, meeting many of his future clients and friends during these years. Good, talented people included trainer Dominic Imprescia, thoroughbred owner Frankie Bertollini of Monarch Stables, and the Martin brothers of Nitram Stables. The Martins and Everard talked horses non-stop at Suffolk Downs, developing a friendship throughout the decade of the 1960s and beyond.

Everard and his wife JoAnne took their talents south to Miami in the 1960s following the re-location of one of the bigger horse stables in Rhode Island. It was at the horse tracks of Florida where Tony extended his client base while developing a reputation as a knowledgeable horseman. With the birth of their son Brian, the Everards settled into Ocala to raise a family and begin a new episode in their lives. Shortly after settling into Ocala, Tony's reputation within the local thoroughbred industry earned him an interview with a wealthy shipping magnate from Ohio who was intent on getting into the horse business. George Steinbrenner, the soon-to-be owner of the New York Yankees in Major League Baseball, purchased 750 acres in Ocala, Florida, calling it Kinsman Farm after the street he grew up on in Cleveland, Ohio. Based upon various recommendations, Steinbrenner tapped the not-yet 30-year-old Tony Everard to become his horse racing manager, providing him a house on the farm to live in when needed. Their business relationship, however, would last less than three years.

Unbeknownst to Steinbrenner, Tony and his wife JoAnne purchased a 70-acre horse training facility in 1970, naming it Another Episode Farm. It was here where Everard would purchase, tame, and train countless thoroughbreds over the next five decades. The 70-acre farm in Ocala saw Joanne running the day-to-day activities, with Tony overseeing the training of horses during his off hours from Kinsman Farm. A slight problem developed, though, once Mr. Steinbrenner found out. The boss summonsed Tony for a meeting the following morning to discuss his employment situation. At the early morning meeting, Tony unapologetically confirmed to his boss what he had heard, but indicating that he had the ability and support to run both farms. After listening, Steinbrenner delivered an ultimatum to Tony: "You can't own your own horses and train mine too."[38] Tony did not flinch at the ultimatum presented, betting and believing in himself at New Episode Farm. Everard was promptly fired on the spot.

Timely Writer may have been Tony's first significant find, but the years ahead confirmed that his vision and skill led to the discovery and development of the son of Staff Writer. One of the more famous horses Everard bought and trained during his decades-long career was a young thoroughbred named Funny Cide. Everard purchased the colt in August 2001 at the Fasig-Tipton[1] preferred yearling auction sale in Saratoga Springs, New York. A horse Tony purchased when many others were scared away, soon developing the colt and creating a legendary story.

Like Timely Writer twenty years prior, even though the colt was a ridgling[2] (born with an undescended testicle), Everard loved what he saw in Funny Cide. Though others had no appetite for the risk of purchasing a ridgling, Everard had a strategy to turn the colt into an elite racehorse and bought him for the bargain price of $22,000. As with Timely Writer, Funny Cide was immediately sent south to the training center in Ocala. Once in Ocala, and before the taming and training of Funny Cide began, Everard drew upon his years of experience to make a quick decision that would forever impact the colt's career. It's Everard's philosophy that waiting and doing nothing with a ridgling does not benefit the colt once he begins the training process. A non-descending testicle will negatively impact a colt's stride, speed, and form. If not gelded, Funny Cide would start training and experience pain and discomfort from the misplaced testicle. To compensate for the pain and discomfort, Funny Cide would reflexively change his natural stride to mitigate the resulting pain. Everard knew, "with ridglings, it's better to go ahead and geld them early.... once they start training around turns, they are moving faster and getting pinched, and it hurts them."[39] Funny, Cide would never have race at an elite level if the medical issue had been left unattended. It was not long after Funny Cide arrived in Ocala before Everard had his colt castrated.

Everard had Funny Cide under his care for the taming and training of the colt in preparation for his two-year-old racing season. Trainer Barclay Tagg of Sackatoga Stables in Saratoga Springs, a colleague and friend of Tony,

---

1. https://en.wikipedia.org/wiki/Fasig-Tipton

2. https://en.wikipedia.org/wiki/Ridgling

often visited Everard's training center looking for the next great racing champion. Barclay was so impressed with the talent of Funny Cide during his visits that one day, he left the training center with the gelding after purchasing him for $75,000.00. During the three-year-old racing season in 2003, Funny Cide became the first gelding to win the Kentucky Derby in over 70 years. After the Derby, New York Yankees owner George Steinbrenner was leaving the facility in an elevator when he recognized Tony's sister Virginia. Steinbrenner bellowed from the back of the elevator, heading down with Virginia in the front, "why in the hell did he geld him!?" [40]

Two weeks later, Funny Cide won the second leg of the Triple Crown, beating all others at the Preakness Stakes in Baltimore, Maryland. Funny Cide was one win away from becoming the first Triple Crown winner in 25 years. With three weeks until the final leg at Belmont Park, the story of Funny Cide and his first trainer captured the media's attention nationwide. The spotlight on Everard and his training facility was non-stop - the telephones constantly ringing with reporters on the other end requesting interviews. Tony's fun and fascinating story about his involvement in the success of Funny Cide brought him well-earned notoriety for creating a champion where few others saw an opportunity. Tony quipped to one reporter during the week leading up to the Belmont Stakes, "I'm getting more media attention than the horse."[41] During the media onslaught of Funny Cide's three-year-old racing season, which included television crews from NBC showing up at Everard's training facility, Everard would point out to people with the belly laugh of an Irishman that his resulting fame only came about because he had the balls cut off the winner of the Kentucky Derby.

Ultimately, Funny Cide became the 17th horse to come up short in winning the Triple Crown, finishing in third place five lengths behind the winner - and two places short of immortality. The wins helped propel Funny Cide to the 2003 Eclipse Award as the top three-year-old colt. As a four-year-old, Funny Cide won the prestigious Jockey Gold Cup in 2004, later finding his way north to compete at Suffolk Downs in the Massachusetts Handicap

– finishing tied for 2nd in a three-way photo finish. Funny Cide retired in 2007 with 11 wins, finishing another 14 times in second or third place while making his owners just over three and one-half million dollars.

Everard's resume includes taming and training countless great thoroughbreds, such as Curlin, Saratoga legend Fourstardave, and Tiz the Law. It was in 2018 when trainer Barclay Tagg sent Tiz the Law South to Everard's training center. Everard, sixty years removed from his boat trip from Liverpool, spent the year taming and training Tiz the Law before returning him to Sackatoga Stables for the two-year-old racing season. As when Everard turned over Timely Writer to the Martins nearly 40 years prior, Tiz the Law went on to win the coveted 2019 Champagne Stakes as a two-year-old and the 2020 Florida Derby as a three-year-old. Tiz the Law would make history during his three-year-old season by becoming the first New York-bred foal in 138 years to win the Belmont Stakes in New York.

It was twenty years before Everard's purchase and training of Funny Cide, and more than 35 years before Tiz the Law, when Tony found a "needle in a haystack." In the early 1980s, people were already commenting on Tony's "uncanny knack for recognizing horses blessed with that runner's look of eagles."[42] He had an innate ability to watch, listen, and develop an untrained horse. Though a horse cannot vocalize thoughts or needs, Everard came to learn how a horse communicates, allowing the trainer to partner with the horse throughout their time together. After Timely Writer was shipped to New Episode Farm in Ocala, Everard began his work with the future champion. After spending the first week with his new tenant, Everard admittedly misjudged Timely Writer's disposition. During Timely Writer's first few days, Everard discovered the colt was brilliant, responding quickly to direction, unusually strong, and fearless – nothing bothered or intimidated him.

The first step in training Timely Writer for Everard and his farmhands was to get Writer "saddled up." A saddle cloth with the saddle on top of it would be placed on the back of Timely Writer with a long leather strap from one side down and under the stomach to the other side. This strapping would hold the saddle securely to Timely Writer. Once the colt accepted the saddle on his back, a farmhand would lay, not sit, across the saddle so Timely Writer could get comfortable with the weight on his back. Timely Writer would then be led around the corral by one farmhand while the other farmhand was still lying across the saddle, guiding him left or right with a tug of the reins leading to the bit in his mouth. Once Timely Writer was comfortable with the equipment and weight on his back, and the reins used to guide him, he was sent to the training stable. This is where Timely Writer would be trained to behave like an elite thoroughbred racehorse.

Everard used exercise riders for the next phase of Timely Writer's development, with some flown south to him from Suffolk Downs. Working with Timely Writer were training jockeys and young troubled teenagers learning to become farmhands, with some living at the bunkhouse on the property. Some teenagers would find themselves at Joanne and Tony's farm for many reasons, including requests from family friends who discovered their children unmanageable or others working full-time as high school was not for them. Joanne and Tony were happy to have the help, as plenty of tasks needed to be completed at the farm. The Everards provided stability, a craft to learn, and mentoring to turn troubled teens into mature adults.

Luke Dufresne from the Boston area was one of those young men at Tony's farm in the spring of 1980. Tony's reputation for training and caring for horses and employees alike was well known due to his continued involvement in the racing industry in Boston for more than a decade after he moved to Ocala. The previous summer, Tony received a telephone call from Luke's father from the Charlestown Street Jail in Boston. The father's residential address had changed for the foreseeable future as he had taken up residency at the county jail – as an inmate. Luke lived with his mother then, who was no more reliable than his father. With no parental supervision, the teenager was only good at getting into trouble. Tony did not know Luke or his father but listened to the father's plea to help the young boy by providing full-time work. Tony's reply was simple, "tell the kid to show -up at my training center on September 1st, and I will put him to work."

Luke Dufresne showed up on September 1, 1979, and Tony put him to work, teaching him the day-to-day chores and working at a horse training facility while also learning how to ride and care for horses. The rebel in Luke was apparent to Tony upon the young man's arrival at the horse facility, with Tony nicknaming him "Cool Hand Luke" after Paul Newman's rebel movie character.

Under the direction of Everard, these exercise riders and farmhands shared the work responsibilities that came with getting Timely Writer comfortable with such things as the feel of another person's legs on each side of his stomach, a jockey in a saddle on his back, along with the novelties of thoroughbred horse racing. The taming process started with guiding Timely Writer in circles to mimic a racetrack oval, before moving on to figure eights for Writer to get accustomed to the reins in the hands of a jockey directing him. As Timely Writer quickly mastered these training exercises, he moved on to other nuances of horse racing, such as being comfortable in a pack with other horses within tight quarters.

As thoroughbreds are bred to run, their instincts are to behave like wild horses, running for daylight without restrictions of fences and rails in place at training tracks. These instincts need to be harnessed to find success racing competitively. The early days of Timely Writer frolicking in the fields with other foals and their mares were in the past. Everard and his farmhands partnered up Timely Writer with other similarly aged thoroughbreds, lining them up on the oval training track. Exercise riders' responsibilities at this stage are to gather a pack of horses, anywhere from six to ten of them, into a group and move them around the oval track in a trotting fashion. Each horse must become comfortable running within the close confines of a group of horses. Speed is not required at this level. Once the horses are relaxed, the jockeys move the speed to a canter. At all times, Everard prioritizes the safety and comfort level of a horse. Competitive thoroughbred racing is not an option if a horse cannot be tamed or taught for any reason.

Peter and Frannie, upon hearing the intermittent success stories from Everard in their weekly telephone calls, began taking trips south to Everard's farm to watch the progress of their promising colt. On every visit to Ocala, the Martin brothers brought an extra suitcase. After all, butchers could not travel without their product. Tony and Joanne, along with anybody else who happened to be around the horse farm, welcomed the luggage filled with racks of ribs. After playing outdoor racquetball by the bunkhouse, all were treated to a late-night barbeque with the best ribs in Ocala.

Timely Writer, without question, was the pack's leader during his time at the training facility. However, the colt had some personality issues that needed to be addressed and managed. Like the majority of great thoroughbreds, Timely Writer was strong-willed. Recounting his days with Timely Writer, Everard remembered how he "was rough to break. He owns his quarters. He was the same when he turned out to pasture with ten other colts. He was *tough*. He fought for his stuff, and he was one of the field's leaders."[43]

During these visits to Ocala, the brothers witnessed what Everard told them about Timely Writer's ability and disposition – both the good and the bad. As Frannie would attest later that day, nobody should underestimate Timely Writer's explosive speed or personality. One morning in Ocala, Frannie and Peter stood nearby watching Timely Writer from behind the corral fencing with a crowd of farmhands. They heard the back and forth between Everard and the exercise rider. Everard sent the exercise rider out with Timely Writer for a light jog within the small corral area - telling the jockey not to take too much on the hold of Timely Writer's reins. The colt liked a loose set of reins. Everard mentioned this as Writer had conveyed his comfort level to other jockeys on his back at the other end of his reins. The rider yelled loud enough for others to hear, "I been on a hundred horses – don't worry about it!"[44] Against Everard's advice, the rider immediately took a tight hold of Timely Writer's reins as he wanted to take control of the colt in the corral area. Timely Writer, feeling the tight squeeze of the reins leading to the hands of the jockey, immediately took his mount to the middle of the infield area, leaning his weight on his front legs and bucking his rear legs upward as high as they could go. Timely Writer was sending his message of discontent to the exercise rider – the force releasing the reins from the jockey's hands while sending the young man nearly ten feet up into the air before quickly falling to the ground. Everard and his assistants immediately thrust the gate open to aid the jockey as he was gasping for air on the ground. The exercise rider was rocking back and forth in great pain while holding an arm broken in three places. As people were running in one direction towards the jockey, a wide-open gate was left behind them. Timely Writer saw daylight and opportunity. Frannie and Peter watched, helpless to do anything, while their horse ran past the oncoming people through the open gate, heading towards open fields and freedom.

As Frannie was observing the chaos before him, Everard yelled in the direction of the injured jockey, "I told you," while Timely Writer was galloping down the road of the horse farm in the other direction. Timely Writer spent the day traveling "down the road maybe seven or eight miles and between trees and everything else." Frannie spent the afternoon watching Timely Writer from the house's porch, the horse enjoying his freedom in the beautiful farmland. Timely Writer would return to his barn six to seven hours later, seemingly making his point about who was in charge. After Timely Writer returned home, Frannie laughed, "he just had a hell of a time for himself."[45] By the end of 1981, with Timely Writer a multiple stakes race winner as a two-year-old, the exercise rider was bragging to people in and around Ocala how he was bucked off Timely Writer and lived to talk about it.

Once word got out to the exercise riders about how Timely Writer must be handled, they moved on to the "ponying" stage with better success. This is the stage where the assistant trainer to the yearlings would take a horse of his own while riding alongside Writer, taking Writer's halter and lead strap as the pair performed a gallop in unison over the dirt track. Writer instantly disposed of this task, letting his handlers know he could ride with a jockey full-time in his mount - as speed and timed workouts were close at hand.

One last task for all racing horses is the introduction of the starting gate. Introducing such a large foreign object to a young thoroughbred often creates stress and anxiety for the horse. The noise, close confines, and activity can create fear and large-scale shock to the nervous system. Some horses cannot get past the introduction of the starting gate and need to be transitioned to uses other than competitive horse racing. Everard and his farmhands introduce the noise of the gate to all yearlings individually and collectively in a group setting towards the end of the process. The yearling is made comfortable within the confines of the training gate, and subtle noise from the gates, such as rattling the front gates together by hand, is introduced daily, with the noise level increasing daily. As the process ends, the horses are raring to go out the front doors of the starting gate, eager to race against one another around the training track oval.

One early observation of Timely Writer was the ease with which he accepted the starting gate. It was as if Writer instinctively knew how to handle the large metal gated area – and the reward of running once released from the confines. Timely Writer would softly enter the open gate, wait for a handler to close the door behind him, and patiently wait for the excitement to come when the front door sprung open. After this task was completed in a quick fashion, speed trials commenced, with Timely Writer having no difficulties running at top speed. Any challenges that arose were limited to the exercise riders not following Everard's orders about the one-year-old needing to be restrained from running at his top speed. As Timely Writer grew by the week, all efforts were made to protect him from himself.

Watching Timely Writer during these months, Everard saw a unique combination of grace, quickness, speed, endurance, intelligence, and heart. With Everard assuming his usual spot along the outside rail of the training track and his eyes trained on the colt, he was intent on watching every stride of Timely Writer circling the track during the early morning hours. During many of these workouts, Ocala's lingering morning mist covered the dirt track below it. Everard marveled as each effortless gallop of Timely Writer produced the quiet sound of hooves. Each stride appeared like the colt was running with only the Ocala morning mist below him. As Tony watched Timely Writer twice around the track, the ease and perfection of Timely Writer's stride were eye-catching – with the scenes of Timely Writer running above the mist forever in his memory.

Tony Everard introducing the training gate to Thoroughbreds.

By February of 1981, Timely Writer was proving he was rounding into a first-class thoroughbred. He was outperforming every task asked of him while continuing to get bigger and stronger. Timely Writer's physical appearance looked more like that of a horse finishing off his two-year-old racing season. He was shockingly muscular. Everard knew he had an elite racing champion. Everard needed the Martin brothers to travel back to Ocala for one more visit before they decided on the colt's future.

During the last visit, the brothers had to decide if they favored the probable future path of Timely Writer's racing career. With Everard by their side and stopwatches in hand, the brothers spent their last morning in Ocala with Timely Writer. It was a morning unlike anything the brothers had witnessed from other horses they owned. Frannie and Peter watched the initial quickness out of the gate, the ease which Timely Writer exerted himself at a high level of speed, and the appearance as if their colt was gliding over the track while working out. They had never seen such a display in one of their own. The brothers saw the recorded times once the click of the stopwatches ended - and had seen enough. It was evident that Timely Writer could take on other elite two-year-old horses in the upcoming season. The brothers were prepared to financially back Timely Writer. It would be a path previously uncharted for the Martins as Timely Writer would be going to racetracks different than those they had traveled throughout New England.

Though the brothers often dreamed, with Frannie now in his 50s and Peter in his 60s, they never believed at this point in their lives that they would be blessed with a horse of such talent. They were uncertain whether Timely Writer would race to the level of talent he possessed, but they could not escape the feeling that they had been gifted a horse from no less than Northern Dancer himself. As Timely Writer was wrapping up his year of training, the brothers knew of the racing history they would be jumping into. It was an industry spoiled by the excitement and performances of legendary horses from the previous decade - and one searching for its next racing legend.

The early years of the 1970s brought with it the long-suffering Vietnam War onto the television screens regularly. Vietnam, combined with the lingering political scandal of Watergate and President Nixon, placed a dark cloud over the spirits of the country. As Seabiscuit carried the country through the great depression in the late 1930s and 40s, multiple horse racing legends brought the country through the difficult times of the 1970s, restoring the sport to the nation's mantel as the most popular. The golden age of horse racing began with a colt nicknamed Big Red dominating the 1972 two-year-old racing season - earning Horse of the Year honors. The country would come to know the phenom as Secretariat. Secretariat became the ninth Triple Crown winner and the first in twenty-five years during the 1973 racing season. It wasn't just that Secretariat won; it was how he did it. Secretariat, who raced under the blue-and-white checkered colors of Meadow Stables and Canadian jockey Ron Turcotte in the saddle, dominated his competitors, sweeping the three races in the spring of 1973 like none other before him. Secretariat's performance before 134,476 people at the 1 ¼ mile Kentucky Derby, with a race time of 1:59 and 2/5, setting a track record that still stands today - becoming the first horse to run the Derby in less than two minutes. Secretariat ran each ¼ mile at Churchill Downs faster than the previous, accelerating through the finish line during the last ¼ of the race. The second leg of the Triple Crown, the Preakness Stakes in Baltimore, Maryland, brought another track record with an official time of 1:53.

As Secretariat prepared for the last leg of the Triple Crown at Belmont Park Racetrack in New York, he appeared on the front cover of three national magazines. *Newsweek*, *Time*, and *Sports Illustrated* all gave their readers plenty of photographs of the red-headed colt to marvel at, including his unique blue and white checkered racing colors Secretariat would wear for the 1 ½ mile Belmont Stakes. Secretariat's performance at the Belmont Stakes on June 9, 1973, is considered by many as the single greatest race by any North American racehorse. On a warm and bright sunny day, Secretariat went off at 1-10 odds before just under 70,000 people. The race was televised live and watched by 15 million households. Secretariat broke out of the starting gate quickly, opening with the fastest half mile in the history of the race. A ten-length lead over his competitors after the first ½ mile continued to grow as Secretariat finished the first mile better than one second faster than every other race run before at the Belmont Stakes. As Secretariat pushed for the finish line, the remainder of the field tired as he opened up a lead of 1/16 of a mile. Through the homestretch, the blue and white checkered jersey of the jockey atop Secretariat was the center of the television screen with no other horses in view. As Secretariat surged towards the finish line, CBS Television announcer Chic Anderson screamed, "Secretariat is widening now! He is moving like a tremendous machine!" Secretariat crossed the finish line ahead of the second-place finisher by an unheard-of 31 lengths. The emotions of people track-side ranged from delirium to stunned silence, with others laughing in awe and disbelief at what they had just witnessed. The length of victory broke the previous winning margin of any Triple Crown race by six lengths. Secretariat's time of 2:24 is the fastest 1 ½ miles ever recorded for a Thoroughbred.

Secretariat's performances turned him into a national celebrity. He gave the country a reason to turn away from the realities of life and invest their time and attention into the sport. Secretariat led off the decade with perfection, but there was a young filly waiting to capture the hearts of the country. The greatest filly this country has ever seen was next in line to capture the country's affection. Her name was Ruffian, so named by her owner, Barbara Janney, because girls could be "ruffians" too. Ruffian was bred by Stuart Janney, Jr. and Barbara Phipps Janney, owners of Locust Hill Farm in Glyndon, Maryland, and arrived on April 17, 1972. She would be the American Champion Two-Year-Old Filly of the Year in 1974 and the

Three-Year-Old Filly of the Year in 1975 – and by all accounts, she was a perfect "10."

Ruffian's jockey, Jacinto Vasquez, once described the beauty of seeing her for the first time with a white star marking perfectly in the middle of her forehead and a beautiful bay coat covering her toned body as she appeared before onlookers. "She was like Marilyn Monroe or Raquel Welsh walking into a room ... she took your breath away."[46] As a racehorse, she was the definition of perfection, having won all ten races she entered. Ruffian held the lead at every mark in every race, setting new stakes records in the eight stakes races she won. She would start and end her career at the historic Belmont Park outside Long Island, New York. An entire nation would fall in love with her - and immortalize her when she passed.

The middle part of the '70s brought more legends to the racetracks each year, with Seattle Slew exploding onto the national scene in 1976. After winning the two-year-old colt of the year in 1976, Slew began his three-year-old campaign at Hialeah Race Track, including a decisive win in March at the same Flamingo Stakes race Timely Writer would win five years later. In a sport forever searching for its next Triple Crown winner in the preceding 25 years, Seattle Slew gave the country its second Triple Crown winner in just four years. As Seattle Slew swept the three races in 1977, a rivalry was brewing in the two-year-old division during the same year.

The rivalry between Affirmed and Alydar lasted over two years, running against each other ten times. Affirmed beat Alydar four times during their first year of competition, earning the Eclipse Award as the best two-year-old colt of 1977. In the mount of Affirmed was a 17-year-old child prodigy named Stevie Cauthen. Cauthen was the son of a Kentucky trainer and earned his first professional win at Churchill Downs as a sixteen-year-old in 1976. While teenagers in Louisville, Kentucky, attended high school in May, Stevie Cauthen was riding in horse races at Churchill Downs. 1977 saw Cauthen lead all jockeys in the country in wins and money earned.

Affirmed and Alydar brought an entire country to its feet each Saturday afternoon in spring and summer of 1978 as people watched the two colts duel during each of the Triple Crown races – one race better than the other. As the pair made their way to the first leg of the Triple Crown, the Kentucky Derby, the eyes of the country were focused on them. Alydar and Affirmed did not disappoint. With trainer John Veitch guiding Alydar and trainer Laz Barrera directing Affirmed, a crowd of 150,000 was waiting for them at Churchill Downs. Due to Alydar winning the Champagne Stakes at the end of their two-year-old season, Alydar was the 6-5 favorite at the Derby. As the two battled down the backstretch, Affirmed held off the late charge of Alydar to win by 1 ½ lengths. The Preakness Stakes set up much the same way as Affirmed set the early pace before Alydar made a move at the far turn. Affirmed held a short lead down the stretch, with Alydar closing from behind at the finish line, losing this time by the length of his neck.

The stage was set for the final leg of their Triple Crown battles at the 1 ½ mile Belmont Stakes. As the two broke simultaneously from the starting gate in front of their competitors, with Affirmed sitting one length ahead of Alydar, they seemed to be in a gear lower than their prior two races over the first ½ mile. With 1 mile to go, though, it was unlike anything witnessed before or since. Alydar's jockey, Jorge Valasquez, pulled the colt up alongside Affirmed for the last mile. As the two competitors raced alongside each other in near synchronicity for the remainder of the race, millions of viewers watched each colt's nose, alternately bobbing up and down in front of the other. Racing up to forty miles per hour, it was impossible to tell which of the two horses was in the lead. The viewing audience was wide-eyed as the two battled for the last ¾ of a mile.

With the two continuing to move together as one in the middle of the home stretch, Affirmed appeared to tire just a bit. Stevie Cauthen, the child progeny that he was, used his left hand to take the riding crop to the back side of Affirmed. It was a move Cauthen never had to use previously – and it caught the colt's attention. Cauthen was able to get Affirmed surging again, with the nose of Affirmed bobbing across the finish line just before that of Alydar - and before the two could exchange leads once again. The sport and the country had its 11th Triple Crown winner. Cauthen, who turned 18 and won the 1978 Kentucky Derby all within the same week, became the youngest jockey to win the Triple Crown. As 1978 ended, Cauthen would become the only jockey to win the *Sports Illustrated Man of the Year*.

As shocking as Secretariat's performance at the Belmont just five years earlier was, the epic battles between Affirmed and Alydar left viewers amazed at the excitement provided and its level of competition. The sport and its attentive audience now had its first-ever back-to-back Triple Crown winners, with another legend around the corner. As the 1979 racing season began, it would bring another colt to the forefront of the country by the name of Spectacular Bid, who attempted a three-peat sweep of the Triple Crown races. Spectacular Bid was coming off a year in which he was the Eclipse Award winner as the best two-year-old colt of the year, capping it with a win at the Champagne Stakes at Belmont Park. Like Timely Writer's path to the Kentucky Derby three years later, Spectacular Bid was shipped from Florida to Churchill Downs after winning the Flamingo Stakes and Florida Derby. Bid would dominate at the Kentucky Derby in front of a crowd of 125,000 and win the Preakness Stakes with ease two weeks later. With a 12-race winning streak in hand, only an injury on the morning of the Belmont Stakes could keep Spectacular Bid from winning the Triple Crown. The injury caused the colt to fade in the backstretch of the race, finishing third and missing the Triple Crown by two lengths. Spectacular Bid would win the 1979 three-year-old colt of the year, adding the Horse-of-the-Year honors as a four-year-old in 1980. He finished off a career winning a staggering 26 of 30 races entered, with career earnings at a then-record $2,781,608.

With the turn of the decade in 1980, three different horses won each leg of the Triple Crown races. The year belonged to Genuine Risk, though, as she came within two places of making history as the first filly ever to win the Triple Crown, winning the Kentucky Derby while finishing second in each of the last two legs of the Triple Crown. The popularity of horse racing was enduring, with racing attendance and television ratings booming. As the 1980 racing season finished, a yearling who could not find a buyer for $4,500 paired up with a couple of butchers from Dorchester. With the winter of 1980 ending in New England and the first season of competitive racing for Timely Writer to come, the new year brought the promise of potential and purse money for the Martin brothers. Bad news for the brothers, though, came with the estimated price tag for the 1981 two-year-old racing season – including $50,000.00 for a full-time trainer, $40 per day for additional costs, and an infinite amount of miscellaneous fees.

As blue-collar workers in a business that required wealth to finance horse racing at the elite levels, the brothers needed a plan to pay for Timely Writer's two-year-old campaign. They needed to find a way to come up with money if they would keep Timely Writer for themselves. Frannie and Peter knew their way around the race tracks, including the types of characters who did business in and around the venues, and some various non-traditional financing options they could choose from. Frannie and his colleagues leaned on their more than twenty-five years of experience in the New England horse racing circuit to craft a plan to secure their future with Timely Writer. It was a plan, though, which came with great risk. A plan that was crafted unlike any other maiden race that had come before Timely Writer's first appearance in June of 1981.

Chapter 5

Timely Writer Takes on the Establishment: From Suffolk to the Spa and Back

When Timely Writer was delivered from Gulfstream Park's stalls in April 1982 to the barns at Churchill Downs in Louisville, Kentucky, he was the best three-year-old horse in the country. However, it was the two-year-old racing campaign of 1981 that first gave birth to the tales of Timely Writer and his crew.

Timely Writer's racing career began differently than other thoroughbreds with his talent level. As Writer was transported from Tony Everard's Another Episode Farm in Ocala during the spring of 1981 for his maiden race, the colt's career commenced with his owners nearly gambling away their prized possession. The two-year-old racing season would end with Timely Writer's value estimated at approximately 6- 8 million dollars (equal to $12-15 million in present-day cash value).

The road to ascension from a no-named colt valued at less than $5,000 in August of 1980 to a champion colt worth millions of dollars first began with Tony Everard transporting Timely Writer north to Suffolk Downs in East Boston. At Suffolk, the now full-time racing trainer Dominic Imprescia was fine-tuning the colt in preparation for his first race. With the track a ten-minute drive from their work, the convenience of the location allowed the brothers to slip away from their meat business for an hour or more to watch Timely Writer's progress. At least one of the brothers would watch Timely Writer's workouts daily as Dominic prepped the colt for his first competitive race. After the workouts, each would share their thoughts and observations upon returning to the business. Conversations during these workouts often focused on the grace and ease with which Timely Writer exploded around the turns of the oval track. As Timely Writer's workouts neared completion, the brothers strategized with trusted friends about which venue would host the first race. The maiden race, surprisingly, though, would not be on their home track of Suffolk Downs.

Timely Writer and his owners' rags to riches story would have never materialized had the brothers not escaped the events they set in motion leading up to the champion's first career race. The brothers' money came from running a meat distribution facility in Boston. Though Frannie and Peter provided for their families, they were not men of wealth. The one valuable asset they possessed in 1981 was Timely Writer. Years of experience in the thoroughbred racing business, and with the guiding hand of Tony Everard, taught them they were holding a once-in-a-lifetime horse - and only a few people knew their secret. In the spring of 1981, before the start of the elite races for two-year-old thoroughbreds, the brothers needed to turn their secret into money to finance an expensive campaign in the year ahead.

Years in the gambling business educated Frannie and Peter on how they could raise cash while keeping Timely Writer their secret a bit longer. Using their network of colleagues in Florida, New Jersey, and the greater Boston area, the brothers and Tony Everard were putting in place the pieces to "cash a bet." In May of 1981, as the City of Boston was pre-occupied with a basketball phenom by the name of Larry Bird, who was in the middle of leading the Boston Celtics to an NBA Championship, the brothers were quietly putting the finishing touches on a financing plan for Timely Writer's first race. The brothers and Tony Everard, whose connections stretched throughout the country with various trainers and horse tracks, found friendly faces at Monmouth Park in New Jersey who could help guide the unknown phenom through his first race.

A claiming race permits the potential sale of every horse in the particular race. Potential buyers on the day of horse racing are limited to licensed owners and buyer's agents/brokers for the horse owners. Claiming races are by far the most common at most horseracing tracks. These types of races are held on the day's racing card as leveled competition and a showcase for horses that are inferior to those in other races. In Timely Writer's hand-picked maiden claiming race, the price for prospective buyers to purchase any one of the eight horses was $30,000.00.

Basic concepts of a claiming race dictate each horse owner agrees by entering the horse in the race that their horse will be sold if another registered owner or agent places a claim on the horse before the race. Claims for a horse in the 1980s were typically in writing, sealed in an envelope, and deposited in a locked box with the racing stewards at the track. The process is done at least 10 minutes before the start of the race. As soon as the race begins, the individual who submitted the claim is the new owner of the horse when the race finishes, with any winnings from the race going to the original owner.

The brothers knew there was little money to make from gambling on Timely Writer by running him in a maiden-claiming race on their home turf of Suffolk Downs. Sending Timely Writer out onto the dirt of Suffolk Downs under the direction of the track's leading trainer, Dominic Imprescia, would not maximize their gambling dollars. Imprescia was successful, experienced, and a well-known trainer throughout New England and Florida. The Martin brothers and their Nitram Stables silks were prominent and respected by local horsemen and patrons in Boston. Too much attention would be drawn to Timely Writer breaking his maiden race at Suffolk with a greater risk of losing him to a claim - especially with Dominic's favorite jockey, Roger Danjean, sitting in the saddle. Even if Timely Writer escaped being claimed at Suffolk, most of the patrons at the track would be placing their money on the unraced colt to win. With the majority of the gambling money on Timely Writer to win, the betting odds would be driven down to near even, resulting in a significant reduction in the brothers' winnings on tickets they were holding.

Execution of their plan began with transporting Timely Writer via an equine van from Boston to Monmouth Park in New Jersey for two weeks of training at the track. As a result of Everard's network, the brothers secured a trainer and a stall for Timely Writer's stay. The trainer, Bill Mullin, had a local jockey named Buck Thornburg, who matched up well within the saddle of Timely Writer. The brothers would forgo entering Timely Writer under the ownership of Nitram Stables, instead choosing to list "Fran Martin" as the owner. Jockey Buck Thornburg would not be wearing the identifiable orange and black silks of Nitram, nor would Timely Writer have his saddlecloth, instead using a basic brown blanket. All efforts were made not to attract any attention from the bettors or potential buyers in the claiming race. All efforts were made to make it appear that Timely Writer was nothing special.

These techniques of gamesmanship were not new to the Martins. One of the stable hands for Dominic at Suffolk Downs was a young man who stood six feet four inches tall and weighed around 350 pounds. Whenever the Martins had a big, strong thoroughbred enter a race, they wanted Dominic to use the hulking young man to walk their racing entry over to the paddock area for saddling. This walk took the horse past the betting crowd lining the walkway. The favorite walker of the Martins always made the horse look smaller - and most bettors hated betting on small horses.

At Monmouth Park on Tuesday, June 9th, Timely Writer was entered by the Martins in the 3rd race of the day. The brothers picked a Tuesday as it was the least attended day of the week at the horse track. In the 3rd race at Monmouth, if Timely Writer were to get claimed, the brothers would receive $30,000.00 for the sale, plus any purse winnings. The win, though, would result in the loss of Timely Writer to the new owner/ claimer. Claiming races had been created to ensure better and fair competition. Theoretically, the horses in each race are valued equally, making the outcome less predictable and attractive to gamblers and potential owners.

One of the most recent stories of claiming horses is a colt named Rich Strike. The thoroughbred was bred at the prestigious Calumet Farms in April 2019. Inconsistent training and racing results led Calumet to enter Rich Strike in a $30,000.00 claiming race at Churchill Downs in Kentucky during his two-year-old racing season of 2021. Trainer Eric Reed claimed Rich Strike as an owner's agent just before the race, securing ownership for the Richard Dawson Stable. Just over one year later, Rich Strike went on to win the 2022 Kentucky Derby at the same track where he was claimed. Richard Dawson took home a winning purse of $1,860,000.00 —more than fifty times the claiming price he paid the previous year.

However, the theoretical flaw in the concept of a claiming race was exposed by the plan crafted by the Martin crew so they could "cash a bet." In Timely

Writer's maiden claiming race at Monmouth, the total purse for the first five horses was a meager $7,000.00. From the total purse, $4,200.00 would go to the winning horse. The winning purse would be further reduced by 10% for the trainer's fee, 5% for the jockey's fee, and other associated expenses such as food and transportation. For an elite horse transported in from Boston, the winner's purse for a maiden claiming race on a Tuesday at Monmouth Park was of no consequence to the Martins.

The phrase "cashing a bet" does equate to collecting money from winning tickets at the racetrack. For sure, Frannie was prepared to place a considerable amount of money through the betting windows at Monmouth Park on Timely Writer to win. However, the key to maximizing their winnings for Frannie and friends was using other avenues to "lay off" additional bets. Massachusetts in the 1980s had various horse and dog tracks spread across the state. As sports gambling was not legal in Massachusetts, sports "bookies" were part of the lexicon at the tracks and numerous other establishments throughout the state. A sports bookie was always found amongst the patrons at each track. Regular track employees and its patrons knew "the book." Nobody, including private security and police officers working the security details at the track, ever bothered the book and his sports business. In fact, many law enforcement officers often placed bets with the local bookies. Whether a person wanted to place bets on professional sports, college sports, or horse races from other tracks, the bookie would take the bet and book it with his bosses. If the bettor won his bet, the person could collect on Mondays. If the person lost, one must pay what was owed, plus a small administrative fee.

In the week before Timely Writer's first race at Monmouth Park, the Martin team spent time spreading around thousands of dollars with various bookies in Massachusetts on Timely Writer to win. Official gambling odds are set at the host horse track based on the total money paid into the gambling pool on each horse for the race. By placing their cash on Timely Writer to win with various bookies, the gambling odds at Monmouth were not driven down. Keeping their money away from the betting windows at Monmouth Park also kept the official odds artificially higher for payouts on the team's gambling dollars placed through bookies, resulting in the winning price that much higher for every $2 bet. As illegal sports bookmaking operations typically paid out winning tickets based on the official results posted at Monmouth Park, the plan as designed would result in a higher payout price for every $2 betting ticket.

Timely Writer and the seven lesser talented horses were making their way to the starting gate at the track for the 3rd race when Frannie's anxiety about losing the talented colt began to sink in. Whether Nitram Stables would lose their prized horse would not be known until after the race concluded. These were the nightmarish possibilities feared in the days leading up to the claiming race at Monmouth. There was at least a one in eight chance that Timely Writer would be bought. If the" cashing a bet" plan had been leaked or an astute buyer picked up on Timely Writer's royal bloodlines, the Martins' horse of a lifetime was gone.

Frannie was sweating from the anxiety overcoming his body as Timely Writer was put into his starting gate. With larger-than-average forearms developed from his years as a butcher, Frannie was continually wringing his hands with the racing program in the minutes before Timely Writer's first race. As Frannie would tell friends and media the following year after inquiries about Timely Writer's first race in Monmouth, he was unaware he could get an ulcer in a day until after he left New Jersey that evening.

The short race went as expected for Timely Writer as he immediately came out of the starting gate ahead of the other entries, in first place after the first turn, and taking advantage of the lower quality entries in the homestretch as he pulled away. Timely Writer's first race saw him winning by 8 ½ lengths, blasting off 5 furlongs in less than one minute. For Frannie, the one-minute race felt like an eternity, with his hands wet from sweating and his fingertips a shade of light black from the ink of the racing program. A photo captured Timely Writer crossing the finish in first place, barely showing the second and third-place horses in the picture.

As Writer crossed the finish line, Frannie's eyes immediately focused on the racetrack past the finish line, searching for the track official who would place the red tag on the horse claimed. As Frannie stood there waiting to identify the horse claimed, he had no interest in the payoff amount for first place. The catholic high school graduate was praying for a favor - needing the red circular tag placed on any other horse. As the winning results and payouts of the race were posted on the tote board in the grass infield for first, second, and third place, the track official was walking over to the horses past the finish line. As Frannie painstakingly watched, the red tag was placed on a horse named Rinley Road.

As Rinley Road was changing ownership hands on the track, Frannie looked over at Timely Writer, letting out a deep breath, now paying attention to the official payouts as posted. The tote board in the grass infield showed that for every $2 bet on the colt to win, $11.80 was returned by the racetrack. Seeing the results, Frannie smiled, knowing his colleagues held *thousands* of winning $2 bets on Timely Writer. After the teller at Monmouth Park was done paying out Frannie's winning tickets in $100 bills, and after his trusted friends collected their winnings from the local Boston bookies the following week, tales from the weekend would be whispered from one to the other in the coming months. In a plan unlike any other, the brothers self-financed Timely Writer's two-year-old racing season on a Tuesday afternoon in New Jersey, taking home the winner's purse plus gambling winnings whispered to be well north of $25,000.00.

With the cashing-a-bet plan allowing the brothers to finance Timely Writer's racing season, another equity partner was no longer needed. The real story of why the Martin crew ran Timely Writer at Monmouth would remain their secret until the following year, with its participants sticking to a script that they did not know what they had in the colt and were lucky he did not get claimed. When asked by a bewildered and quizzical journalist during Timely Writer's three-year-old racing season why a horse of such talent was entered in a claiming race, Tony Everard paused before answering with a sly smirk. In his thick Irish brogue, a twinkle still in his eyes from that day in June, Tony conceded the reason was simple, though the plan a little more complicated. As Everard explained, the boys needed to "cash a bet." "We decided to run him for a tag (claiming price) right away. We wanted to get some money in the kitty. He didn't have black type (stakes winners) in his family, and when you've got horses like that, you can run them for $25-$30,000 and it's really hard for somebody to claim them."[47] The following year, after Timely Writer's win at the Florida Derby in April of 1982, the Monmouth race was "seen in some circles as proof positive that the stable was interested in cashing a bet."[48] Everard and the Martins, unsophisticated as the racing elite may have believed, knew how to play the claiming business a bit better than the first owners of Rich Strike at Calumet Farms.

The Martin crew's plan worked to perfection. Timely Writer broke his maiden race without calling attention to himself, allowing the Martins to bring in the extra money so desperately needed to finance a racing campaign a bit different from their usual years in the New England and fair racing circuits.

In reviewing the racing chart of the 3rd race the following morning, the summary depicted that the new owner of Rinley Road spent $30,000.00 on a horse that came in 7th. The purse payout for 7th place was zero dollars. Less than twelve months after the Monmouth race, history would show that on that fateful day in June of 1981, the buyer of Rinley Road passed on the favorite for the 1982 Kentucky Derby. Rinley Road would enter thirty-six races in his career, earning just under $16,000.00 in purses. Timely Writer would double that amount in his second career race.

Monmouth Park, New Jersey - Timely Writer blazes to victory at his maiden race in the cashing a-bet plan.

Prior to Timely Writer leaving Monmouth, jockey Buck Thornburg marveled at the horse he rode. Not knowing the secrets well kept, Thornburg told the Martins to bet a hundred on the colt the next time, "no matter who he runs against or what town he's in."[49] After sharing some advice with Frannie, jockey Buck Thornburg, and trainer William Mullin would never again see Timely Writer in person.

Once his maiden was broken, the game plan for Timely Writer was to move up to the next level of horse racing - stakes races. The brothers knew where they could find such a race. As unfamiliar as Frannie was with Monmouth Park, he knew the friendly confines of Suffolk Downs, returning Timely Writer to the comforts of home. The brothers entered Timely Writer in the 47th running of the 50,000 Mayflower Stakes on Independence Day, July 4th. In a state where the Pilgrims landed the *Mayflower* in Plymouth, Massachusetts, the Mayflower Stakes had been the premier two-year-old race in New England since the inception of Suffolk Downs in 1935, with many of the country's top horses entered during the early years of the track. In the years before he captivated the country, the legendary Seabiscuit was one of the horses who appeared at the Mayflower Stakes during its first running in 1935.

Timely Writer would need to conquer top-level talent from New York and New Jersey as they chased a purse of $50,000.00. One of the horses entered included Herschelwalker, who was shipped into Boston by the Whitney family. The 12-horse race was the 10th of the July 4th event, with Timely Writer not considered one of the top three favorites, going off at 9-1 odds to win. Complicating matters for Timely Writer was that he would start the race from the disadvantageous 11th gate in a short 5 ½ furlongs race.

Also sharing the billing on Independence Day at Suffolk Downs was the annual John Macomber Memorial Handicap. The Macomber Handicap covered one mile and 70 yards over grass turf for three-year-old horses. Entertaining and controversial New York trainer Johnny Campo, who went by the self-proclaimed moniker the "Fat Man," brought a horse in for the

Macomber. Campo had stormed onto the national stage some 90 days prior as he was fresh off a near Triple Crown sweep in the spring. Under Campo's direction, Pleasant Colony surged to wins in the Kentucky Derby and the Preakness Stakes before coming in third at the Belmont Stakes - Campo's home track.

Campo arrived in Boston, bold and braggadocio as ever, with a horse bred at Buckland Farms in Louisville, Kentucky, by the name of Johhny Dance. The rotund conditioner had earned a reputation as loud, crude, egotistical, and insulting, among other adjectives. Born in Harlem, New York, Campo moved from one difficult Italian neighborhood to another before being raised in Ozone Park, Queens – located just down the street from Aqueduct Race Track. Despite a prickly personality, nobody doubted Campo's work ethic around the horse track. After dropping out of high school, where he had a view of Aqueduct Race Track from his classroom window, the big man went to work at the track. Campo spent years working his way up from horse walker to groom to assistant trainer and then working on his own as a trainer.

Campo was known for pulling up to the horse barns in his Mercedes, exiting the car in his muscle t-shirt, barking orders to his people, and walking around the barns smoking cigars while checking on his horses. The trainer in him, though, produced. Campo boldly predicted in 1970 that he would become only the second trainer to produce 100 winners in New York. He went on to accomplish what he predicted before the decade's end. A *Sports Illustrated* featured article in 1979 let their readers know about Campo's story and talents, making the case that a kid from the streets of New York City might be the best trainer in the country.

In the spring of 1981, Thomas Mellon Evans, owner of Buckland Farm, called upon Campo to take over the training of a problem horse named Pleasant Colony. Campo brought in his entire team, transforming the colt with a physical makeover, changing the horse's diet, and adding weight and muscle while training him for distance and durability. On April 18, 1981, two weeks before the Kentucky Derby, Pleasant Colony went off at 12-1 odds and won the Wood Memorial at Aqueduct -Campo's backyard. While accepting the trophy, Campo was telling the media it was "fucking easy, that's what it was.... [a]nd we're going to Kentucky and beat those motherfuckers, too."[50]

Campo told everyone leading up to the Kentucky Derby that his horse was winning it – and he did. After the blanket of roses was placed on Pleasant Colony, ABC's Jim McKay, wearing the same *Wide World of Sport* gold blazer he would wear interviewing Dominic Imprescia at the 1982 Flamingo Stakes, went over to speak with Campo. Unable to keep a straight face, McKay asked with a smirk, "you're always a very quiet man. You wouldn't hazard a thought on this would, you." Campo took McKay's bait, responding, "I kept telling everyone this horse was going to win...We won easy." As McKay wondered how Campo could predict the future, Campo shot back on live television, "I'm a good horse trainer, pal.... and don't ever forget it!"

Whether the city of Boston was ready for the New Yorker and whether patrons could bear to see him win their Macomber Memorial Handicap race at Suffolk Downs on July 4th was not something to be considered as the city prepared for its annual fireworks later that night over Boston Harbor.

Suffolk Downs may not have been Campo's home turf, but it served as the backyard for Frannie and his three older brothers since they were teenagers in Dorchester. The Martins' horses, mostly claimers, had been racing at the East Boston track for 20 years. The brothers also knew that a second convincing win at the Mayflower could propel them to venues never before traveled. Though Suffolk Downs was not nearly the caliber of talent at Hialeah or Gulfstream Park, the Mayflower Stakes was a significant upgrade from Monmouth Park and a purse of $7,000.00. With a $50,000.00 added purse for the Mayflower Stakes, owners of the winning horse would receive over $30,000.00. In previous years at Suffolk, the twin billing of the Macomber Handicap and Mayflower Stakes would draw over 50,0000 people. However, the state of affairs in thoroughbred racing in New England during the early 1980s saw just over 10,000 people come through the turnstiles on the last official day of the 1981 summer racing meet.

Thirteen horses entered the field for the Mayflower. Also entered for the race was a horse named Tom the Riverrat, which was owned by the Martins's good friend Franki Bertollino of Monarch Stables. The last time Timely Writer and Tom the Riverrat saw one another was in a barn they shared at Tony Everard's training facility in Ocala. Staying around to watch the talented two-year-olds was trainer Johnny Campo. Campo had just finished accepting congratulations for his MacComber stakes win, with Johnny Dance finishing just 4/5 of a second off the track record.

Riding in the saddle for Timely Writer was jockey Roger Danjean. Danjean, with trainer Dominic Imprescia directing, shared a history of success at Suffolk Downs. Both respected each other's skill set and trusted one another. The same combination teamed up at Suffolk two weeks prior, winning the $162,000 Massachusetts Handicap. The short 5 ½ furlong distance in the Mayflower Stakes would require Timely Writer to jump out quickly if he would be competitive in the large field. With the starting gates bursting open, Danjean managed to get Writer out of the gate quickly, dropping him back to 4th as Writer headed a bit wide before the beginning of the last turn. As Writer came surging out of the turn, Danjean tugged hard on Writer's reins in order to get the colt into the middle of the track and head towards the finish line. Coming out of the far turn, Danjean urged the colt ahead of the rest of the pack. At the top of the homestretch, a minor duel with a colt named Ring Proud remained before Timely Writer crossed the finish line one length ahead of his nearest competitor.

The favorite, Herschelwalker, finished in a disappointing 6th place. Despite it only being Timely Writer's second career start and wrestling with Danjean to go outside while the jockey was pulling him back to the middle of the track, Writer missed a 42-year track record by 1/5 of a second. Though it was the second win in a row for Timely Writer and a significant pay raise from the winner's purse for the Martins, the afternoon belonged to trainer Dominic Imprescia – much to the delight of the crowd and the media. Rather than focusing newspaper headlines on the local horse winning, the journalists also had fun taunting a particular New York trainer. The *Providence Sunday Journal's* headline read "Campo Shares Suffolk Stage." Mike Welsh from the

Daily Racing Form similarly led with "Campo had to Share Billing." Sam McCracken from the *Boston Globe* was kinder with "Timely Writer, Johnny Dance Win."

Imprescia's win at the Mayflower, coupled with a win in the Massachusetts Handicap earlier in the year, earned him the honor of becoming the first trainer in the history of Suffolk Downs to walk away with both stakes' races in the same year. The accomplishment added to Imprescia's resume after being named Trainer of the Year honors at Hialeah Park over the winter. The steady leadership of Imprescia directing Timely Writer from his home park in Boston contrasted with Campo's management style at Belmont Park in New York. As both trainers and horses left victorious over the holiday weekend, fate would find the trainers and horses competing against one another the following year.

As the Martin crew kept Timely Writer away from the locals and continued to stay quiet with the expert procrastinators, Timely Writer was not given much thought as a favorite for the race. Since Timely Writer was not viewed as a serious challenger for the race, with only one race in New Jersey, the owners and friends continued to reap the financial rewards of their gambling bets. The win by Timely Writer paid an eye-opening $21.40 for every $2 winning ticket. Emboldened by the victory at Suffolk, the Martins turned their attention to the next phase of their plan. The Martin crew looked northwest for its next race - to one of the country's oldest and most prestigious racetracks. Having never previously run a horse at a New York racetrack, the brothers would dare to bring Timely Writer on the four-hour drive to Saratoga Springs, New York.

People have been traveling to Saratoga Springs as a destination for over 200 years. Its very name pays homage to the nearby mineral springs believed to carry medicinal properties. Tucked away in the northeast corner of New York, thoroughbred racing first began in the state's rural area in the summer of 1863. With the track's original management and ownership group struggling to maintain credibility, local investors led by William Collins Whitney purchased the property in 1901, making significant improvements to the facility while bringing respectability to a race track later nicknamed "the Spa."

One of the many allures of the Saratoga Race Course includes the intimate settings at the venue, where patrons are permitted to get within arm's length distance to the horses and jockeys. Visitors to the track often line the horizontal white wooden rails, watching the magnificent animals stroll their way down the path from the horse stables to the paddock area for the mounting of jockeys. Along the tree-lined path, adults can be seen leaning on the top wooden rail separating them from the thoroughbreds, their attendants, and jockeys. As they watch from above the rail, children are ducking below the top and second rail, arms extended, waiting to slap hands with the jockeys as they pass. One row back from the rail are picnic tables dotting the grounds where families and friends have camped out for the day, unpacking meals from the large beach-style coolers wheeled in with them from the parking lots.

The charm of the intimate settings found in and around the grounds at the Spa is matched by the environment outside the main gates in the surrounding neighborhoods. As patrons leave the race track gates, many head towards the nearby grass parking lots, leaving their parked cars in the care of trusted homeowners. A wave goodbye to the parking attendant/homeowner or a word with the young boy or girl sitting in a beach chair at the edge of the grass lot ends the day of racing as the cars slowly exit the grass yards, doubling as parking lots for the two-month racing season. Within walking distance, or a short drive from the grass parking lots, are parks, restaurants, watering holes, hotels, and the historic Broadway Avenue, where shopping stores have lined the street for two centuries.

Horse racing during Saratoga's weeks-long summer meet is often the best in the country, and it annually showcases historic thoroughbred stakes races. The Travers Stakes has been running since 1864 and, like the Triple Crown races, is limited to three-year-olds. It is held in August every year, two months after the final leg of the Triple Crown at Belmont Park, and is affectionately known as the "The Mid-Summer Derby." Many viewing it as the 4th leg of the Triple Crown racing season.

In August of 1981, with Timely Writer's entry in the 79th running of the Saratoga Special, the Martins would venture to Saratoga Race Course for their first time – and for a race won by Timely Writer's great-great-grandfather Native Dancer some forty years prior. The 8th race of the day on Monday, August 3rd, covered 6 furlongs with a purse of $50,000. Waiting for Timely Writer at the Saratoga Special was the formidable Conquistador Cielo, and there was a rematch with Herschelwalker from the Mayflower Stakes the month prior. Conquistador Cielo was under the direction of Hall of Fame trainer Woody Stephens, jockey Eddie Maple, and owner Henryk de Kwiatkowski. Conquistador Cielo's owner purchased the colt the same year as the Martins bought Timely Writer – only the price was a bit higher at $150,000.00. The race included several talented jockeys, with jockey Jorge Velasquez riding He's an Angel. Jockey Angel Cordero, Jr., was in the mount of Lejoli, and a young Canadian jockey named Jeffrey Fell was riding Rich Saul. A news article in the days beforehand spoke to the prospects of the ten horses entered. The article, naturally, was dismissive of Timely Writer, questioning his ability as "the fans are likely to be a bit wary of his credentials until he shows his form [at Saratoga]."[51] It seems a win at the top 2-year-old stakes race in New England was of no consequence for the elite talent at Saratoga.

As Timely Writer made his way down the path to the paddock area for the mounting of the jockeys, Frannie and Peter were awaiting his arrival, looking at the faces of the crowd standing across and outside the fencing of the historic venue. Once jockey Roger Danjean was atop the mount of Timely Writer, the pair made their way onto the dirt track and over to the starting gate, where the colt settled into his position with ease, patiently waiting for the gates to explode open. Once the track official hit the button releasing the gates, Jockey Danjean immediately fought for position in the middle of the pack of racing entries. As the short race quickly developed, Danjean searched for an opening through the middle of the pack to get

Timely Writer to the lead. As Danjean approached the first of two turns in the 6-furlong race, he was tugging tight on the reins of Timely Writer to get him to squeeze through an open space that had developed in between horses. Timely Writer refused to take the space, though, arching his neck and throwing his head in the air towards his right side. Timely Writer's body language forced the jockey to pull the colt to the right after the first turn, bringing the colt to the open running area outside the pack. With the second turn quickly approaching, Danjean needed to get Timely Writer moving to make up the distance created from the time spent traveling to the outside of his competitors. Danjaen was pushing Timely Writer into an extra gear from the outside as they headed towards the finish line. Writer complied and increased his speed, but with the shorter race, too much ground was left to make up. The pair settled for a disappointing third place, two lengths short of winning. Timely Writer's first loss came at the hands of first-place winner Conquistador Cielo and 2nd place finisher Herschelwalker.

Imprescia walked over to Danjean after the race, listening to the jockey explain the difficulties encountered, including how Timely Writer reacted when asked to go between horses in the middle of the track. After listening, Imprescia had a couple of ideas about what to work on before the next race. He was bringing Timely Writer back to Suffolk Downs to make some adjustments before racing again at Saratoga. Imprescia planned to put a "blinkers hood" on Timely Writer during additional training, monitoring whether it improved Writer's focus. Also being discussed was a change in the colt's racing style.

A blinker hood over a horse's head keeps the animal focused by its unique design. The hood is put on the horse with cut-out openings for the ears and eyes. The openings for the eyes have a blinder running along the eye socket's outer area, which minimizes peripheral vision. The design is tailored to keep a horse from being distracted and spooked during racing. Any horse using the blinker hood, however, also needs to feel comfortable with the accessory if his running form and speed are to improve.

In addition to listening to the words of jockey Roger Danjean after the Saratoga Special, Dominic reflected on what he observed from Timely Writer during the race. Writer was insistent about moving to the outside of the track, refusing to go through the middle of horses in the center of the track. Writer also appeared it was from the outside of the pack where he looked at ease - hitting the homestretch for the finish line with explosive late speed from the outside during his one appearance at Saratoga. Dominic was also mindful that in the Mayflower Stakes at Suffolk Downs on July 4th Timely Writer drifted to the outside of the racetrack before posting a time less than one second from the track record. A disappointing 3rd place finish in New York was of no consequence as to what Dominic thought of Timely Writer's potential and ability. Years of experience taught him he had a unique and talented horse – who may be trying to tell others something. Late gaining speed from outside the pack on the last turn is an unusual place for a horse to win a race. It is difficult for a horse to win from this area of the track as more ground is required to be covered, but Dominic had seen enough out of Timely Writer and remembered the comments from Tony Everard. A change in running style was needed if Timely Writer would find greater success.

Timely Writer returned to his hometown track in East Boston between races, with Dominic adding the blinker hood accessory to Writer's training sessions. Dom had the stopwatch on Timely Writer as he wore the new ensemble, working him at six furlongs. Timely Writer was indifferent to the extra equipment covering portions of his head. After reviewing the times at each distance, Dom later commented to the press, "[r]right then I knew we had a real shot to win the big one."[52] Dom's target, which he referenced as the "big one," was the Hopeful Stakes at Saratoga Race Course

As Timely Writer trained well with the blinker hood and continued to show great talent in workouts at Suffolk Downs, the Martins decided he was ready to return to Saratoga. Timely Writer was entered into the 77th running of the Hopeful Stakes, scheduled for Saturday, August 22, 1981, with a purse totaling $75,000 and a course covering a distance of 6 ½ furlongs. The visual appearance of the larger-than-usual two-year-old Timely Writer returning to Saratoga with the orange and black blinker hood was nothing short of intimidating.

During the summer racing season, the Hopeful was the first Grade 1 stakes race for two-year-old thoroughbreds. It serves as a summer showcase for the top horses in their age group. The field of entries for the Hopeful Stakes included unbeaten and heavy favorite Out of Hock - who was going for his fifth straight win. The horse had soundly beaten excellent horses in his four previous races – all runaway victories by a combined 34 lengths. Out of Hock had never trailed at any point of any race and, with good reason, bettors sent him to the gate as the favorite at 4-5 odds. On the other hand, Timely Writer came into the Hopeful without fanfare, publicity, and with no expectations - viewed by racing experts as a long shot. Betting odds at post time had Writer a distant 6-1. Bettors recognized Timely Writer's home turf listed in the racing program and were not impressed with his resume.

The crowd at the Hopeful was the 4th largest in Saratoga race course history – making 1981 the best-attended year in the track's history. The entry Maynesian had an impressive team with 33-year-old Nick Zito as the trainer and Ruffian's jockey Jacinto Vasquez in the saddle fresh off a win at the Sanford Stakes in Saratoga ten days earlier. Fast-rising jockey Jeffrey Fell from Canada was riding Pavarotti on the outside of the eight entries in the field. A jockey originally from Dorchester by the name of Gregg McCarron was riding Sitka. Future Hall of Famer Angel Cordero, Jr. was on Lejoli. Danjean was on Writer for the second straight race, starting from gate number three.

As the racing gates sprung open with the sound of the bell for the start of the Hopeful, the early lead found Maynesian jumping out of gate number one quickly. Out of Hock was the only other speed horse capable of keeping pace with Maynesian for the first ½ mile and stayed in his shadow, never more than a length behind. Danjean, as directed by Dominic, was changing riding styles and strategy with Timely Writer. Dominic gave the directive before the race to get Writer outside the pack upon exiting the gate. For the first ½ mile of the race, Writer was purposefully settled in on the outside of the pack in 8th place out of the eight entries.

Turning for home at the top of the stretch, Out of Hock took over the lead from Maynesian and looked to have enough energy left in the tank to finish off the field for his fifth straight win. Out of Hock held the lead at the top stretch and on his way to the first-place finish many expected. The colt was increasing his lead to two lengths with just 1/8 of a mile left to the finish. However, the jockey for Out of Hock could not see what was transpiring behind him. Danjean had begun turning Timely Writer loose from the back of the pack through the last turn and into the top of the home stretch. Timely Writer's speed coming through the last turn from outside the pack made him look like a projectile slingshot forward - allowing him to swoop past each horse in front of him.

As the eight horses raced through the last turn and into the middle of the track for the stretch drive, Timely Writer covered ground at a speed rarely seen by patrons at the Spa. Writer continued his move through the homestretch, blazing by Out of Hock with 1/16 of a mile left to the finish line. Writer's dash left onlookers with the impression that the undefeated Out of Hock, standing in place at the 1/16 pole, cemented into the depths of the dirt track while the colt from Boston was running away from the heavy favorite. Timely Writer drew further ahead with every stride, crossing it in first place with a miraculous 4-length victory.

As journalist Landon Manning observed from the track rail, "the crowd of 35,363, fourth largest in Saratoga Race course's history, looked on in disbelief as Timely Writer came on with a rush in the homestretch to win going away." The upset by the horse from Boston and how he did it over the heavy favorite, humiliating Out of Houck in the home stretch, left the crowd stunned at the performance. The shock of it all led Manning to write, "Timely Writer's win sounds like something out of a movie – a colt, only recently out of the claiming ranks, defeating an unbeaten counterpart."[53]

Track patrons and employees stared at the tote board, waiting for the official winning time of the race to be posted, with the board confirming their disbelief. Timely Writer, in just his fourth-lifetime race at a track nearly 120 years old, ran the 6 ½ furlongs in 1:16.20 seconds, equaling the time of one legend at the Hopeful, 1973 Triple Crown winner Secretariat, and within 4/5th of a second from breaking the course record set by another legend - 1978 Triple Crown winner Affirmed. A 50-cent copy of *The Saratogian* newspaper the following morning included the front-page headline, "Timely Writer wins 77th Hopeful Stakes." Another headline read, "77th Hopeful Stakes A best-seller for Timely Writer."

In post-race comments, Dominic spoke about the form Timely Writer displayed during the Hopeful. "This colt is beautiful; he's got the best temperament of any horse I've ever been around.... His stride is so smooth... he just glides. He does things Roger doesn't even realize are happening. This colt definitely can go long." Dominic stated the obvious to all who witnessed the race. The win "puts him in the two-year-old championship picture."[54]

Timely Writer, with his blinkers' ensemble, shocks the racing establishment with a win at the Hopeful Stakes in Saratoga Springs.

In an article on the Monday after the race, Russ White of *The Knickerbocker News* summed up the drama and comedy that unfolded during the Hopeful Stakes. "So, two meat men get themselves a horse and think so much of him they enter him in one of the country's most prestigious stake races for two-year-olds, the Hopeful. The Hopeful has been a stepping stone for the Triple Crown races. A horse without fame and without a name, Timely Writer, now must be regarded as a colt to watch."[55] Danjean warned people after the win, '[t]his is no fluke."[56]

The excitement and interest in Timely Writer in Boston and New England increased exponentially after the win at the Hopeful. The story also began spreading across the country - as far as Oklahoma and Washington. Timely Writer's sire, Staff Writer, who never ran a thoroughbred race in his lifetime, had taken up residence in Hagerman, Idaho. Staff Writer had been purchased from Sunshine Stud in Reddick, Florida, as a young stallion. His buyer, Donald McFadden, who did not have the farm facilities to board a stallion, made arrangements for Staff Writer to stand at the farm of a friend in Oklahoma until McFadden could build out the required barns. Before the Hopeful Stakes, the stud fee for Staff Writer in Oklahoma, a state known for breeding quarter horses to outfit rodeos and working ranch horses, had been set at $2,500.00. After the win at the Hopeful, McFadden negotiated a syndication agreement for Staff Writer at $40,000 per share while retaining 25% of the horse.

With the summer racing dates at Saratoga ending on Labor Day weekend, the New York Racing Association (NYRA) began its fall racing season at Belmont Park in Elmont, New York. Frannie was well aware that the Champagne Stakes in October at Belmont Park, which typically serves as the final two-year-old end-of-the-year stakes race to determine the two-year-old horse of the year, was within reach. The one concern Peter and Frannie had about their racing team, though, as they headed back to the Boston area from Saratoga, was whether a change was needed with their regular jockey as the talent and importance of each race was increasing.

Shortly after the win at the Hopeful, Frannie and Peter began discussing the need for a different jockey on Timely Writer. The brothers' concern was that Danjean's inexperience could cost Timely Writer wins at Belmont Park. In contrast, other more experienced and talented jockeys were better suited for the challenging races ahead. However, discussions with Dominic on this topic were saved until they returned to the barns at Suffolk Downs.

Once the first week of September began, with Frannie watching the workouts of Timely Writer at Suffolk Downs, he went to the barns to discuss his thoughts with Dominic about replacing Danjean in the mount. Once the topic was broached, however, disagreement between the trainer and Frannie was immediate. Knowing Dominic was loyal to Danjean and that the jockey had two key wins atop Timely Writer, Frannie expressed his concerns that Danjean's experience was limited to the New England racing circuit and unproven at Belmont Park's elite races. Frannie also indicated that despite Timely Writer nearly breaking track records at three different venues, Danjean wrestled with his ride during his three races in the mount. Frannie believed Danjean should be sitting in the saddle like a glove atop Timely Writer, simply sticking to the plans of the race and directing the colt where he needed to go. Frannie wanted an experienced jockey who had been through the stress and demands of racing at Belmont Park. Dominic wanted to stay with his rider from Suffolk.

Frannie was a bit surprised that Dominic was not in agreement and pushing back on the idea that they needed to switch jockeys quickly, so he brought Peter into the loop on where Dominic stood on the issue. With the owners of Timely Writer not sharing the same opinion with their trainer on such an important issue, the jockey for Timely Writer was unsettled as the fall racing season at Belmont approached – and the first signs of a fractured relationship were lingering as they made their way to the big money races and the end of the racing season awards.

Chapter 6

The Champagne Room: Timely Writer & the Martin Brothers Conquer New York

After successfully breaking his maiden in Oceanport, New Jersey, conquering Suffolk Downs in East Boston, and winning the Hopeful in Saratoga Springs, the fall racing schedule put together for Timely Writer found the team moving from upstate New York to the state's furthest parts east. Just outside of New York City, the elite Belmont Park Race Track, located in the town of Elmont, sits less than 15 miles from the eastern edge of Manhattan. A moderately sized suburban town, it is considered the gateway to Long Island as it divides a city of millions from one of the most affluent areas in the United States.

With its 1 ½ mile course, Belmont Park is the largest race track in America. The race track is deep in history, beauty, and the depth of its dirt track. The green ivy walls of the exterior stands outline an entrance to a tunnel where the horses and their riders enter from the paddock area on one side, exiting onto the dirt track on the opposite side. Once on the dirt track, the proximity of the horse track to the patrons sitting in the grandstands is immediately noticeable. The second and third levels of the grandstand hover over the ground below, creating an intimate sporting event for its participants. The track's impeccably groomed beach-like dirt surface, nicknamed "Big Sandy," resembles that found ocean side in nearby Long Island. Like the beaches in Long Island, the Belmont track surface is deep and tiring – only the strong survive the length of the race and dirt track of the Belmont Stakes. It is the only venue in the country where immortality in thoroughbred racing is achieved if the third and final leg of the Triple Crown race is conquered.

The grand opening of Belmont Park on May 5, 1905, brought over 40,000 people to the venue, many traveling by horse, horse-drawn carriage, trains from Long Island, and the "horseless carriage"—the precursor to the modern-day automobile. Since then, it has been considered one of the grandest estates across the country for thoroughbred horse tracks.

At Belmont Park in the decade before Timely Writer made his way to the race track in 1981, thoroughbreds Affirmed, Secretariat, and Seattle Slew cemented their legacies by sweeping the final leg of the three Triple Crown races. Winning the Triple Crown comes after the culmination of the three most intense and challenging races. The journey begins at the Kentucky Derby over the course of 1 and ¼ miles on the first Sunday in May. A win at the Kentucky Derby asks the winning horse to repeat two weeks later at the Pimlico Race Course in Baltimore, Maryland, at the Preakness Stakes. Finally, if a horse is good enough to win and survive the first two legs of the Triple Crown, he and his team are staring at what appears to be a nearly unconquerable 1 ½ mile race at Belmont Park. There is a reason why the Belmont Stakes is the last of the three Triple Crown races – it is the longest and most challenging to win. As of 2023, only 13 horses have won the Triple Crown. Another seventeen horses won the first two legs before falling short at Belmont. On those 13 occasions when the Triple Crown has been won at Belmont Park, the celebration of the thousands in attendance is electric and unexplainable.

As the 1981 summer racing meet in New York finished in Saratoga, the annual fall pilgrimage for the best thoroughbreds, jockeys, and trainers brought the Martins to Belmont Race Track. Timely Writer was in the top three races for two-year-old horses offered at Belmont. The first race on Timely Writer's fall racing card was the 92nd running of the 7 furlongs Futurity Stakes on September 12th. "The Futurity marks the first of three prestigious events for the beginning males at [the 1981] Belmont meet. The following pair are the $50,000.00 Cowdin also at seven furlongs, two weeks [from the Cowdin] and the 125th Champagne Mile, Saturday, Oct. 10th." [57] The Champagne is run on the last day of the racing schedule, with a field of entries representing the best two-year-old thoroughbreds in the country. The winner of the Champagne is regularly regarded as one of the favorites for the Kentucky Derby during the following three-year-old racing season – and is often crowned as the two-year-old colt of the year.

With the purchase of Timely Writer in 1980 for $13,500, the Martins never anticipated their meager investment would be racing at Belmont Park in 1981. The idea of paying the $25 nomination fee before the start of the year for entry into the 92nd running of the $100,000.00 Futurity never crossed the brothers' thinking. For Timely Writer to secure a starting gate in the field of entries, the Martins had to cut a check for $10,000.00 as a supplemental entry fee. Far more problematic, though, was that the Martins and Dominic did not resolve their disagreement over their jockey. The first-ever appearance for the Martins and Timely Writer at Belmont Park found Roger Danjean in his usual role.

Fresh off his prior win at the Hopeful in Saratoga, Timely Writer was established as the favorite for the first time on September 12th. As the starting gate was rolled onto the dirt track awaiting the eight-horse field for the start of the Futurity, Timely Writer was going off at odds of 4-5, returning $2.80 for every $2 winning bet. The 8-horse race would match obscure jockey Roger Danjean against three future Hall of Fame jockeys, with Angel Cordero, Jr., Eddie Maple, and Jorge Velasquez looking to beat the favorite. The start gate draw for Timely Writer found him in the favorable outside gate number eight. An immediate concern in the paddock area as Timely Writer was getting saddled up for the start of the race was that he was "washing out" in his first competition at Belmont Park. In plain language, Writer was anxious and sweating as he prepared to walk to the starting gate. Washing out typically results in a horse expending unnecessary energy before the race.

The 6 ½ furlongs race before a crowd of 24,000 people saw old nemesis Herschelwalker and Irish Martini out in front of the pack with the opening of the starting gates. The experienced Valasquez knew how to handle a low-cost colt with his ride aboard Irish Martini, who was purchased at auction for $7,500.00. as he battled Herschelwalker right to the finish line. Irish Martini and Valasquez pulled off the win as they battled

Herschelwalker to the finish line, winning by the length of a nose. Timely Writer, not showing his usual finishing sprint, came in a disappointing 3rd, 2 ½ lengths behind the winner. Danjean confirmed the venue change affected Timely Writer, commenting that when he swung Timely Writer into the middle of the homestretch after coming off the final turn, Timely Writer did not have the energy to catch Irish Martini.

Danjean, who never finished out of the money in his four races aboard Timely Writer, with two first-place finishes and two third-place finishes in less than 90 days, was sent back to Suffolk Downs in Boston after the race. Canadian Jockey Jeffrey Fell, who was scheduled to ride Pavarotti in the Futurity before the colt was scratched, had reached out to the Martins through his agent after losing to Timely Writer at the Hopeful in Saratoga. Fell let it be known that he wanted to be the full-time jockey for Timely Writer. Earlier in the year, Fell had been the jockey on Pleasant Colony during the colt's win at the Wood Memorial at Aqueduct in New York. Within the month after his win aboard Pleasant Colony, the owner and trainer Johnny Campo switched to their full-time jockey, perhaps costing Fell wins atop the eventual Kentucky Derby and Preakness Stakes winner. From what Fell saw of the two-year-old Timely Writer, he thought the colt was superior to the three-year-old Pleasant Colony. Any union between Fell and Timely Writer would have to wait, though, as the Cowdin was less than two weeks away, and Fell had already committed to riding Talc Plot. Making matters worse for Fell, the Martins had signed up the great Angel Cordero, Jr. as Timely Writer's jockey for the Cowdin. Although Cordero was scheduled to be the jockey for the well-respected and undefeated two-year-old Deputy Minister, his owners chose not to race their colt in the Futurity or the Cowdin.

On September 24th, the Cowdin saw four future Hall of Fame jockeys in the race, including Angel Cordero, Jr., in the saddle aboard Timely Writer. The pre-race favorite was a horse named Another Bid, whose jockey was Hall of Famer Bill Shoemaker. Shoemaker, though, was injured in a pool mishap vacationing in Acapulco the week prior. Shoemaker's injury left its owner, Hawksworth Farm, scrambling to find another jockey. Hawksworth Farm replaced one future Hall of Fame jockey with another in Stevie Cauthen. The 6 ½ furlongs race left Timely Writer with a difficult gate 1 entry. Sharing the metal gate wall next to him was 1978 Triple Crown-winning jockey Steve Cauthen. Old nemesis Hercschelwalker was further down in gate 7 of the 9-horse field. Out of Hock, who last saw Timely Writer blowing past him in the Hopeful, was in gate 8. Long shot Native Raja, going off at 37-1 odds, was looking for some luck of the Irish with one of the McCarron brothers in the mount - Gregg's younger brother Chris. Fell and Talc Plot found themselves in gate 5, adjacent to Dorchester's Chris McCarron in gate 6.

Brothers Chris and Greg grew up in Dorchester in a tight Irish family. While the Martin brothers from Dorchester were toiling away running Nitram Stables at Suffolk Downs during the 1960s and 70s, Gregg McCarron overlapped his time there with the Martins. It was at Suffolk where Gregg perfected his craft in the saddle. Chris, seven years younger, would often go from Dorchester High School to Suffolk Downs to watch his brother ride professionally, having to sneak in over the fence as he was not the required 18 years of age to get in. With a freckled face to match, the curly-haired redhead learned well by watching his brother throughout his early teens at Suffolk Downs. Chris was a rags-to-riches story himself when, in 1974, two years removed from Dorchester High School, he won the Eclipse Award as the Outstanding Apprentice Jockey, setting a record for wins by a jockey in a season. McCarron broke the record with win number 516 of the year by outracing his brother Gregg, with their father Herb in the stands, having flown in that morning from Logan Airport in Boston to watch history at Laurel Race Course in Maryland. In the prior year, Chris had also added to his trophy collection, winning the Eclipse Award for Outstanding Jockey in 1980.

The depth of talent of jockeys in the Cowdin was unlike that seen at Suffolk Downs regularly. The Cowdin would be Fell's third race of the year against Timely Writer, all ending with Fell watching Timely Writer from behind when crossing the finish line. In a battle of Hall of Fame jockeys, it was the talented Dorchester kid stunning the Cowdin field, beating second-place finisher Timely Writer by 4 ½ lengths. Native Raja paid $77.60 to win on every $2 ticket. Timely Writer, in gate 1 for the 7 furlongs race, had a brutal trip around the track over the short distance. As he tried to get Timely Writer to the outside to run, Cordero found himself cut off three times on the inside rail by his competitors. Although Timely Writer did not finish first, the brothers left optimistic. Though Timely Writer was shut off multiple times during the race, the colt found a way to grind out a second-place finish in a prestigious race.

Timely Writer's "stumbles" in both the Futurity and Cowdin Stakes with 3rd and 2nd place finishes were disappointing. Still, more was expected of Timely Writer after the type of performance he exhibited in winning the Hopeful. The Writer crew, looking forward to the end of the year Champagne Stakes, were still searching for a full-time jockey. Once jockey Angel Cordero received word that the Canadian horse Deputy Minister was transported from north of the border, Jeffrey Fell was granted his wish as the regular jockey for Timely Writer as the Champagne Stakes approached.

The New York Racing Association (NYRA) schedules its annual super card for the final Saturday of Belmont Park's Championship fall meeting. CBS Sports Saturday lined up a 90-minute prime-time horse racing program for the country on Saturday, October 10th. The national television audience spent their late afternoon watching Belmont Park's two biggest stakes races on the closing day of their racing season. The Champagne would be the undercard, set to run at 4:00 p.m. The prestigious $500,000 Jockey Club Gold Cup, with a staggering $300,000 to the winner, was scheduled to run 30 minutes after the completion of the Champagne.

The Jockey Gold Cup, run over 1 ½ miles, typically determines the older Horse of the Year award. John Henry, a six-year-old gelding, with Willie Shoemaker as the jockey, was the favorite for the race and would win the race handily. Once purchased in a claiming race for $1,100, John Henry became the first horse to break $3 million in career winnings with the win. Challenging John Henry in the race was Ogden Phipps' 5-year-old mare Relaxing. Since the age of 35, Phipps had been the Chairman and Chief Executive Officer of the NYRA since 1976. He had grown up in the thoroughbred industry since birth, as his family traced its lineage back to his great-grandfather Henry Phipps – the business partner of steel tycoon Andrew Carnegie. The grandfather of Phipps, Henry Carnegie Phipps, was named after the steel magnate. Grandmother Gladys Mills Phipps, owner of the Wheatley Stable, partnered with Odgen's sister Cynthia to bring the country the finest filly ever in Ruffian.

In pre-Breeder Cup racing days, the 1-mile Champagne Stakes was the ultimate end-of-the-year race for two-year-old colts and talented fillies, which typically determined the two-year-old colt of the year. Winners of the Champagne produced the 2-year-old champion in 15 of the prior 17 years – just under 90% of the time. The Champagne Stakes first ran in 1867, with the Champagne of 1981 offering a $150,000.00 purse - $90,000.00 going to the winner.

A crowded field of 13 horses was considered the best two-year-old horses in the country - two of which were undefeated, having won a combined 11 races in a row. Another entry in the Champagne was from the horse farm of Tony Everard's old boss, George Steinbrenner III. Steinbrenner, owner of the New York Yankees since 1973 and winner of back-to-back World Series championships in 1977-1978, was busy during the afternoon as the Yankees were in a battle for their playoff lives against the "Brew Crew" from Milwaukee. The first pitch in the Bronx was scheduled for 4:10 p.m. Steinbrenner would not be able to be in both places simultaneously, but he had one of the country's best jockeys in Eddie Maple, in the mount on Count Francescui.

The overwhelming favorite in the race was what many believed to be the best filly since Ruffian 8 years earlier. Before Dawn had an unblemished record in her first five races, the backing of the great Calumet Farms and trainer John Veitch by her side, with Jorge Valasquez as the jockey. After Before Dawn won convincingly at the $135,000 Matron Stakes for two-year-old fillies on September 20th, Veitch had decided three weeks prior that their girl would race against the boys. After the win at the Matron, with many believing Before Dawn was "a 2-year-old filly of uncommon talent," Veitch entered her against the talented colts. Veitch thought Before Dawn was of such uncommon talents that she was the one to change history - as no filly had won the Champagne in 55 years. Bill Leggett of *Sports Illustrated*, President of the New York Turf Writers Association, gushed after watching Before Dawn at the Matron, "right now I'm making her the 6-5 favorite for the 1982 Kentucky Derby."[58]

Before Dawn entered the starting gate as the 4-5 favorite. Deputy Minister, the much-hyped horse from Ontario, Canada, who was a perfect six for six going into the Champagne, came into New York as a formidable opponent. Some experts were critical of his record, though, with five of the six wins coming north of the border at Woodbine Race track. Others also thought, especially the Boston crowd, that Deputy Minister had been ducking stronger competition who had raced at the Futurity and Cowdin. There was no question that Deputy Minister, who shared the same grandsire as Timely Writer in legendary Northern Dancer, was a good horse, but he needed to prove his mettle against elite, talented two-year-olds. Despite the concerns, Deputy Minister, with jockey Angel Cordero, Jr. in his saddle, was installed as the second favorite by the bettors. In addition to Before Dawn and Deputy Minister, their full-time jockey Jeffrey Fell would have to contend with Irish Martini, who beat Writer by 4 ½ lengths a month prior at the Futurity. In the week before the race, the Martins could not find Timely Writer's name in discussions as a potential contender in any of the newspapers in New York.

Before Dawn was assigned starting gate position number three, which was a horrible position for a filly at Belmont, as the dirt along the rail is regarded as deep and tiring. A filly of Before Dawn's size would have to battle with others along the inside of the rail. She would need to break quickly and head to the center of the track if she had a realistic chance of beating the colts.

Jack Whitaker, working the race for CBS Sports Saturday, opened his television broadcast announcing the 2-year-old horse of the year honors would come from the winner of the Champagne. The pre-race hype lived up to expectations from the moment the starting gates sprang open. Despite a bad start from the gate, Before Dawn was 4th after the first ¼ of a mile. Legendary jockey Bill Shoemaker had Native Raja in first, with Timely

Writer some distance behind in the 11th spot. Jockey Jorge Valasquez was doing great things in the saddle of Before Dawn as the race moved along, directing her into open space some distance off the rail. This move by Valasquez let his filly make up the earlier lost ground, pushing Before Dawn in front of Native Raja at the ½ mile mark.

As the race developed, Fell strategically positioned Timely Writer on the outside of the pack as they held tight in 7th place – stalking Before Dawn from before hitting the final turn. Fell played possum with Timely Writer and the rest of the field from this spot. CBS television cameras struggled to find Timely Writer in their lens as the middle of the race developed. In a racing move Fell had witnessed in person at the Hopeful in Saratoga, albeit from behind, he let Timely Writer loose before the beginning of the last turn. In a breakout performance in front of his first national television audience, Timely Writer's orange and black silks were now in full view of the television cameras, blazing from the right-hand side of the television screen to the left as he was making his way past six of the best two-year-old horses in the country.

As Timely Writer surged around the final turn at Belmont Park, with Before Dawn and Deputy Minister in sight, Tony Everard was home in Ocala watching the race live on television from his sofa like a proud father watching his child at a high school sporting event. Timely Writer had not yet caught the two undefeated favorites, but Tony knew what others watching did not at this moment - the race was over. Tony knew how the story would end – as he helped write the script earlier in the year.

Timely Writer continued to surge through the end of that last turn at Belmont Park as Tony's thoughts flashed back to one late morning during the spring at Another Episode Farm. A moment in time forever etched into his memory of the young two-year-old colt whipping around the one-mile track in Ocala. Tony was standing in his usual position on the track's dirt, just inside the rail at the end of the homestretch, his body turned leftward and staring towards the beginning of the final turn as Timely Writer made his way through it. The colt surged through the final turn at the end of the one-mile track at a speed the trainer had not seen before on his farm. Not believing Timely Writer could sustain the same level of speed through the homestretch to the finish line, Tony watched Timely Writer increase his pace as he approached. As Tony watched, Timely Writer surged past the proud trainer, with Everard quickly pivoting his body to his right to keep watching. Tony stood watching and thinking that the colt's late surging speed was as fast as any he had seen, with a stride as smooth as any that had ever passed before him.

For those patrons in the stands at Belmont Park looking leftward, Timely Writer could now be seen at the top of the homestretch making his way towards the crowd and finish line. With Timely Writer heading towards him, the fifty-five-year-old Frannie "felt his heart pumping so fast [he] thought it was going to jump out of [his] throat."[59] After finishing his move around the last turn towards the finish line, Timely Writer caught Before Dawn just before the 1/8 pole marker. Coming out of the final turn, Before Dawn had beaten back the challenges of stake winners Irish Martini and Native Raja. However, Jockey Jorge Valesquez, trainer Scott Veitch, and her owners never saw Timely Writer coming. Before Dawn was driving at the top of the homestretch, many believed the filly was about to win her 6th race in a row, cementing the two-year-old horse of the year award and drawing comparisons to the legendary Ruffian. Before Dawn had 1/8 of a mile remaining before winning the Champagne and being declared the favorite for the 1982 Kentucky Derby. None of the people watching, though, knew what Tony Everard knew.

Timely Writer soared past Before Dawn while making his way through the finish line – stealing away the championship while posting a one-mile time of 1:36.40. The winning time, with Timely Writer strategically running slower in the shadows of the leaders until the final turn, was faster than the 1977 champion Alydar and just short of the mark set by Seattle Slew in 1976. Fran and Peter could have cared less that Timely Writer missed the track record, with the 65-year-old Peter philosophizing about the day. "When you've been in this business as long as we have, and have owned as many mediocre or worse horses as we have, at places like Lincoln and Scarborough Downs, time is of no essence."

After winning the Champagne Stakes, the whispers around the track about Timely Writer's greatness had grown to entire conversations, with individuals telling others, "I have never seen a horse run like that."[60] Other experienced track journalists observed, "It was one of the most convincing Champagne victories in the 110-year history of the historic 2-year-old one-mile classic."[61] "Simply stated, it was a day that will live long in the memory of anyone there. The drama on that afternoon was the equal of any sports entertainment package this year."[62] After the race, Imprescia declared Writer "the 2-year-old champion ...... and he beat a darn fine filly." [63]

Experts and supporters of the fantastic filly were stunned and disappointed in Before Dawn's second-place finish. It seemed the only colt she couldn't handle was this horse from Boston and his unknown owners. Observers reveled in the fact that the "tenacious shipper from Suffolk Downs had come over from Boston to put seven rivals more familiar to the NYRA circuit in their places." With the win and victories in the two most critical juvenile races in the pre-Breeder Cup days, Timely Writer had disposed of three elite horses at the Hopeful and Champagne, who totaled sixteen races without a loss before taking on the horse from Boston.

Champagne Delight – Mary, Fran, Peter & Jeffrey Fell stand behind the trophy and bottles of champagne.

After the winner's circle celebration, the Martin family took the champion's trophy and the pair of one-gallon Moet champagne bottles with them as they accepted an invitation from the New York Racing Association. The family celebrated at the "Champagne Room" at Belmont Park. Dinner and drinks were served to the champions with the hoisting of champagne glasses as the family gave thanks for what had been accomplished. Mary Martin, an eye-witness to the nearly 30 years of hard work and struggles of her husband and brother-in-law, put it best as they sipped champagne poured from their over-sized champagne bottles, "I can't think of anything nicer to happen to us but to win this race. It means so much to Fran. He's been in the business for 28 years and has had mostly cheap claimers, but he spent a lot of money trying to get a good one."[64]

In the Champagne Room, the two brothers reflected on where they were sitting and who helped to bring them to the table – Tony Everard. Everard was not only the visionary who recognized greatness at a breeding farm in the middle of Florida but also a magician of a trainer who turned the discovery into an elite champion. From the riches of their winning purses, the Martins would quietly show their appreciation during the winter of 1981, purchasing and delivering a new Cadillac and farm equipment to Tony at New Episode Farm. Everard had thousands of wealthier clients once Timely Writer was done with racing, but only a few owners showed their appreciation in such a manner. More than 40 years later, Everard reflected on the gift from the brothers, knowing they never told anyone of their holiday gift.

As he sipped champagne with Mary and Peter, Frannie also shared his opinion on who he believed to be the most underrated trainer in the country – Dominic Imprescia. Frannie told the media that his trainer was so good he "could train a donkey to run." Though the two-year-old racing season challenged the relationship with their trainer, with the issue of Timely Writer's jockey lingering from Saratoga through the races at Belmont Park, there was no doubt about their loyalty and respect for Dominic's abilities. Many more challenges for the group lay ahead in 1982, including multiple owners looking to purchase 50% of Timely Writer - some demanding that Dominic be replaced as part of the sale.

After a dominating win in a showdown against undefeated rivals, and with the winter months coming, the owners and trainer believed there was nothing left to prove for their colt. Only rest was needed for Timely Writer as he was eventually shipped south for the winter to the warm barns in Florida. Fran and Mary returned to their home in Quincy and Dorchester for Peter, all getting ready for a busy holiday season at the meat business. The media attention increased exponentially for the brothers as they now owned one of the elite thoroughbreds heading into the three-year-old racing season and a probable trip to the Kentucky Derby. Newspapers and television stations nationwide began to tell the fairy tale story of the rags-to-riches owners. The national attention started immediately after the win at the Champagne, with the Sunday newspapers spreading the story about the brothers' dramatic win in headlines above the top fold in the sports sections. The Monday morning headline on the front page of the *Daily Racing Form* proclaimed, "Timely Writer Scores." On Thursday of the same week, a half-page article appeared in *Sports Illustrated* magazine. Congratulatory telephone calls, cards, and gifts arrived at their homes in the weeks after the win, including a remarkably accurate hand-drawn caricature of the two owners.

As Timely Writer was resting and readying for spring racing, the story spread from coast to coast, with the Boston media market leading the charge. The Sunday *Boston Globe* published a human-interest story on October 25th, running a multi-page article with a headline entitled, "*Two Butchers, a horse, a dream: The saga of Timely Writer and the Martins heads for Kentucky.*" A photograph under the headline showed Frannie and Peter from inside their meat freezer, with the biggest smiles across their faces, the pair posing while wearing their white butchers' coats and racks of ribs hanging in the background.

The story was also making its way onto the television screens throughout New England. A young sports reporter with incredible storytelling talents had recently returned home to work for Channel 4 News in Boston. Bob Neumeier, or "Neumie" as he was affectionately called, was a 1968 graduate of Weymouth High School - a 20-minute car ride to Suffolk Downs. Neumie graduated college at Syracuse University in 1972, finishing with a Bachelor of Arts degree in broadcasting and television. At 25, he became the voice of the Hartford Whalers of the National Hockey League. After finishing a five-year television broadcasting career in Hartford, Connecticut, the now 31-year-old Neumie was returning home.

Neume was joining the sports department for the most popular news television channel in Boston and throughout New England. In the days when full-time sports channels were not yet dotting cable television and in an era where families sat down together in the early evening hours to listen to the national and local news stories of the day, sports commentators were some of the leading characters at the news stations. In the decade of the 1980s, regional news stations had a captivated audience - though die-hard sports fans were forced to sit through the first fifteen minutes of the day's news before witty sports commentators took over the show in their allotted 5-minute segment. The sports segments were a roller coaster ride of sorts, with the free-wheeling sports commentators in the news studio supported by on-site reporters, providing in-season scores, highlights, and human-interest stories.

As a sports commentator who had perfected his craft by age thirty, Neumie was a gifted storyteller with a second-to-none personality. Educated in the art of journalism, witty, humble, and quick thinking, Neumie could spin a sports yarn like no other. In the television news of the 1970s and 80s, and having grown up in the suburbs of Boston, the young Neumie was pure gold on television tubes in Boston.

The fairy tale story of Timely Writer and his owners proved a perfect match for Boston's newest sports reporter. After the Champagne Stakes win by Timely Writer in New York and the probable 2-year-old Horse of the Year award, Neumie's story about the champion and his owners would be broadcast throughout New England's six states. News crews with their television cameras were dispatched for interviews at the offices of Keyes Supply and Suffolk Downs. Interviews with trainer Dominic Imprescia were conducted trackside at Suffolk Downs. Television cameras and crews spent the afternoon at Keyes Supply in Boston, interviewing Peter and Frannie in their office. The camera crew taking footage of the inner workings of the Martin brothers' business. Archived video footage of Timely Writer's wins at the Hopeful Stakes in Saratoga and the Champagne were retrieved by the editing room of the news station for preparation and production. Neumie and his crew brought the printed story to life for their viewers, creating a love affair for all of New England.

The four-minute segment aired the week after the win at the Champagne Stakes, with sportscaster director Bob Lobel introducing the story as "one straight out of the movie *Rocky*." Lobel's comparison to the fictional Rocky Balboa character was not one of hyperbole. As he sat in the sports director's seat from the Boston news station, the commentator knew the New England region loved an underdog story, and Lobel had one heck of a story to share with his audience. Tales of underdogs overcoming odds first began in the Boston region of the country – the forefathers of Lobel's audience driving out the strongest army in the world from Boston. Knowing his audience loved underdogs, Lobel tied in the contemporary underdog with a reference to the Rocky Balboa movies in the cinemas.

Rocky first arrived in the cinemas in 1976 - a role and character that appeared in sequels which captivated the country for over two decades. As Lobel teased the story to his audience, the Martin brothers and Timely Writer were a comparable tale of underdogs - though not a fiction story created for the movie screen. After the Rocky Balboa comparison, Lobel swung the story to Neumie, with the Weymouth resident narrating the news production for the next four minutes – dropping in the forever-quotable brothers within the segment. At one point while being interviewed, Frannie laughingly shook his head sideways, telling viewers, "Only in America could this happen."

After interviews with the brothers, the camera crew's footage from earlier in the week was shown throughout the story, including blue-collar employees from Kyes Supply sharpening their commercial-grade knives before breaking down the racks of ribs sitting atop the countertops for packaging and resale. In a precursor to his debut on the national television scene in the spring of '82, Frannie's son John found his way into the background of newsreel footage taken at Kyes Supplies. The news segment finished with video footage of Timely Writer blazing down the home stretch from his recent wins at Saratoga and Belmont, the roar of the crowd heard in the background, with Neumie pronouncing that the favorite for the 1982 Kentucky Derby was resting comfortably in the barns at Suffolk Downs awaiting his transport van south to Florida for the winter.

Frannie's patriotic reference to "only in America" was spot on - only in America could two butchers and their real-life fairly-tale story compare to the fictional Oscar Award-winning movies of Sylvester Stallone. By the end of Neumie's real-life tale, the entire viewing audience from the six states of New England was rooting for Timely Writer and the Martins as 1982 approached. New Englanders, who typically enjoyed a bowl of clam chowder during the winter months, longed for the taste of Mint Juleps served at Churchill Downs in the coming spring as they prepared to watch their newly adopted horse at the Kentucky Derby.

Brothers and butchers from Dorchester conquer Florida while their story spreads across the country.

Chapter 7
The Eclipse Awards: Celebration . . . and Corruption

The Eclipse Awards serve as the annual recognition for excellence in the horse racing industry. Winning an Eclipse Award in horse racing is equivalent to winning an Oscar from the Academy of Motion Pictures Arts and Sciences in the movie industry. The awards are named after an 18th-century British racing champion, so named due to the colt's birth during the solar eclipse on April 1, 1764. Seemingly energized by the sun, Eclipse won every one of his races during his 26 starts. The colt's stud career was also lights out, producing 344 first-place finishers while establishing himself as one of the best stallions in the history of Thoroughbred racing. "As a stallion, he proved so successful that he appears somewhere in the pedigrees of most Thoroughbreds even today."[65]

Eclipse Awards were first established in 1971 to celebrate the top horses and individuals nationally in various categories within the thoroughbred business. Voters come from three separate thoroughbred organizations within the industry: the National Turf Writers Racing Association (NTRA), the NTRA racing secretaries, and staff from the Daily Racing Form. Before its formation, each of the three groups of voters held separate elections and annual awards, with many years producing inconsistent and puzzling results.

Horse racing awards had been in existence for over 125 years before the 1981 racing season. In the 90 years preceding the 1981 Eclipse Awards, every colt who had won the Hopeful and Champagne Stakes, two of the three premier races for two-year-old horses, went on to win the Two-Year-Old Horse of the Year Award. For 90 consecutive years, this formula was as good of a predictor as any mathematical equation. It defied logic that the force and fury Timely Writer imposed upon his competition during the 1981 season, with stakes wins at Suffolk Downs, Saratoga Race Course, and Belmont Park while never finishing less than third against elite competition, would end with anything but the recognition he and his racing team deserved.

Eclipse Award winners are announced during the holiday season with a banquet held after the new year - always at a swanky hotel. The $125 per person black-tie dinner banquet for the 1981 racing season was scheduled at the Fontainebleau Hotel in Miami Beach on February 5, 1982 – 60 days before the Florida Derby for 3-year-old colts at Gulfstream Park – and just 30 minutes south of the horse track. The only whispers about any competition for Timely Writer as the Two-Year-Old Colt of the Year came from the camp and supporters of Canadian bred Deputy Minister. Reeling from his collapse at the Champagne Stakes in early October, Deputy Minister's new ownership team sought to salvage the colt's credibility.

From his foaling through the 2-year-old racing season, the Canadian colt's ownership group could not match the stability of the Martin family. Deputy Minister's foaling began with Mort and Morjah Levy - owners of a small breeding farm in Ontario called Centurion Farms. Their farm had just one breeding mare by the name of Mint Copy. After saving enough money, the couple had the good fortune to breed Mint Copy with Vice Regent, the union-producing Deputy Minister, in 1979. Ownership of Deputy Minister changed for the first time during the summer of the colt's two-year-old season, with owners Mort and Morjah selling 50% of the colt to Bud Wilmot and Kinghaven Farms before the Champagne Stakes. The sale was reported at less than $500,000 and included the complete transfer of decision-making control of Deputy Minister to Bud Wilmot.

Bud, a former chairman of the Canadian brewery Molson Industries, founded Kinghaven Farms in 1967 and oversaw its development into one of Canada's best racing and breeding farms in less than fifteen years. Before purchasing Deputy Minister, the farm had extended its footprint further south in the horse racing business by buying a 660-acre farm in Ocala, Florida. In a move much criticized by the Canadian press, Kinghaven Farms turned its back on the local full-time jockey and trainer of Deputy Minister, firing both before the Champagne Stakes at Belmont Park.

With Timely Writer shutting it down after the Champagne win, the new owners of Deputy Minister saw an opportunity with four weeks left to go in the racing season. Despite the associated risk of continuing to run a young developing colt, the new owners and trainer took an aggressive approach with Deputy Minister. From October 11th through November 5th, Deputy Minister was entered into two more races - totaling 3 in 26 days. After the loss at Belmont Park, the new ownership team entered Deputy Minister in the $200,000 Laurel Futurity on October 24th in Maryland. Also booked, and an interesting choice for the Canadian owners, was a racetrack known as the "Big M" - Meadowlands Race Course in East Rutherford, New Jersey. The Young American Stakes at the Big M would host Deputy Minister on November 5th for his final race.

Deputy Minister survived his race at the Laurel Futurity in Maryland, winning by a nose over the inexperienced Laser Light, who was making his second career start along with six other lesser-quality entries. A businessman named Robert Brennan watched the race during the evening program. Brennan, not yet 40 years old and a resident of New Jersey, made the trip to watch Deputy Minister race. Brennan later commented on seeing Deputy Minister for the first time, "I had seen him win the Laurel Futurity. He made a brilliant move on the inside that night. I remember being very impressed." [66]

With an accounting degree from Seton Hall University and born and raised in Newark, New Jersey, Brennan appeared to be a hometown success story. Brennan founded First Jersey Securities in 1974, building a business that included offices in 20 different cities, with clients totaling more than 100,000, and a helicopter, which transported him from his home in New Jersey to his office on Wall Street in New York City. The businessman built his empire by buying "penny stocks" of distressed companies and selling them to his clients at highly inflated prices throughout the 1970s and 1980s. The business platform for First Jersey Securities involved salesmen who utilized high-pressure techniques to sell shares in worthless companies to unwitting investors. First Jersey Securities was run with two other businesses owned by Brennan, Hibbard Brown, and LC Weyard & Company. The scheme by Brennan involved the two brokerage firms working to manipulate the penny stock prices upward, showing stock prices in First Jersey Securities' portfolios were rising. Once the penny stocks hit a specific price, the two brokerage firms would sell their shares to their benefit and the detriment of the clients at First Jersey Securities. In the decade before the real-life character of Jordan Belfort from *The Wolf of Wall Street* began defrauding clients of hundreds of millions of dollars, Brennan had already started his criminal enterprise. Brennan would spend his ill-gotten gains from First Jersey Securities by funneling money into horse racing stables, a breeding business, horse farms, and eventually racetracks. Most important for Mort and Morjah Levy was that Brennan had millions of dollars of other people's money at his disposal.

Similar racing results at the Big M, which included an appearance by Brennan once again, followed twelve days after the Laurel Futurity with Deputy Minister's entry in the Young American Stakes at Meadowlands Race Track in New Jersey. Deputy Minister once again outraced Laser Light and a horse named Royal Twister. Watching Deputy Minister from his owner's box at the Big M was Robert Brennan. The Big M was the home turf of Brennan's racing stable, which he had aptly named Due Process. Brennan's name for the stable was born from his perceived injustice at the hands of the Securities & Exchange Commission (SEC). Brennan's battles with the SEC first began in the year he formed his company and grew to involve various legal difficulties - including one suspension for improperly selling mutual funds to his clients. Brennan, when asked about the reason for the literary legalese of his stable, responded, "Because that's what I never got from the SEC – due process."[67]

As he watched Deputy Minister from his owner's box at the Big M in November 1981, Brennan's venture into the horseracing business only began in January of 1980 at the Hialeah two-year-old sales in Florida. In Florida, Brennan purchased a filly, naming her Newkidontheblock. Brennan then poured 20 million dollars into his horse racing empire, including a 420-acre farm in New Jersey and a 320-acre farm in Ocala, where he would stall approximately 170 horses. As it turned out, though, Brennan's ability to spend other people's money happened to be illegal. A decade later, one federal judge characterized Brennan as "nothing but a crook."[68] Chick Lang, the General Manager of Pimlico Racetrack, told people he thought Brennan was a "snake-oil salesman from New Jersey, with the face of a choirboy, the confidence of a safecracker, and the finesse of a riverboat gambler."[69]

With the end of Deputy Minister's two-year-old racing season at Meadowlands Racetrack, the colt's record stood at 8 wins in 9 races, though many of the wins were against far lesser competition. The races against inferior talent began with Deputy Minister's maiden race at Woodbine Race Track, located north of the border in Ontario, Canada. The track was Deputy Minister's home turf, where he spent five of his first six races before taking on Timely Writer at the Champagne. Though Timely Writer broke his maiden against a bunch of nobodies at a claiming race in Monmouth Park, his next six races included five stake races at Suffolk Downs, Saratoga Race Course, and Belmont Park. He took on talented horses such as Herschelwalker, Conquistador Cielo, Out of Hock, Irish Martini, and Before Dawn - none of the thoroughbreds finding their way north to race at Woodbine.

Awards season for Timely Writer began with the New England Turf Writers Association announcing their 41st annual Awards Banquet at Lombardo's restaurant in East Boston on Monday, November 16th. The Martin brothers brought their families to the Italian restaurant near Suffolk Downs. Their dear friend Frank Bertolino and his family joined the Martins at the gala. The Bertolino family was sitting at a table of 10 adjacent to the Martins. The night was spent eating spaghetti and meatballs, swapping horse stories, and discussing their dreams for the following year. Frannie and Peter took the stage at the night's end, accepting the award for the champion Two-Year-Old Colt of the Year. Frank Bertolino also took the stage as he was presented with the Outstanding Contributions Award for New England Thoroughbred Racing. Boston television news station Channel 4, which had broadcasted stories about the success of Timely Writer and the Martins during 1981, was also represented at the awards banquet. The news station's popular sports director, Bob Lobel, was present to accept the Television Achievement Award in horse racing.

Also honoring Timely Writer in the month following was the Florida Thoroughbred Breeders' Association, with the group presenting the Martins the trophy for the Florida Bred Two-Year-Old Colt of the Year. Although the Martins were deeply honored with the awards coming out of New England and Florida, they had their eyes focused on the national prize. The culmination of the annual horse racing awards would come with the announcement of the Eclipse Award winners on December 22, 1981.

With Deputy Minister's win at the Big M in November, the politicking for the Two-Year-Old Colt of the Year began from his new home in New Jersey. A campaign was set in motion to clear the memory of Timely Writer's 8 ½ length drubbing of Deputy Minister at the Champagne Stakes. People directly involved with Deputy Minister were determined to be on the stage accepting the Eclipse Award for Two-Year-Old-Colt of the Year at the Fontainebleau on February 5th. One Eclipse Award voter who knew of the politicking behind the scenes was *Miami News* sports journalist and national turf writer Art Grace. Despite whatever gifts or bribes were sent his way, Grace never changed his vote for the Two-Year-Old Colt of the Year. Grace warned Floridians, "There is a concerted publicity campaign in progress to sneak Deputy Minister ahead of Timely Writer in the Eclipse Award voting for the 2-year-old champion."[70] Bumper stickers and pamphlets were distributed to the masses, reading "Deputy Minister – a helluva horse." The campaign was shameless as trainer Dominic Imprescia was even marketed, with one of the bumper stickers mailed to him by Louis Raffetto, Jr. - the racing secretary and Eclipse Award voter from Laurel and Hialeah racetracks. Holding to his beliefs, Art Grace explained, "there is no way I am going to change my vote. When Timely Writer came from 11th in the Champagne and blew by everybody – including Deputy Minister and Before Dawn (both unbeaten at the time) to win by 4 ¾ lengths... it was all over as far as I was concerned. The fact that Deputy Minister came back to win the Laurel Futurity by a nose over Laser Light, who was making the second start of his life, and then won the Young America, does not balance his eight-length loss to Timely Writer. Deputy Minister was 8 for 9, but his first six victories were in Canada against horses which do not offer much of a yardstick."[71]

As other journalists would admit, more than bumper stickers were distributed to voting members. "The 1981 Eclipse awards, and the connections of one of the two leading contenders for the championship of that particular division have responded by sending bottles of whiskey to certain turf writers whom they consider key to the voting. Horses used to be awarded championship status based on ability, on their superiority over their peers, not on whether their connections were clever enough or wealthy enough to bribe the voters." Laurel Race Course in Maryland was even distributing free windbreakers to patrons with the same moniker imprinted on them as the bumper stickers.

Winning the Eclipse Award for Two-Year-Old Colt of the Year is akin to winning a multi-million-dollar lottery ticket. An owner collecting winnings from purses distributed from horse races is one thing, but stud fees after retirement are a far different money maker. When the great thoroughbred Alydar was put out to stud at four, he serviced more than 100 mares yearly at $250,000 per appearance. By 1980, breeding syndication agreements had been popularized within the thoroughbred racing industry. Lord Avie had won the Eclipse Award as the champion Two-Year-Old Colt. Before Lord Avie's three-year-old racing season started, his six owners assembled a $10 million breeding syndication agreement where each of the 40 shares cost $250,000. A clause in the agreement also stated if Lord Alvie won the Eclipse Award at the Three-Year-Old Colt of the Year, each shareholder owed an additional $100,000 – another $4 million in addition to the $10 million already paid to the six owners. Once Lord Avie became a stallion at the age of four, all income generated from each of his stud appearances would be distributed to the shareholders of the syndication. Winning the prestigious Eclipse Award and the millions of dollars in stud fees that inevitably come with the award are always central thoughts in the minds of horse owners. It is the type of money that motivates individuals to make decisions that are not otherwise considered.

Deputy Minister's new ownership team took the pursuit of the Eclipse Award to a different level as they "marketed" voters. It seemed an open secret about what Deputy Minister's team was doing and why. The *Baltimore Sun* reported on the morning after Deputy Minister's win at Laurel that "the struggle for year-end honors is almost as important to racehorse owners as the races that elevate them to such titles." Deputy Minister had lost his luster after the Champagne, "so it was important to everyone for him to win yesterday. The Laurel Futurity had a winner's purse of $110,782 but the victory could turn out to mean millions more when it comes time to syndicate him."[72]

After the November 5th win at the Meadowlands, Mort and Morjoh Levy were approached by a buyer about selling their remaining interest in Deputy Minister. The potential buyer had been watching Deputy Minister from not so far away in the month prior – and was prepared to pay the price for the remaining 50% of the colt much higher than that paid for the first half. Though the formal announcement would not be made until after the new year, the sale price and conditions were already being negotiated.

Winners of the 1981 Eclipse Awards were announced on the evening of Tuesday, December 22nd, including near Triple Crown winner Pleasant Colony as the top Three-Year-Old Colt. Before Dawn was the top Two-Year-Old Filly, John Henry, a six-year-old gelding and winner of the Jockey Gold Cup at Belmont in October, won the Horse of the Year. Looking through the listings of winners, most readers paused at the Eclipse Award winner for Two-Year-Old Colt - Deputy Minister. As the *Miami Herald* expressed the following morning, "Deputy Minister was the surprise choice as Eclipse Award winner over Timely Writer in the division for two-year-olds."[73] During the same morning, Frannie Martin, after fielding numerous telephone calls throughout the night from people within the industry, showed his frustrations with the injustice done to Timely Writer. Frannie, always one to speak his mind with journalists from any horse publication, newspaper, or magazine, gave the horse racing establishment a verbal thrashing. As he spoke with *Boston Globe* sports journalist Bill

Griffith, Frannie started slowly, growing angrier the more he spoke. From his meatpacking business in Boston, Frannie expressed his feelings about the award being presented to a horse other than Timely Writer. In an industry the brothers had been involved with for over thirty years, he expressed it was the biggest disappointment of their lives.

Frannie's error in judgment was his wrongly held belief that the process used by voters to determine winners of the Eclipse Awards was beyond reproach. He thought the awards process in place would "be played on the level, straight down the middle."[74] However, the principles instilled in him from growing up in Dorchester faced the cold reality of a sports industry dominated and controlled by men different than Frannie and his family. As the interview with Griffith continued, Frannie addressed the thoughts lingering in the minds of many about how this could have happened, telling the sports journalist, "Money and power did the talking in this award."[75] Referencing the history of the Eclipse Award in the 90 years prior, Frannie asked rhetorically, "you tell me why [Writer lost]."[76] The answer was evident to Frannie as Timely Writer outraced the undefeated Deputy Minister, Before Dawn, and Out of Hock in the biggest stakes races of the year. Frannie's last statement to Griffith went right at the establishment. "A lot of people in Florida and Kentucky are shaking their heads today. A lot of people know it wasn't fair. And a lot of people know money was involved." [77] Frannie did more than suggest that votes for the Eclipse Award had been bought - he flat-out stated it. Frannie and many others knew certain people were prepared to do what was needed so the owners of one horse would win the award.

An angry trainer, Dominic Imprescia, told the press shortly after Deputy Minister was announced as the winner, "Wait until the Flamingo, Timely Writer will prove them wrong."[78] Critics of the award were plentiful, with commentary lasting into the following year. The horse from Boston even received support from journalists in New York as one declared Timely Writer as "the best 2-year-old in the land last year.... and the overwhelming favorite to sweep the triple crown classics."[79] For differing reasons, many journalists believed that Timely Writer and the Martin crew were not treated fairly. One school of thought was that the horse racing establishment was not fond of the background the Martins brought with them. The thinking was "they held it against Fran and Peter Martin that they [were] local meat wholesalers who [didn't] exactly hob-nob with the DuPonts."[80] Another belief was that "they held it against Dom Imprescia that he [was] a veteran Suffolk trainer who has succeeded while working up to his elbows in claimers."[81]

Denying Eclipse Awards to owners not from within the horse racing establishment was not new to the sport. The Martin crew only need to think back five years prior when a Boston sports icon was similarly treated. Former Boston Bruins goalie Gerry Cheevers, and the team's head coach during Timely Writer's racing seasons in 1981 and 1982, had owned a two-year-old colt named Royal Ski in 1976. Royal Ski was disregarded in a very similar manner as Timely Writer – if not worse. After pouring through the Thoroughbred sales catalogs in 1975, looking for a one-year-old to purchase, Cheevers settled on a colt he would later name Royal Ski, paying a modest purchase price of $20,500. `

Royal Ski began his two-year-old season with wins in his maiden race at Pimlico Race Track on June 22, 1976, followed by a first-place finish at Suffolk Downs in the Mayflower Stakes on July 5th. After leaving Boston, Royal Ski raced another seven times, including a second-place finish at the prestigious Grade 1 stakes race Arlington Futurity and a first-place finish at the Grade 1 stakes race in Laurel Futurity on October 30th. Royal Ski finished his season on November 13th, winning the Grade 3 Heritage Stakes race. As the announcement for the Eclipse Awards' winners approached, Royal Ski had been battled-tested, racing against top-level talent throughout the country. Royal Ski's season totaled nine races in eight different states during his two-year-old campaign, with six wins, one second-place finish, and one third-place finish. The successful season ended with Royal Ski as the leading money winner for his age bracket, with total earnings of $309,000.00

Despite Royal Ski's impressive year, certain New York Eclipse Award voters were touting Seattle Slew as the top colt in the division. Seattle Slew, bred by a Kentucky Racing Commissioner named Ben Castleman, had been unraced but training in the summer of '76 at Saratoga Springs and putting up fast times. The colt had developed later than most his age, requiring additional training before beginning his two-year-old campaign. An injury over the summer also pushed Seattle Slew's first race back from August in Saratoga to late September at Belmont Park, where he would remain for the fall racing season. Over 30 days, Seattle Slew left the starting gate three times at Belmont – which was the totality of his racing season. On September 20, 1976, the colt won his maiden race at 6 furlongs by five lengths. On October 5th, Seattle Slew won by 3 ½ lengths in a 7 furlongs Allowance conditional race – the race against entries whose pre-race requirements were set as non-winners of two races. In his third and final race on October 16th, Slew's trainer entered the colt in the prestigious one-mile Champagne Stakes. The colt blew away the field by just under ten lengths while setting a track record. The winning purse for Slew totaled $82,350. Adding the smaller winnings from his prior two races, Seattle Slew's annual earnings totaled $94,550. After the Champagne, as with the decision of Timely Writer's owners five years later, the owners of Seattle Slew shut the young colt down.

As a statistical comparison of the two competitors vying for the Eclipse Award for Two-Year-Old Colt of the Year in 1976, Royal Ski finished his season running three times more than Seattle Slew (9 to 3), earning more than three times in purse money, and with twice as many wins (6 to 3) – including a total of 4 stake wins to 1. One Eclipse Award voter, in explaining his choice of Royal Ski, published an article in the *New York Daily News* after the voting was finished but before the awards were announced. "Royal Ski was my 2-year-old champ among the colts and geldings. The decision was made – and it was a difficult one – on 1976 performance, not 1977 potential. Gerry Cheevers' colt negotiated two turns, running short and winning the Futurity over Timonium's five-eighths track and running long in winning the Heritage at Keystone and the Remsen at Aqueduct. Seattle Slew, the hometown favorite, was an impressive winner of his three late starts, galloping away from everything in sight in taking the Champagne at Belmont. But second choice Seattle Slew has never been around two turns." [82]

In the face of the clear numerical advantage Royal Ski possessed, including the breadth of his campaign over the calendar year, Eclipse Award voters from New York and throughout the East Coast were declaring the award a close competition – pointing to Seattle Slew's win at the Champagne Stakes as the difference maker. The rumors of an award competition closer than some may have thought proved accurate when, on December 15th, it was announced the Eclipse Award for Two-Year-Old Colt of the Year was Seattle Slew. Unlike Frannie, Cheevers never aimed his ire directly at Eclipse Award voters and the racing establishment. However, his words a month prior reflected sentiments from a professional athlete struggling to come to terms with a potentially flawed awards process. In an interview just weeks before the award was announced, Cheevers spoke from logic and principal, "it doesn't seem right that the New York colt (Seattle Slew) should win the Eclipse Award just for winning the only three races it's run. My colt has won two 1 1/16th mile stakes and raced well at eight different tracks throughout the country. He's won two earlier stakes and proved he can run well on either the front end or come from out of it."[83]

After the 1976 Eclipse Awards were announced, others were not as gracious in choosing their words as Cheevers. Trainer Smiley Adams, whose horse Run Dusty Run was a candidate for the award with six wins in 9 starts and earnings of $268,241, asked perplexedly, "how could they give the title to a horse who had run only three times, won less than $100,000, and ran only in New York?"[84] Though plenty of people questioned the voters' rationale for handing the Eclipse Award to Seattle Slew in 1976, the voters' logic was simple – the colt dominated his competitors in the prestigious Champagne Stakes at Belmont Park.

The folly of the voting process laid bare in awarding the 1976 Two-Year-Old Colt of the Year was further exposed five years later when the same group of voters reversed its logic in giving the same Eclipse Award to Deputy Minister. In handing Deputy Minister the 1981 award for the Two-Year-Old Colt of the Year, the majority of voters rationalized it based upon the breadth of the Canadian's racing season while ignoring Timely Writer's season and dominating win at the Champagne Stakes – which had been the logic used for Seattle Slew's Eclipse Award. Using the logic employed by the Eclipse Award voters in 1976, the Eclipse Award of 1981 should have gone to Timely Writer. In contrast, using the voters' logic for the award in 1981, the 1976 Eclipse Award should have gone to Royal Ski. Logic from one year cannot be reconciled with the other year in justifying the Eclipse Awards given to Seattle Slew and Deputy Minister. History and facts were on Frannie's side when he blasted the corruption of the voting process in the Eclipse Awards in December of 1981. A review of the voters' logic from the 1976 and 1981 Eclipse Awards exposes a sport operated by those on the inside to the detriment of others on the outside. A review of the historical data going back to 1891 further supported Frannie's scolding of the establishment.

Frannie need not have looked too far to identify suspects behind the campaign to unseat Timely Writer for the 1981 Eclipse Award. Officially, the Levys sold their remaining 50% of Deputy Minister on January 21, 1982, for a reported $5-6 million dollars. Not surprisingly, the buyer was Robert Brennan - the gentleman sitting in the stands watching Deputy Minister at the racetracks in Maryland and New Jersey. Weeks before the official announcement of Deputy Minister's purchase, Brennan's team of veterinarians spent time performing their due diligence on his investment. Medical evaluations of Deputy Minister included thorough physical exams with a series of X-rays for their review. Although he was not yet an owner of the colt, Brennan was keeping Deputy Minister close by - with the medical reviews conducted at Brennan's stable located at Meadowlands Racecourse. Despite Canadian Bud Wilmot owning 50% of Deputy Minister, and Deputy Minister's home turf across the border to the north, the colt never returned home to Canada that year - staying at Brennan's horse barn throughout.

With Deputy Minister's new ownership team in place for a new year of racing, the colt was vanned to Hialeah Race Track for boarding at Brennan's Due Process Stable. Shortly after the colt's arrival, a Canadian television broadcasting company was dispatched to the Miami stable. The crew recorded nearly every move of Deputy Minister, chronicling the champion's path to the Kentucky Derby scheduled for May 1st. Shortly after the colt arrived at Hialeah, Brennan immediately put Deputy Minister back into competitive racing mode, choosing to enter the Canadian colt in the $30,000 Bahamas Stakes on Tuesday, January 26th.

In contrast to the frantic racing schedule of Deputy Minister during the fall season of 1981 into the new year of 1982, Timely Writer rested in Boston and at Tony Everard's farm in Ocala, slowly growing into his three-year-old frame. The Martin brothers spent their time working at their meatpacking plant, fighting through another cold winter in New England, sharing the holiday times with their friends and family at their small cape-style home in Quincy, and turning down million-dollar offers for their colt. Wintering in Miami went exceptionally well for Timely Writer. Dominic Imprescia, and the Martins knew what they had in their colt as they patiently waited for the start of the three-year-old racing season. The Timely Writer team let everyone who was listening, including Boston Globe sports columnist Michael Madden, know that they would win it all in the coming year.

From Miami, as Timely Writer rested and before the Martin brothers joined him down south, Dominic told people that despite losing the Eclipse Award, they would not have changed a thing from the prior racing season. The Writer team was all about the best interests of their colt and staying focused on the next racing season. Reflecting on the previous year's end, Dominic commented, "If I had to do it all over again, I'd do the same thing. I would not keep him in training longer just to win a statue." "Stopping this colt did him a lot of good . . . [I]look at how much weight he's put on and how he's developed. He's been here in Miami since November 1st and had a good chance to come into himself. He had a couple of months of long gallops, and now he's ready to get serious."[85]

As the men predicted, Timely Writer won the two Florida stakes races, exhibiting power and grace similar to previous Triple Crown winners making their way through the Sunshine State to Kentucky for the first Saturday in May. Almost as predictable was an injury to Deputy Minister. The colt fractured his ankle on January 26th during the Bahama Stakes at Hialeah Park, forcing him to skip the upcoming Triple Crown races. As the owners of Deputy Minister collected their trophy for the 2-year-old colt of the year at the Fontainebleau Hotel on February 5th, their colt's future was in doubt.

Before heading north after the Florida Derby win in April, Frannie had one last place for his family, friends, and colleagues to visit in the Sunshine State. In a city filled with hundreds of restaurants, hotels, and resorts, and with the prohibitive favorite for the Kentucky Derby in his stable, Frannie knew where the Timely Writer crew would spend their Florida Derby victory party. With a smirk on his face, Frannie made a telephone call to book a banquet room at the Fontainebleau Hotel in Miami Beach for their celebration. By all accounts, the Martins thought a dinner celebration for the Florida Derby champion at the Fontainebleau in April was far more meaningful than the Eclipse Award banquet held at the same hotel two months prior. As Frannie would sing the words of his favorite crooner later that night in Miami Beach, "If I can make it here, I can make it anywhere."

In the week following the win at the Florida Derby, the groundskeepers at Gulfstream Park put their final touches of Nitram Stables' orange and black colors onto the miniature statute of the jockey standing in the center of the walking ring at the paddock area. The stable colors of the Florida Derby champion would cover the statute for the next twelve months until the crowning of a new champion in April of 1983. Later that night, Timely Writer left Florida by way of an airplane transport, heading for Churchill Downs and the Kentucky Derby with "the respect of the American racing community as the best of his generation going into the classic campaign."[86]

Chapter 8
Tragedy: Part I

———

"Many of the sport's most influential people - people devoted to the improvement of the breed and dedicated to the integrity of the game – have seen their horses draped in roses at Churchill Downs after winning the most important race in North America. There is no place here for people who would run a champion for a claiming price in order to cash a bet. The sport might never recover from such an embarrassment. "[87]

The clock was ticking, and the calendar pages were turning as the rags-to-riches story of Timely Writer and his owners neared the final chapter. It was Tuesday morning, April 20, 1982. Eleven days before the 108th running of the Kentucky Derby. Eleven days until Timely Writer, his trainer, his jockey, and his owners would seize their chance at immortality in a horse race first contested in 1875. A win at the Kentucky Derby would culminate in a fairy tale story first authored when Tony Everard and the Martin brothers made the life-altering purchase in September of 1980. Wednesday, April 21st, would mark three years to the day Timely Roman foaled a young unnamed colt in a quiet pasture on a horse farm in Ocala, Florida. The 1982 Kentucky Derby was a race Timely Writer and his owners were seemingly destined to win.

In the morning hours of April 20th, without the aid of a rising sun, Dominic and his son carried out their usual pre-dawn duties at their rented horse stall on the cherished grounds of Churchill Downs. It was the father and son's first visit to the barns of Churchill Downs. It was the accomplishment of a lifetime for Dominic Imprescia, Sr., and, as he was sharing it with his namesake, he was wishing every day went slower than the one before it as the calendar was closing in on that first Saturday in May.

It had been a long and challenging journey to Churchill Downs for the 63-year-old veteran of World War II, who, upon his return from the war, began work as a used car salesman in Fitchburg, Massachusetts. Decades after leaving the car business and taking up a full-time job as a horse trainer, beginning every work day in the darkness before dawn, Dominic had finally made it in thoroughbred racing. Dominic's life-long goal to be fulfilled on Saturday, May 1st with the saddling of Timely Writer in the paddock area at Churchill Downs. The trainer's dreams played out before him as he slowly dressed Timely Writer with his racing equipment and blinkers hood. Once saddled, Dominic would lend a quick hand to the bottom of Jeffrey Fell's riding boot, providing the necessary aid in hoisting Fell into the saddle of the Florida Derby winner and the morning line favorite for the Kentucky Derby. A tap by Dominic to the colt's back side sends the pair down the path leading to the race track. The jock and his colt making their way onto the dirt track with 140,000 people standing and joining the Martins as they serenade Timely Writer and the rest of the entries with the lyrics of "My old Kentucky Home." Imprescia, with a tear of joy in each of his eyes, is sporting the rose-colored sports coat his wife Ethel bought him in Louisville to match the beautiful bed of red roses that would be placed over the back of Timely Writer in the winner's circle. The former used car salesman, singing the lyrics he knew from memory, watching his colt, the best three-year-old thoroughbred in the country, slowly pass the grandstand towards the starting gate for the beginning of the Kentucky Derby.

Timely Writer, along with five other Florida Derby entries, had been transported from Florida to his stall in Kentucky by way of an equine aircraft in the days before the morning of Tuesday, April 20th. The group of colts had been brought in two weeks before the May 1st Kentucky Derby. Timely Writer and his team, in Churchill Downs for the first time, arrived earlier than most to get acquainted with their new surroundings. Before the transport, jockey Jeffrey Fell, who rode the near 1981 Triple Crown winner Pleasant Colony two weeks before the colt's 1981 Kentucky Derby win, declared Timely Writer "the best 3-year-old I've been on."[88] Though many racing entries would not arrive until the week of the Kentucky Derby, Timely

Writer was at Churchill Downs in preparation for "the most exciting two minutes in sports." As the Kentucky Derby's prohibitive favorite, media cameras followed the colt from the moment Timely Writer arrived at Churchill Downs.

Jeffrey Fell was flown on a private airplane charter in the early morning hours from New York into Louisville on Sunday, April 18th, for Timely Writer's first full weekend. Fell arrived at Churchill's barns from the airport by private car transport for Timely Writer's first full workout. A quick change into his riding clothes at the barn left Fell patiently waiting for Timely Writer at the track rail. Fell passed the extra minutes speaking with the assembled media writers at the rail - as they all awaited the workout of the prized colt. Timely Writer's arrival was worth the wait as he breezed through the 7-furlong distance in one minute and twenty-six seconds, with media photographers snapping pictures of the champion while journalists hurriedly took notes. Afterward, the usually reticent Fell was singing the praises of Timely Writer to the awaiting media with an overwhelming confidence heard in his voice and words, hinting at a probable first-place finish at the upcoming Kentucky Derby.

After Timely Writer was done with the workout, the jockey and colt parted ways, with Fell heading back to the airport for an afternoon of racing at Aqueduct Race Track. Timely Writer returned to the barn for a cold shower courtesy of a nozzle-free garden hose – the colt chomping at the constant water flow whenever it came near his wide-open mouth. After the cool-down, the champion colt was tucked back into his stall for the day. Dinner was provided sharply at 4:30 p.m. – the thoroughbred served his standard meal of grain and oats.

Jeffrey Fell and Timely Writer breeze through a workout at Churchill Downs

Monday, April 19th, a scheduled day off for Timely Writer, was an uneventful day of rest for the colt, with his handlers noting the evening meal of oats and hay had once again been delivered at 4:30 p.m. As the evening hours passed, Writer, always one to attack his meals, could be seen picking at his grain during the evening hours. Dominic thought the behavior was unusual for Timely Writer and rang up track veterinarian Dr. Alex Harthill at his office. Dr. Harthill, working in the equine building just across the gate to the stables, walked quickly over to the stall of Timely Writer.

Timely Writer, with Dr. Harthill and Dominic watching from the stall door, started pawing at the floor. As he observed Timely Writer's behavior, one concern Dr. Harthill shared was the colt was showing some minor signs of colic. Dr. Harthill entered the stall to administer a further examination. After completing his review, and as only a precautionary measure, Dr. Harthill gave Timely Writer three-quarters of a gallon of mineral oil as a laxative to flush out any obstruction in the intestines. Talwin was also administered to sedate the colt through the night, and Banamine was administered as an anti-spasmatic to prevent vomiting. A short time after receiving the three medications, Timely Writer slept through the night without difficulty.

As darkness lingered on the Tuesday morning of April 20th in New England, Frannie traveled north to New Hampshire to meet with clients at various hotels and restaurants. Frannie was intent on getting ahead of his work, sitting with clients and putting together their meat orders for the remainder of the month and through the first week of May. Frannie, Mary, John, Maryellen, and Janice would leave for Louisville within forty-eight hours. Peter was in Boston managing the operations at Keyes Supply, running the business for another week before leaving for Louisville. Mary was at the family home on Argonne Street in Quincy, sipping coffee with her Irish scone for breakfast before organizing matters for the family and their trip to Kentucky.

While the Tuesday morning in the Boston area was just another spring morning for the Martin family, Timely Writer was lying flat on the bedding of his stall at Churchill Downs – unable to rise. Something was wrong. Dominic Jr., despite prodding the colt, could not get Timely Writer to stand. The colt was staring straight ahead, occasionally moving his big brown eyes upwards, making eye contact with the trainer's son. Though words could not be spoken, Timely Writer communicated to his assistant trainer that something was wrong with him. Never witnessing Timely Writer in such a compromised state, Dominic Jr. rushed out of the stall to the other end of the barn to get his father. Dominic Sr. rushed back with his son, quickly kneeling next to Timely Writer, rubbing his hands over the colt's legs and stomach area. Considering the information Dr. Harthill shared the night before, it did not take long for Dominic to know he needed to act quickly. Dominic's years of experience taught him that Timely Writer was probably suffering from colic, and it appeared to be worsening. Dominic knew he needed to get Dr. Harthill back to the stall. They would need to find a top equine surgeon and hospital if the condition were severe. If they did not act quickly, the overwhelming favorite for the Kentucky Derby would die a painful death at his stall in Churchill Downs.

Thoroughbreds are gifted with beauty and strength, rising to their feet within the hour of birth, though a delicate digestive system forever burdens them. The average person hears "colic" and thinks of babies and burping. Hardened and experienced horsemen hear the term, and horrific thoughts run through their minds. Equine experts know all too well that colic causes the fragile intestinal system of a horse to twist into knot after knot as the horse awaits his or her fate. The diet of the magnificent animal is constantly monitored. Mixing improperly cured hay into a horse's diet or changing the type of feed can create deadly gases and cause a blockage within the intestines. Although uncertain at the time, as Timely Writer was on the floor of the stall, a fatal gas was already developing within his intestines. Time could not be wasted.

An early morning emergency phone call from Dominic led to Dr. Harthill returning to the stall shortly after 5:00 a.m. As the doctor returned to the barn, and despite the medication provided the night before, Timely Writer was now regurgitating. The colt was losing vital fluids through the constant vomiting, and since Timely Writer was not drinking, his excreting liquids were not replaced. Dr. Harthill, with Timely Writer lying on the floor of the stall with his trainers trying to soothe him, began inserting a nasogastric tube down the colt's throat to decompress the stomach. Timely Writer, though, was manufacturing fluids within his intestines faster than Dr. Harthill could withdraw them with the tube. Dr. Harthill, convinced an intestinal blockage was to blame, administered additional anti-spasmodic medication to replace the oil regurgitated from the previous evening. An intravenous line was also administered to Timely Writer to replace lost fluids.

As Dominic and the doctor waited to see if Timely Writer would improve over the next few hours, the trainer had the difficult task of calling the Martins to keep them informed of what was happening. Uncertain where Frannie may be, Dominic knew where he could find Peter – managing the business at Kyes Supply. An early morning telephone conversation with Peter at 8:00 a.m. provided news that Timely Writer may have colic, and the racetrack veterinarian was monitoring the situation.

Tuesday morning turned into the lunch hour, and with no improvements in Timely Writer, Dr. Harthill scheduled a telephone conference with Dr. Reed and Dr. Loren Evans at the University of Pennsylvania's New Bolton Clinic. Dr. Evans was one of the country's leading veterinary scholars and practitioners. Dr. Harthill summarized the symptoms and events to the two nationally known equine experts, beginning from the previous night. All agreed an equine van was needed at the barn to transport the colt out of Churchill Downs to a suitable clinic. However, the mechanics of scheduling and transporting a thoroughbred of Timely Writer's value to an equine clinic is unlike hailing a taxi for a ride to the hospital. First, Dr. Harthill needed to speak with the insurance company holding the policy the Martin brothers had purchased at the beginning of the year. Fortunately, the ever-practical accountant Peter Martin had decided to insure their multi-million-dollar asset. Although the premium for the policy was steep, at $300,000.00 for the year, the brothers purchased a surgical and fatality policy before the start of the Florida races. After much discussion with the insurance carrier, it was agreed Timely Writer would be transported to Haggard, Davidson, and McGee, one of the most respected veterinary centers, located on Newtown Pike in Lexington, Kentucky – some 80 miles away.

Dr. Harthill ended his phone call with the insurance company and rushed to the barn to debrief Dominic on the plan. After listening, Dominic headed to the other end of the barn to phone racing officials at Churchill Downs to relay that he needed an equine van rushed to the horse barn for the medical transport of Timely Writer. Dominic's next phone call went to Peter. Dominic was blunt with Peter, opening the conversation with "we're in trouble."[89] As Dominic spoke with an update, a chill was overcoming Peter.

After Dr. Harthill gave Dominic his assignment, he returned to his office for a phone conference with Haggard, Davidson, and McGee. Dr. Harthill gave the doctors advance notice that he and his patient would arrive in an equine van from Churchill Downs later that afternoon. After repeating many of the same conversations he had with Drs. Reed and Evans and representatives from the insurance company, Dr. Harthill let the doctors know the patient they would be working on was the favorite for the Kentucky Derby. As a result of the telephone call, the lead surgeon at the clinic, Dr. Paul Thorpe, assembled his team of Dr. Linda Robbins and Dr. Allen Simpson, who prepped the surgical room and readied for the colt's arrival. With the telephone call to Churchill Downs for an equine transport, along with the calls to the equine center and the Martins in Boston, rumors were slowly spreading that something may be terribly wrong with Timely Writer.

Dominic had the task of telephoning Peter Martin a third time before leaving Churchill Downs, letting Peter know that Timely Writer was sick enough that running the colt in the Kentucky Derby was unlikely, as an invasive surgery into the stomach area of Timely Writer was probable. The brothers, days away from fulfilling dreams they shared in their younger years, were praying for Timely Writer's survival. The panic in Kentucky had spread to Massachusetts.

As the equine van rushed to Timely Writer's barn, the colt was carefully brought to his feet and guided into the van for transport by Dominic and his son. Dr. Harthill set his medical bag to the side of Timely Writer in the holding area of the van for the 80-mile trek across the picturesque roads of horse farm country. Dominic Sr. told his son he needed to ride in the transport van with Dr. Harthill as the medical assistant. Dominic Sr. needed to drive Dr. Harthill's car - following the van, his son, and his colt. As the 80-mile journey began just before 3:30 p.m., Timely Writer's symptoms were getting worse as the van exited the gates of Churchill Down, with his body temperature rising to dangerous levels and coughing up fluids.

With the equine van limited by its travel speed along the winding rural roads, time was the enemy of Timely Writer. As the first half of the journey prodded along, poisonous fluids continued to collect inside the stomach area of Timely Writer, with the van's movements challenging the stability of all the occupants throughout the ride. Timely Writer's coughing up of fluids worsened as the trip endured, with its foul smell trapped in the floorboards for the duration of the journey. Dominic Jr., who grew up around horses and horse tracks at his father's side, had never before witnessed a thoroughbred in such a compromised condition. Dr. Harthill, so concerned about Timely

Writer's medical situation as they neared the forty-mile mark, inserted a new intravenous line into the colt to keep him from dehydrating before surgery.

With Dominic Jr. helping, Dr. Harthill fed Timely Writer quart after quart of intravenous bottles throughout the last 40 miles. As Dominic Jr. held a full intravenous bottle in one hand, Dr. Harthill handed off each empty bottle in a quick exchange with the colt's assistant trainer. One quart after another, once depleted, was thrown to the floor of the van by Dominic Jr., with the younger Imprescia reaching into the medical bag time and time again for another full intravenous bottle. Dominic Jr., who was holding Timely Writer still for the cameras in the winner's circle at the Florida Derby just weeks prior, was now comforting the champion on the floor of a van as Dr. Harthill tried to keep the colt alive for the remainder of the transport.

Dominic Sr., from Dr. Harthill's car's front driver's seat, helplessly watched the van's rear as he traveled behind it, unable to see his son and the doctor working from the vehicle's floor. The trainer could only catch glimpses of his son as he occasionally stood after throwing another empty intravenous bottle to the floor, then bending out of sight to pick up another full bottle. Dominic Sr., too distracted to notice the beauty of the rolling green horse pastures and white wooden fences along the way, believed the ride to the clinic would never end. Dominic's dreams of Churchill Downs were replaced by fear as he drove behind the van to the clinic - believing the story of Timely Writer may end in tragedy once the van reached its destination. As the doctors at the clinic would later concede, the chances of Timely Writer surviving the transport to the hospital were "touch and go."

With the final five miles of the trip approaching, Dr. Harthill's experience taught him about the level of pain Timely Writer was experiencing. The source of the medical disorder within Timely Writer was located somewhere within 115 feet of his small and large intestines. With this type of colic condition, "a horse produces 120 liters of gastric juices a day. . . If the fluid becomes blocked and can't move down and out the intestines, fluid builds up, forcing the abdomen walls of the horse to swell enormously and painfully."[90] With the end of the transport near, Dr. Harthill's new concern for Timely Writer was that with everything the colt's body was going through, his patient would slip into septic shock. As with humans, a horse's body reacts when death is imminent. With death near, the body goes into survival mode and shuts down its circulatory system, forcing a drop in blood circulation and pressure. "Deprived of oxygen and nutrients, the organs begin to fail. If the shock isn't treated, the horse will eventually lose consciousness, the heart will stop, and the horse will die."[91] Laying on the floor of the transport van, without the medical services found at the equine clinic, Timely Writer would die from septic shock.

Upon entering the driveway at the equine hospital shortly after 5:00 p.m., Dominic's father parked the car and hurriedly ran to the van's rear, springing the doors open. Timely Writer, with the empty jugs of intravenous coming to a rolling stop around him, willed himself to a standing position upon opening the van doors. With the distinct orange and black blanket draped over him, Timely Writer exited the van much like he had done on hundreds of occasions. To the amazement of those watching from the hospital, the Kentucky Derby favorite "stepped off reasonably briskly."[92] Dr. Harthill walked with Timely Writer into the rear entry of the hospital – the doctor had now been by the side of his patient for more than twelve straight hours.

Dominic Jr., able to gather himself once Timely Writer was turned over to the staff of doctors, spoke with his father privately. A trainer at his father's side since birth, Dominic would tell his dad of the near-death events he witnessed within the van. Dominic Jr. estimated Timely Writer had regurgitated more than 20 gallons of fluids during the ride, with Dr. Harthill administering well over thirty jugs of intravenous fluids back into the colt. As he would repeat to everyone in the following days and weeks, Dominic Jr. told his father, "[Timely Writer] would not have made it without Dr. Harthill. I guarantee Dr. Harthill saved this colt's life."[93]

Timely Writer was guided into the emergency area of the equine hospital, still coughing up fluids. Dr. Thorpe and his team in the room prepared to do everything they could to save the colt's life. The doctors thoroughly examined Timely Writer and agreed that exploratory surgery was needed.

"[T]hey feared that a tumor or some other obstruction was blocking Timely Writer's intestines."[94] As the doctors prepped the colt for surgery, Dr. Thorpe left the room to speak with Dominic.

When Dr. Thorpe approached, Dominic was still talking about the day's events with his son in the hall. The father and son paused their conversation, turning towards Dr. Thorpe to hear him utter the words, "we've got to open him up."[95] Imprescia, Sr. did not respond immediately, looking past Dr. Thorpe as he searched for wisdom and words. Knowing his answer would end the dreams of the Martins, the Timely Writer racing team, and a nation of followers, Dominic could not look into the eyes of the doctor, uttering just six words as he stared straight ahead, "do what you got to do."[96]

Dominic took some time to gather himself afterward, then located a telephone at the facility to make his fourth phone call of the day to Peter. Sitting at a desk covered in newspapers and magazine articles about the great Timely Writer, Peter held the phone in his right hand as Dominic talked to him. As Dominic continued to speak, Peter's forehead was buried in his knife-scarred left hand, his left elbow supporting him as it dug into the top of the stack of magazines and articles. With tears in his eyes and lips pressed together, while choking back his emotions, Peter struggled to hear Dominic explain the reasons for the emergency surgery, only hearing that the doctors were doing it in order "to save the horse's life."[97]

With Timely Writer sedated, the first phase of the surgical procedure started with the insertion of a tube into his nose - a surgeon pushed it further and further down his throat until it entered the stomach area. The continuing problem for Timely Writer was that his body was producing gastric fluids faster than the doctors could handle. Doctors were pumping gastric fluids from the stomach of Timely Writer through the tube, running out his nose at a furious rate in an attempt to gain control over the imbalance that had been building and not moving since at least the morning hours. At the same time, doctors were as concerned about the fact that Timely Writer was continuing to lose fluids, with the resulting septic shock a strong possibility.

Once again, additional quarts of intravenous liquids were administered to fend off Timely Writer going into a critical septic shock.

Dr. Thorpe, with his support team strategically placed in and around Timely Writer, made a surgical incision across the stomach area measuring just under one foot in length. Once Dr. Thorpe cut into Timely Writer's abdomen, the doctors then inserted a needle attached to a suction device into the stomach area to remove the remaining excess fluids. The team of doctors, as they began to move into the intestinal area of the colt, were expecting to find Timely Writer was suffering from a mechanical blockage. They were searching for a loop or kink in the intestine which was causing such extreme symptoms.

It took some time for the doctors to move carefully through the more than one hundred feet of Timely Writer's intestines to find the affected area. When the doctors located the area, there was oddly no mechanical blockage. Timely Writer was suffering from what was called acute gastroenteritis. An area in the small intestine of Timely Writer was inflamed, causing the colt to lose the forward propulsion of food. The blockage had grown to the size of a balloon within the small intestine. Once located, the medical team spent close to an hour working in the area - a suction device slowly extracted the contents of the inflamed area of the small intestine. Once doctors had sufficient confidence that the area was cleared and cleaned, Timely Writer's incision was sewn up with 20 sutures. A muzzle was placed over the mouth of Timely Writer before he awoke – to prevent him from eating anything but small portions of hay - to be fed to him every two hours through the night and early morning hours. The still unconscious horse was transferred over to a recovery barn for monitoring.

As Timely Writer rested, his sitters for the night were Dr. Simson, a medical intern from Australia, along with a designated security guard for the prized colt. The two men stayed in the barn's tack room through the morning hours, one checking on Timely Writer every few minutes. The doctor and the security guard passed the time watching the black and white television set, adjusting the antenna sitting on the flat top of the television tube while changing the limited number of channels back and forth, watching a movie and a talk show simultaneously. As the pair passed their time together through the dark of night, they marveled at Timely Writer's ability to survive the near-death event while discussing the fragility of horses.

Dr. Thorpe, understanding the importance of the moment and his famous patient, made himself available to the media right immediately after surgery. The doctor did not mince words as to Timely Writer's near-death situation, telling gathered reporters, "If we hadn't operated when we did, his stomach would have ruptured, and he would have died."[98] Doctors were telling people in the immediate aftermath that the surgery saved Timely Writer's life - but only for the moment, as he remained in critical condition.

More information about Timely Writer's chances of survival would not be known until the morning when doctors would assess if their patient's digestive system was adequately functioning. Like the doctor and security guard passing their time through the early morning hours, all required more waiting. Dr. Thorpe drove to his home to get some sleep before returning to the clinic. While Dominic stayed near Timely Writer throughout the day and night in Kentucky, the Martins were home in Quincy feeling isolated, helpless, and sleepless. As Tuesday passed midnight, the calendar marked three years to the day Timely Roman foaled an unnamed colt in Ocala, Florida. Timely Writer was fighting for his life rather than celebrating his date of birth. Near-death upon his arrival at the equine clinic, Timely Writer's chances of surviving post-surgery were set by doctors at just over 50%.

Dominic, his eyes red and swollen, his voice shaking, addressed the newsmen parked outside the clinic for the night. "He's definitely out of the Derby.... But the important thing right now is that he came out of this OK. We only have to hope that he will pull through OK, that is the most important thing. It's just too bad he couldn't have had his big day. I'm sure he would have won the Derby. I've been saying that all along after the Champagne."[99]

With the arrival of Thursday's morning hours, Timely Writer showed no signs of discomfort. Dr. Simson, an equine stomach specialist who had been with Timely Writer throughout the night, upgraded Writer's chances of living to approximately 60 to 70%. Doctors Harthill and Simson would later opine that the probable cause of the illness was bad grass or mildewed hay – leaving the barn at Churchill Downs as the prime suspect. Dr. Thorpe returned to the clinic Thursday morning and consulted with Dr. Simson. Both doctors examined Timely Writer and agreed with the chances of his survival. An hour later, at 7:30 a.m., Dr. Thorpe observed Writer passing excrement - proof that the colt's digestive system was working.

An unshaven Dr. Thorpe exited the recovery barn where Timely Writer would call home for the next week, making himself available to the still-gathered media. Staring into the rising sun as it projected onto the roof of the barn where the champion colt was recovering, the weary doctor told the press, "Timely Writer is going to be just fine,"[100] announcing his chances of survival at 95% and higher.

A few hours later in the day, Dr. William Reed made himself available to the media from his home in New York. The doctor spent his time with the press marveling how Timely Writer survived the near-death experience. Dr. Reed was "delighted but not really surprised."[101] As one of the leading equine veterinarians in the world, he explained why nothing about Timely Writer shocked him anymore. Dr. Reed had spent significant time studying Timely Writer in the prior six months, with exclusive access to the colt. The expert equine veterinarian was uniquely positioned with his private access and interaction with Timely Writer. The doctor had watched Timely Writer at the race tracks and his stall when nobody was around. Dr. Reed described Timely Writer as a unique and unusual thoroughbred, a mix of strength and intelligence, who did not waste energy during his activities. As he explained, this level of intelligence "makes him a good patient."[102]

Dr. Reed explained in a language that the average person could understand how this once-in-a-generation horse could recognize that he was sick and needed help. Timely Writer knew intuitively that the distress he was experiencing differed from his regular daily routine on the race track. As time passed during the 80-mile transport, with Timely Writer violently ill throughout, the colt refused to direct his energy negatively – never becoming anxious or nervous. The colt lay patiently in the transport van while he was going through the ordeal, conserving his physical strength long enough to allow doctors the time to help him. For sure, brilliant doctors saved Timely Writer's life. Still, Timely Writer had an innate sense and purposeful intent throughout the ordeal, combining his intelligence with his strength and athleticism, which allowed him to overcome the near-death event. These same skill sets shined on the race tracks during the prior two years. As Dr. Reed explained the morning following the surgery, Timely Writer was the one unique horse who could win a fight against the probable death facing him.

On Thursday morning, Frannie returned home early from New Hampshire after Peter delivered the tragic news over the telephone the previous day. He was returning telephone calls with friends, supporters, and the media. Peter went to work at Kyes Supply in his usual fashion. Peter's cousin, Isabella Totovian, drove to the Kyes Supply office from her Watertown home to search for Peter. Like so many people, Isabella was emotionally involved with the story of Timely Writer and the Martins for nearly a year. As she walked through the business area, Isabella found Peter coming out of the meat locker. Isabella couldn't hold her tears back as she spoke with Peter. Though Peter knew the answer before he asked the question, he wondered why she was crying. Isabella told Peter she had been dreaming of seeing Timely Writer at the Kentucky Derby. Peter told his cousin that he, too, was a dreamer with Timely Writer, but the key in life was not to get too high off the ground. Showing a smile and a wink to Isabella, Peter told his cousin she would get nosebleeds if she got too high off the ground anchoring her feet.

In the ensuing days, the brothers refused to duck from people or the press after Timely Writer's injury. Both brothers had gone on their journey with Timely Writer, their eyes wide open. Years of experience had taught them about the fragility of a thoroughbred; Frannie often talked with people about how the beauty of the animal is second to none, but the beauty is anchored by a skeletal system and physical makeup that lends itself to injury and worse.

As others turned towards the brothers to soothe their sorrow and the unexpected tragedy now written into their script, people observed: "[t]o their credit, they reacted with great strength and dignity."[103] Despite their grace in public, any reasonable person would be hurt. A young and talented trainer named Wayne Lukas, who was new to the thoroughbred circuit and who stood to benefit with Timely Writer scratched from the Kentucky Derby field as he was training the Santa Anita Derby winner Muttering in California, shared condolences with the Martins and spoke of a similar loss he had previously experienced just one month prior.

Lukas had recently started training thoroughbreds after spending a decade of success training quarter horses from 1968 to 1978. Lukas' first big win with a thoroughbred horse was at the Preakness Stakes in 1980 with a colt called Codex. The trainer was convinced he had the 1982 Kentucky Derby winner in Stalwart sitting in his barn in California. Just weeks before Timely Writer's illness, Lukas noticed something wrong with Stalwart's leg in the middle of March. Further examination revealed Stalwart suffered from a bowed tendon, and surgery was needed. Stalwart and Lukas were six weeks from the Kentucky Derby when their dream was ended. Lukas was devastated and found himself in a daze in the immediate aftermath. Sounding like a man who thought he might never win the Kentucky Derby, Lukas commiserated with what the Martins were going through. "All my life I waited for a horse like this and he finally comes along and then he was gone."[104] Though they had never met, Lukas felt the Martins pain, "you wait all your life and hope and dream . . . and then you wake up and your horse has a problem. When it happens, your guts knot up. It's absolutely devastating."[105]

The stories of Timely Writer's victory over death quickly spread from the recovery barn straight to the media. As the early hours of the morning on the East Coast grew longer, and with the West Coast waking up to radio and newspaper reports of Timely Writer's survival, reporters and newscasters across the country were broadcasting that the prohibitive favorite for the Kentucky Derby and Triple Crown was now out of the race after fighting for his life. As news of the tragedy spread throughout the country, surviving death would engender Timely Writer to the public that much more. Though the story of Timely Writer's fairy tale did not reach its expected conclusion, his story and legend would continue to grow throughout 1982 and after.

The unspoken question, though, which lingered in the minds of many after the invasive surgery, was whether Timely Writer would be able to race again. After the dust settled the morning after successful surgery, plans were put together later in the day for Timely Writer's recovery and rehabilitation. Most people and experts in the racing industry believed Timely Writer surviving the near-death experience was one thing, but racing at an elite level once again was another. Many people believed Timely Writer would never run again; if so, he would never regain the elite form he once possessed. On Thursday, April 22nd, the *Daily Racing Form* put thoughts to print in the opening paragraph of their headline story, "there is some question if the Flamingo and Florida Derby winner …. will ever race again."[106]

There was good reason to be skeptical about future success, as the history of horse racing was littered with many unhappy returns. In the spring of 1982, one need only walk over to the Boston Garden and listen to former hockey goaltender and present head coach of the Boston Bruins. Gerry Cheevers had earned a reputation as a "money goalie" during the early '70s when he anchored the best hockey team the city of Boston has ever witnessed, including two Stanley Cup Championships and a record 32-game undefeated streak during the 1972 season. Cheevers also earned respect on the Thoroughbred racing circuit, having a stable of over twenty horses by the end of the decade, including a horse he purchased for just over $20,000 as a leading contender for the 1977 Kentucky Derby.

Cheevers first big horse, Royal Ski, ended his two-year-old season much like Timely Writer's - somehow losing out on the Eclipse Award. Royal Ski's three-year-old season began with him and Seattle Slew established as the favorites for the Kentucky Derby. In December of 1976, Royal Ski was shipped to Florida in preparation for the three-year-old racing season, focusing on winning the Florida Derby as his team prepped for a run at the Kentucky Derby. In January of 1977, Cheevers began reaping the benefits of his talented colt, selling a one-third interest in Royal Ski for $1 million, keeping two-thirds for himself and controlling interest.

By February of 1977, with Cheevers in the middle of another hockey season, the Royal Ski trainer was reporting to Cheevers that his horse was ill with a virus that would not leave his system. At some point, as the illness lingered, more severe symptoms hit Royal Ski, and he became feverish, experiencing diarrhea and losing weight. Over a critical 10-day period, the colt's fever hit 104 degrees with a weight loss of 200 pounds. Veterinarians were monitoring Royal Ski daily. Royal Ski escaped the worst of the illness, but it became evident that Royal Ski would not be ready for the Triple Crown races. Cheevers would not compromise the future of Royal Ski, pulling him from the spring and summer racing season, dissolving the syndicate, and returning the one million dollars.

Cheevers watched the Kentucky Derby from his hotel room in Montreal that first Saturday in May 1977 as he prepared for game 1 of the Stanley Cup finals against the Montreal Canadians. Cheevers told the media he was "disappointed about not being in the Derby.... but I'm cocky and arrogant enough to think I'll get another shot someday."[107] Cheevers could only watch from his hotel room in Montreal as Seattle Slew, who many believed was inferior to Royal Ski the year prior, won the Kentucky Derby. With no other horse to challenge him, Seattle Slew won the Preakness and Belmont Stakes to become only the 10th Triple Crown winner. Cheevers and the Bruins would lose to the Montreal Canadians in the 1977 Stanley Cup final, with Cheevers retiring after the 1980 hockey season, becoming head coach of the Bruins.

As the last week of April 1982 turned to the first Saturday in May 1982, with Timely Writer recovering from surgery and real questions unanswered about his future, the media turned to the now Boston Bruins head coach for his experiences about what may lie ahead for the Martin brothers. Cheevers' words and experience offered little promise for the future.

Veterinarians for Cheevers spent time looking over Royal Ski after he recovered from the illness. As Royal Ski was declared fit to resume racing by doctors, he was put on a rehabilitation program at Rockingham Park in the summer of 1977. Trainer John Lenzini put Royal Ski through a standard program for his road to full recovery. However, Lenzini's experiences with rehabilitating horses gave him reason to pause while watching Royal Ski in training. The more Lenzini watched, the more he knew the horse would never be the same. Royal Ski "never wanted to train. He didn't want to go to the track…. He was affected more mentally than physically."[108] Royal Ski would race twice more in 1977, winning once at Rockingham Park in New Hampshire, but only due to a disqualification of the first-place finisher, and once more at Laurel Park. Cheevers and Lenzini, though, were not fooled by the limited success. Cheevers saw Royal Ski "just wasn't the same horse." After his three-year-old racing season, Cheevers would never race or own Royal Ski again, retiring the colt to stud and selling him to a breeding syndicate for $1.2 million. In the week leading up to the 1982 Kentucky Derby, Cheevers, who knew the Martin brothers from Suffolk Downs, commiserated with what they were going through. "No question it was a big disappointment; I can understand how Timely Writer's people feel."[109] As the Martins prepared to travel south from Boston to Churchill Downs for the 108th running of the Kentucky Derby on May 1st, 1982, they, too, were wondering if Timely Writer would ever race again.

Rather than letting himself be a victim of the event, and with Timely Writer out of immediate danger, Frannie chose to find a moment of levity when a reporter asked if something like this had ever happened to a horse he owned. Frannie recalled a nag of a horse from years prior, "I had one other horse with colic, but he wasn't worth 40 cents. In fact, he could have had colic every day, and it wouldn't have bothered him."[110] With so many in the public wondering if the Martins would be attending the Kentucky Derby after such an emotional let-down, the reporter asked Frannie whether, despite the setback, he would be attending the race. Without any doubt in his mind, and in a split-second response to the question, Frannie shot back, "you bet I'll be there. I'll be there if I have to ride a bicycle."[111]

Chapter 9
Kentucky Derby Week: Bittersweet Emotions.... and Suspicions

Dear Timely Writer,

I am very sorry that you are not feeling well! I hope you feel better by fall so you can win all those races. You are a far better horse than all those others. Even my daddy says you would have won the Derby. But when you get well, you will win them all and I will cheer you on. Get well soon!

Love, Carmelita Stafford from Nicholasville, KY.

"It was going to be such a sweet storybook tale. Two hard-working brothers whose only recreation came from buying one or two cheap horses a year, were going to outdo all the rich society staples and win the big one."[112] The Martins' dreams and storybook tale was shattered, and the emotional pieces needed to be picked up. A grieving public let Timely Writer and his family know they could find strength in numbers.

Carmelita, whose father in Kentucky believed the Boston-based horse was the best in the country, was one of the numerous people sending get-well notes, cards, and letters of encouragement to Timely Writer after surgery ended the dream. June Johnson was the office manager at Haggard, Davidson, and McGee Equine Surgery Clinic. June played a prominent role in running the office at the clinic where Timely Writer lay recovering - and the one sharing Carmelita's letter. June was the point person for the clinic who was fielding the requests for interviews from newspapers due to their famous patient and his story. As June shared in her interview during Kentucky Derby week, no horse had ever received a single letter as a patient during the time the clinic had existed before Timely Writer's arrival.

There were no protocols regarding incoming mail directed to their patients at the clinic. Ms. Johnson, as a result, took it upon herself to add an additional title to her work responsibilities – Mail Room Director. In reality, she was in charge of managing and organizing Timely Writer's mail. The need for the new title resulted from the level of mail arriving at the Clinic addressed to their famous patient, who was neither capable of picking up his mail nor literate to read it if delivered. Many of the mailings, as evidenced by the handwriting and sentiments, came from the hands of young and old alike. Well-wishes and condolences knew no age, gender, or economic boundaries. Letters arrived from a Boston film critic addressed to "Mr. Writer," a postcard from a woman on Cape Cod in Massachusetts; letters sent from states as close as Pennsylvania, Tennessee, and Michigan; and from the opposite coast of California.

During the workday, Ms. Johnson spent her spare time reading the mail to Timely Writer. One wealthy woman from Louisiana sent Timely Writer six handwritten messages - all read to the patient. The Louisianan also made a point to travel to Kentucky on the Wednesday before the Kentucky Derby, bypassing Churchill Downs as she headed straight to the equine Clinic. The mode of transportation for the adoring fan was a limousine driven by her chauffeur. The native from Louisiana hoped to visit with Timely Writer and get a photograph taken with him. Frannie, who had arrived in Kentucky the previous morning, was at the clinic during the afternoon visiting with Timely Writer when the colt's visitor arrived. Upon hearing about the visitor, Frannie greeted the lady in the office area. Gracious and thankful for her concern, Frannie had to decline the wealthy visitor's request, explaining Timely Writer was in such an irritable mood after a week of recovery that "if you go in there, he'll tear you apart."[113]

Frannie, Mary, and Peter arrived on Tuesday of Derby week. John, Maryellen, and Janice were left behind to "watch over the house." As Peter expressed before leaving, he could not put into words the pleasure Timely Writer had not only brought to the Martin family but also to the city of Boston. The one regret the Martins collectively felt was that the people of Boston had lost out on the Kentucky Derby. Peter lamented, "I just feel sorry for the people of Boston. . . because he *was* the Kentucky Derby winner." [114] Peter, Frannie, and Mary divided their time in Kentucky over the four days between Derby parties in Louisville and the equine clinic some 80 miles away. As they showed in Miami the month prior, the Martin family was a group not to turn down a good party. The various parties also served as a welcome distraction, helping to ease some of their loss and pain.

During the early morning hours on Friday, the brothers and Mary took the 80-mile drive to the equine clinic for a scheduled meeting with Drs. Thorpe and Reed, who had visited with Timely Writer for the 2nd time in three days. In the immediate aftermath of the surgery, Dr. Thorpe told the brothers that it would be three months before Timely Writer could return to training under the most ideal conditions. In the doctor's best-case scenario, if rehabilitation went well, Timely Writer could resume training sometime in mid–August, leaving the fall racing season at Belmont Park as the only legitimate option for a comeback. The doctors shared some optimistic news during the Friday morning meeting, some ten days after Timely Writer's surgery. Both doctors assured the Martins that there had been no internal damage, and Timely Writer's appetite and energy were excellent as the colt began his rest and rehabilitation. With some good news, the Martins returned to Louisville for the Friday night events.

As the Martins spent their morning at the Clinic, Phyllis George, Miss America of 1971, and Kentucky Governor John Y. Brown, Jr.'s wife, hosted the Governor's Breakfast at the Kentucky Horse Park. Sixteen thousand people attended the breakfast in the park where, for the first time, alcohol was served at the morning event. The first lady of Kentucky opened the breakfast on the main stage in the park by greeting her guests seated at the tables. "How're you doing?" Getting a tepid response, Phyllis retorted, "If you're not doing better than that, maybe there should be a little more bloody in that, Mary."[115] The Friday morning breakfast served as the opening primer for the festivities in Louisville over the next 36 hours.

The Governor and his wife finished their morning breakfast obligations as hosts, making their way to an early afternoon party as guests of Mr. and Mrs.

Cornelious Vanderbilt Whitney. The party was an invite-only affair with 300 attendees at the couple's horse farm. The couple greeted the guests at the Whitney estate at the tunnel entrance to the farm's party room. After passing through the greeting line, guests were brought into an anteroom where ten uncorked champagne bottles for consumption stood upright at all times in a huge silver bowl. Engraved on the outside of the bowl was "Belmont Stakes – 1906." The Belmont Stakes winner some 75 years prior was Burgomaster - a colt bred by one Whitney and owned by another Whitney.

Guests of the Whitneys at the luncheon included celebrity television newscaster Barbara Walters, author William F. Buckley, and the Chairman of Occidental Petroleum, Armand Hammer. After some time in the champagne room, guests went outside, where a swimming pool greeted them at the center of the manicured grounds. Fair-type booths dotted the estate's property, where vendors, such as fortune tellers, welcomed the guests, providing an afternoon of entertainment. Past the enormous pool, a butterfly-themed party extended across the grounds, with the party supported by a beautiful warm spring day.

With the afternoon party finishing at the Whitney estate, many of the 300 guests made their way to a party at the Governor's mansion, where dinner was served to the 400 invited guests. The invitations to the party spoke of an event promoting the economy of Kentucky - though it seemed anything but. An outdoor tent greeted guests at the mansion, complimented by a horseshoe bed of red roses at the front entrance. Guests mingled with artist Andy Warhol on one side and country singer Waylon Jennings on the other. Also seen in the crowd were the Italian and French Ambassadors to the United States of America. Owners of the racing entries for the Kentucky Derby mingled within the crowd as well. Multi-millionaire Nelson Hunt, who had been in the horse racing business for 28 years, was a guest at the party, marking the first time that one of his horses made the field of entries at the Kentucky Derby.

Dinner tables were placed throughout the tent, with one table of ten boasting a live panda bear sitting at it. The panda was a gift from Mary Lou and Sonny Whitney to the Governor and his wife. An enormous gift card in the center of the table read, "It's Derby Week. Bear Up!"[116] As the Governor's Derby dinner party finished, many guests rushed home to change clothes for an evening dance party hosted by Anita and Preston Madden at their Hamburg Place Farm.

Hamburg Place was home to Preston Madden since his birth. Madden's family tree traced its lineage back to the first governor of Kentucky through his grandmother. Not content to rest on the many privileges provided to him at birth, Preston began working on the family farm at an early age. The young boy's early years led to his love of riding horses. At the age of sixteen, Preston's riding skills were exemplary, becoming a National Steeplechase Champion. By 1956, Preston managed the family's 2,000-acre farm, founded in 1898 by his grandfather. The farm had been home to five Kentucky Derby champions, including the first Triple Crown winner, Sir Barton.

Guests at the Maddens' Kentucky Derby party in 1982 would leave never forgetting the night. One Thousand three hundred of Maddens' closest family members, friends, and owners of the Kentucky Derby entries were regaled in an outdoor tent covering hundreds of yards. Under the tent was a decorated haunted forest with a band and dance floor centered in the middle. Stuffed animals such as bears, raccoons, and game birds were scattered about the forest. The forest also included a real-life witch stirring a black cauldron of "potion" while atop a ten-foot-high platform. Under the platform was a stuffed deer with antlers. Mixed into the antlers were drink cups filled with the witches' brew for the taking. As the dancing continued past midnight, it was officially the first Saturday in May – post time was 17 ½ hours away. Churchill Downs would see 141,009 people pass through the gates for the Kentucky Derby on May 1, 1982, all of them knowing that any horse could win without Timely Writer in the field.

With Timely Writer's absence from the Kentucky Derby field, Saturday morning's newspaper headlines throughout the New England states reflected the loyalty of the region's sports journalists. Upon the newspaper delivery trucks pulling away from the loading docks during the early morning hours at the various print companies, dropping off pre-wrapped bundles of the day's papers at the homes of neighborhood newspaper boys & girls for delivery, customers opened their neatly folded-up newspapers left at their front doors. Newspaper headlines staring back at them announcing the 1982 Kentucky Derby Day: "Meet the No-Class of '82," and "It's Anybody's Race in a Nobody Field."

The wealthy may dominate the exclusive invitation-only parties during the week, but the middle class sets the standard on the day of the Kentucky Derby. Derby Day for the general public starts during the early morning hours as patrons make their way through the entrance to the grass infield. This oval area of the interior of the race track manages to stuff approximately 80,000 people within the rails. With a Mardi Gras-like atmosphere similar to that hosted every February in New Orleans, Louisiana, the enclosed area is a festival with a population larger than the great majority of towns throughout the country. The guests at the grass infield mingle and party throughout the day while the country's best thoroughbreds race around the track every thirty minutes for viewing and gambling pleasures.

As Churchill Downs does not permit the patrons in the grass infield to bring alcohol into the venue, the challenge is to sneak alcohol through security instead of paying for the pricey drinks offered at the track. May 1st, 1982, began for seasoned Derby Day infielder Chuck Magera by placing two kegs of beer hidden into a 30-gallon garbage barrel, then covered on top with crushed ice and steamed crabs. Once Magera smuggled his cold steamed crabs through security, he and his friends celebrated as they pre-gamed for mud wrestling events, water slip and slides, and sprint races across the tops of the port-a-potties - which had been conveniently placed one next to the other by the staff. Other patrons in the infield included a still-dressed newlywed couple and a group of friends who smuggled Kentucky Whiskey into their bags of Seal-A-Meals.

As the infield crowd looked across the dirt track, they only needed to look up at the 4th floor to find "millionaire's row." The V.I.P. section at Churchill Downs includes some of the wealthiest people in the country - with females of all ages covering their heads with the fanciest and most exorbitant hats found at any location. Guests at the 1982 Kentucky Derby included former President Gerald Ford, comedian Phyllis Diller, newsman Walter Cronkite, newswoman Barbara Walters, the music group Fifth Dimension, country singer Waylen Jennings, sports stars such as professional basketball player Dan Issell, and baseball Hall-of-Famer Stan Musial from the St. Louis Cardinals.

Frannie, from an owner's box above the finish line, in between receiving greetings from well-wishers, spoke with various journalists about the bitter-sweet emotions they were experiencing during the week of festivities. "I'm awfully glad we came. It would have been so easy to stay home and say to hell with it. People have been wonderful to us; we have had a lot of fun here this week. The parties are starting to take their toll. Mary and I have never been to a Derby. It really is a 'happening,' like they say."[117]

The *Boston Globe* dispatched long-time thoroughbred racing journalist Sam McCracken to Louisville for Kentucky Derby Week. Part of his assignment for the newspaper was to write a human-interest story on the Martin family and their day at the Derby. Fifty-six-year-old Sam McCracken, a Dorchester native, had worked for the *Globe* in one capacity or another since he was 20 years old. Renowned throughout the country as one of the best journalists of his time, McCracken set up shop with his notepads and typewriter in room 300 at the Galt House in Louisville — the hotel room serving as his office for his work week.

Sam had been attending Kentucky Derby week for years. Sam knew everybody, and everybody knew Sam. During the week, Sam would typically wake at 4:00 a.m., leaving for the horse barns to chat up jockeys, owners, grooms - and the horses. As Sam admitted, "I never met a horse I didn't like." [118] After the races, Sam returned to room 300 to work on his articles and, when done, dinner with his colleagues. After dinner, any number of people followed Sam back to the hotel, where they made their way to the restaurant and bar. Their late-night hours were spent singing songs and enjoying one another's company. Publicity director Edgar Allen of Churchill Downs observed, "Of all the writers who came to the Derby, there may have never been one quite like Sam."[119]

On the morning of the Derby, Sam spent his day with Peter, Frannie, and Mary at their seats above the finish line. In speaking with Mary, as she was sipping her Kentucky Mint Julep, with the fresh mint dangling along the crushed ice cubes, she turned and told Sam that when the pre-race song "My Old Kentucky Home" begins playing while the horses are led onto the track, she will be shedding some tears. Frannie, the doting husband, assured Mary that things would be fine, asking her not to cry. Frannie warned Mary, though, as she turned back to her drink, be careful drinking that Kentucky Mint Julep – "the way we've been going, I wouldn't be surprised if these twigs of mint are poison ivy."[120]

It wasn't all bad karma for Frannie on Derby Day, winning his first bet of the day after placing a $50 wager to win on a horse named Amy Joy, who went off at 11-1 odds. Frannie was keen on the jockey, Phil Rubbicco, who he saw race several times at Suffolk Downs. Frannie's instincts served him well as Rubbicco led Amy Joy to victory and a payout of nearly $25 for every $2 winning ticket – putting more than $600 winnings into Frannie's pocket. As Fran and Mary sat with Sam, an unknown patron recognized the owners of Timely Writer, yelling over to Frannie about who he liked in the Derby race. Frannie's immediate, quick-witted response depicted one of his most endearing qualities - loyalty. Shouting back, Frannie yelled across the owner's boxes, "who else, - Jeff Fell."[121]

As the racing entries for the running of the 108th Kentucky Derby made their way onto the dirt track, heading past the owners' boxes towards the starting gates, the University of Louisville marching band began playing the music for Kentucky's state song. With more than 140,000 people singing the lyrics to "My old Kentucky Home," Mary joined the chorus. Mary was true to her word, with her husband on one side and her brother-in-law on the other. With tears in her eyes, a mint julep in her hand, and a beaming smile, Mary sang the words she knew by heart.

With the racing entries loading into the gates, Timely Writer remained back at his recovery stall some eighty miles away, shuffling over to a suspended hay bale to eat his prescribed dinner for the evening. Timely Writer's breakfast and dinner menus included one quart of grain in the morning and one quart at night. With Timely Writer's medically excused absence from the field of racing entries, journalist Paul Moran from the *Fort Lauderdale News and Sun Sentinel* had his wish granted from six weeks earlier. On March 28, 1982, various newspapers carried Moran's elitist view that "there is no place here for people who would run a champion for a claiming price to cash a bet. The sport might never recover from such an embarrassment."[122] As Frannie's suspicions regarding the cause of the medical disorder inflicted upon Timely Writer, it appeared others may have shared Paul Moran's views.

The field of remaining entries for the Kentucky Derby totaled 19 horses for the 1 ¼ mile race. Timely Writer's absence from the field, combined with that of Distinctive Pro and Deputy Minister, left a Kentucky Derby without the top three horses in the three-year-old division. Somewhat predictably, long shots came in first and second. Going off at 21-1 odds was Gato Del Sol, who had not won one race in his three-year-old campaign. Gato Del Sol started the first ¼ mile of the race in dead last, spending the remainder of the race plodding past most of his contemporaries before the final turn. Gato Del Sol made his final move at the top of the backstretch, overcoming second-place finisher Laser Light, who had gone off at 18-1 odds and finished 7th to Timely Writer at the Florida Derby just a month prior. In winning the Kentucky Derby, Gato Del Sol clocked in at a pedestrian 2 minutes, 2 and 2/5 seconds. The favorite of the morning odds makers, Air Forbes Won, finished a disappointing 7th.

The headline story of the day was one of Kentucky's favorite sons, Arthur Hancock III, owner of Gato Del Sol, who claimed the Kentucky Derby trophy for the first time. Hancock, well-liked by all, was a renegade of sorts. His father, A.B. Hancock Jr., founded the dynasty known as Clairborne Farm in 1910. Hancock Jr. passed in 1972, having never won the Kentucky Derby. Rather than remain with Clairborne Farm after his father's passing,

Arthur ventured out on his own, creating Stone Farm. Arthur took home the Kentucky Derby trophy his father could never capture with the win.

The Martins remained in their box seats at Churchill Downs, watching the festivities in the winner's circle. In a ceremony dating back to 1896, a bed of red roses was placed across the back of the 1982 Kentucky Derby winner Gato Del Sol, his owner Arthur Hancock proudly standing nearby accepting the owner's trophy. With Mary and Peter by his side, Frannie stood in the owner's box watching from a distance with mixed emotions. It was a surreal moment for the three of them – watching others take what many thought belonged to them. Privately, Frannie remained suspicious about how Timely Writer became sick. After all, how could Timely Writer go from the overwhelming favorite for the Kentucky Derby, shipped to Churchill Downs with other competitors from the Florida Derby, yet be the only horse stricken by colic? Dominic Imprescia, Jr., the assistant trainer, had wondered aloud the morning after the surgery, "[h]ow could all of this have happened? He had been as healthy as you want a horse to be up until that Monday at 5:30 p.m. Jeff Fell came in Sunday to work him, and he went dynamite. He ate up his whole meal soon after that, and he was really feeling great."[123] After surviving the surgery, Dr. Alex Harthill placed the blame on Timely Writer's near death on uncured hay from the stalls of the barn.

Frannie told a few trusted friends and family members he did not believe Timely Writer's illness was terrible luck. Frannie later told people in Boston, "I think I should have been down there as a guard. But I had to go back and forth to attend to our meat business. If I had it do over again, we would have brought in our own hay and water and gone over it with a microscope."[124] Frannie was passionate about sports, particularly Thoroughbred racing, and a historian of it as well. He knew his family and their colt were outsiders in a sport controlled by local state racing officials, elite owners, and loyalists. He also knew the concerns of others for his family and their colt as outsiders.

Frannie remembered the chaos and shenanigans surrounding the 1968 Kentucky Derby winner. The most controversial finish of any Kentucky Derby race began shortly after the colt, with an owner with ties to Boston crossed the finish line. The Boston newspapers also had a memory of the not-too-distant past. The *Boston Globe* ran a front-page story in its sports section on the morning of the 1982 Kentucky Derby entitled "*The Boston Jinx*." In an article by *Globe* columnist Michael "Mad Dog" Madden, the journalist began the story with a lyric from American poet Ogden Nash: "Here's to Dancer's Image, Who beat the loaded dice; He's the only horse in history, To Win the Derby twice."[125] Madden's not-so-subtle reference to the controversy involving the 1968 Kentucky Derby, laid out in his column on the morning of the 1982 Kentucky Derby, brought back lingering memories that racing officials at Churchill Downs would rather not relive.

It was fourteen years prior when the 1968 Kentucky Derby was held with the unwelcome backdrop of racial unrest in the streets of its city. Racial issues had lingered over the city from the previous year. Civil rights activist Dr. Martin Luther King, Jr., to call attention to the housing discrimination occurring throughout Louisville, led peaceful demonstrations during Kentucky Derby week of 1967. Derby officials were not at all pleased with the racial issues brought to their doorstep - their venue and city were used as center stage for Dr. King's civil rights demonstrations. Events of 1967 served as the pretext for the unprecedented controversy surrounding the finish of the 1968 Kentucky Derby. Legal issues surrounding the race's actual winner and related court litigation would last another five years. The underlying political and racial undertones, however, would last for decades.

As the two-year-old racing season ended in the fall of '67, a thoroughbred named Dancer's Image was among the few horses considered a favorite for the upcoming 1968 Triple Crown races. Dancer's Image was a well-respected colt as he had royalty in his bloodlines – his sire, the legendary stallion Native Dancer, would later be part of Timely Writer's lineage. The owner of Dancer's Image, Peter Fuller, was the son of the former governor of Massachusetts. Fuller was born and raised in Boston, a graduate of Harvard College, and later a member of the board of trustees at Boston University. During his years as a trustee in the mid-'50s, Fuller met a student and a Dorchester resident named Martin Luther King, Jr. King was studying for his doctorate in theology at the university. Fuller developed a friendship and admiration for Martin Luther King, Jr. during the student's time at the school.

With the three-year-old racing season underway in 1968, Dancer's Image won the prestigious Wood Memorial, throwing himself and his owner into the discussion as a favorite for the Kentucky Derby. For Fuller, the news that came on the evening of April 4, 1968, from Memphis, Tennessee, that Dr. Martin Luther King, Jr. had been assassinated left the Bostonian stunned. As Fuller and the nation mourned the loss of Dr. King during the first and second week of April, Dancer's Image won the Governor's Gold Cup in Bowie, Maryland, securing his entry in the field of participants for the Kentucky Derby. Without bringing attention to his generosity, Fuller gifted his winner's purse of $60,000.00 from the Governor's Gold Cup to Dr. King's widow, Coretta Scott King.

Three weeks later, with 12 wins over the previous 12 months, Dancer's Image made his way to the Kentucky Derby as one of the few favorites. It was during the time leading up to the Derby when a local media member heard the story about Fuller's generosity to Coretta Scott King. The story of the gift, which was viewed by the great majority of people with admiration, brought out closeted bigots. Death threats, threatening telephone calls, and intimidating letters became commonplace for the Fuller family. Even acts of violence were carried out against the Fuller family, with one of the storage barns in New Hampshire burned to the ground.

Fuller's racing team for the Derby included well-known veterinarian Dr. Alex Harthill. Dr. Harthill cared for most of the prominent horses at Churchill Downs, earning the nickname "Derby Doc." Dancer's Image, like his grandfather before him, Native Dancer, had tender ankles. Harthill treated the soreness in the ankles of Dancer's Image with Butazolidin ("bute"). Bute for horses is similar to aspirin for humans. It is not a performing-enhancing drug, and the great majority of states had already legalized it, though the rules in Kentucky stated bute could not be in the horse's system within 72 hours of the race.

Dancer's Image, a favorite of the Kentucky Derby entries at odds of 7-2, came from last place to first during the race, crossing the finish line as the winner of the 1968 Kentucky Derby. The family celebrated in the winner's circle, given the owner's trophy, and watched as the garland of roses was laid across the back of Dancer's Image. Immortality had been achieved by Dancer's Image and his owners, with historic pictures taken from the winner's circle. The Fuller family and friends celebrated and partied as they joined an exclusive circle of winners – or so they thought. On the night of May 4th, in an amateur laboratory at Churchill Downs, a chemist for the state of Kentucky tested a urine sample from Dancer's Image. The sample was to have tested positive for "bute," with the chemist confirming the result at the state laboratory.

On the evening of Tuesday, May 6th, three days after the running of the Kentucky Derby, the president of Churchill Downs, Wathen Knebelkampt, announced the positive test. The Kentucky Racing Commission ordered Dancer's Image to drop to last place in the field of entries, with Forward Pass from the historic Calumet Farms in Kentucky declared the winner. The reaction from the Fuller camp was outrage. Dr. Harthill conceded he treated Dancer's Image with bute after a training session on the Monday before the Kentucky Derby – which would have allowed the drug to clear the colt's system within 72 hours of the Derby. Fuller, blindsided by the announcement, retained a local Louisville attorney and appealed the resulting decision of the racing commission to the state court. "The uproar made the cover of *Sports Illustrated*, and rumors ran wild about how the lax security at Churchill Downs conspired to create an opportunity for the horse's feed to be tampered with or how the urine sample was intentionally tainted."[126]

As a result of the lawsuit, Judge Henry Meigs of the Superior Court of Kentucky reviewed over 2,000 pages of evidence and testimony from the three weeks of hearings before the Kentucky Racing Commission. On December 11, 1970, Judge Meigs reinstated Dancer's Image as the winner of the Derby, finding the chemical tests "cannot be accepted as adequate to support the commission's decision."[127] Judge Meigs, within his ruling, was critical of the testing procedures in place and further indicated other expert evidence contradicted the chemist's opinion as to whether bute was in the system of Dancer's Image. Rather than leave the decision alone, though, the Kentucky Racing Commission chose to appeal it.

It would take nearly five years for the litigation in Kentucky to finish, with the Appeals Court reversing the lower court and awarding first place and $122,000.00 in prize money to Forward Pass. Having spent $150,000 in legal fees, Fuller withdrew from further appellate litigation on April 4, 1973. Less than one year after the Appeals Court made their finding, the Kentucky Racing Commission legalized bute for use in thoroughbred racing.

Peter Fuller and Dr. Alex Harthill stood firm throughout their lives that the state chemist, the Kentucky Racing Commission, and the appellate courts of Kentucky were not even-handed in how Dancer's Image was treated after he crossed the finish line first. On the 20th anniversary of Dancer's Image's ill-fated win in Louisville, Fuller sat down for an interview with the *Los Angeles Times*, explaining, "It hurt me being the outsider; I was the new guy in the game from abolitionist Boston."[128]

Fuller was critical of the barn and stall areas at Churchill Downs, as the security system was neglectful – and as reported by others in the article. Whether or not bute was ever in Dancer Image's system during the Derby race was argued about amongst the so-called experts in Kentucky for many years. Fuller believed "it was impossible for him to get a fair decision in Kentucky because of Calumet's strong position in the breeding business there. Lucille Markey, the grand dame of Calumet, vowed never to run another horse in Kentucky if the courts did not award Forward Pass the Derby Victory." As the Martins spent Kentucky Derby Week in and around Churchill Downs, Peter Fuller expressed his sympathies for the family in the Boston newspapers, "I genuinely feel for the Martins. The first thought that popped to mind when I heard about Timely Writer was that there is a hex hanging over Boston horses."[129]

Before leaving Churchill Downs, knowing in all likelihood that this would be their only trip to the Kentucky Derby, the Martins took one last look at a place and an event that people forever dreamed about. The blue-collar brothers from Dorchester and Suffolk Downs had finally made it to the Kentucky Derby. Whether Timely Writer's illness involved something more sinister than bad luck, Frannie never directly voiced his thoughts outside his circle of closest friends. Though the dream of their younger years was cruelly interrupted, the Martins knew they gave it one heck of a ride and visited places they had only previously talked about. As he returned home north, hoping for a return to racing for Timely Writer, Frannie would not question the fate that had befallen his family. As the kid from Dorchester and St. Mark's explained, "who was he to question the guy upstairs."[130]

Upon returning home from the Kentucky Derby, the Martins were met with an overflowing mailbox of letters and cards. In the weeks ahead, Peter, Fran, and Mary spent time responding with handwritten notes of appreciation to every well-wisher. One card of note came from a young girl named Elizabeth Tobey from Hingham, Massachusetts. One of the many families in Massachusetts following the story of Timely Writer and his owners was Elizabeth and her family from nearby Hingham. Elizabeth ("Lizzy"), her brother, and her parents were less than thirty minutes from Suffolk Downs. Elizabeth was one of the many teenagers brought into the sport of thoroughbred racing due to Timely Writer's success and feel-good story. The big wins in Florida increased Lizzy and the family's interest as Timely Writer prepared for his near-certain win at the Kentucky Derby. Liz, like so many, was despondent when the horse from Boston nearly died. Like many others, Liz was one of the many people who sent condolence letters and wishes to the Martin family.

Within the month of the family's return to their home in Quincy, Mary penned a note on behalf of Frannie to Elizabeth. The kind note telling Liz, "Timely Writer thanks you for your wishes! He is doing very well and will go on to prove what we already know – he is a truly great and gallant horse! Enclosed is a picture showing him "doing his thing." Frannie's confidence in Timely Writer's return to championship racing was underlying the note's tone. More than anyone, Frannie knew the type of athlete he had been around for nearly 18 months. He knew Timely Writer had the strength, talent, and heart of a champion to mount a comeback, which many thought impossible. Before the month of May ended, Frannie knew Timely Writer would return.

Chapter 10

The Comeback: Heart of a Champion

"Champions are made from something they have deep inside them - a desire, a dream, a vision. They have to have the skill, and the will. But the will must be stronger than the skill." — Muhammad Ali

In the spring of 1982, many believed Timely Writer was rivaling the level of talent that would match the accomplishments of Triple Crown winners Seattle Slew and Affirmed in 1977 and 1978. Timely Writer, however, was denied his bid at immortality when he was unexpectedly struck with a life-threatening illness days before he was the prohibitive favorite to win the Kentucky Derby. The illness also cost him the remaining two legs of the Triple Crown - the Preakness and Belmont Stakes. Timely Writer's popularity, rising in the weeks before the Kentucky Derby, began increasing in the immediate aftermath of surviving the near-death experience as "the story of the colt's surgery captured the hearts of racing fans everywhere."[131]

One week after surgery, Timely Writer was transported to Dr. Reed's Mare Haven Farm near Louisville, Kentucky, for much-needed rest and recovery. Timely Writer had shed 160 pounds during the immediate aftermath of surgery. The weight loss, about 15% of his body weight, was noticeable. On-lookers could see Timely Writer's rib cage peering through an area where layers of muscle were previously interwoven and bursting through his beautiful bay-colored skin. For the few people permitted around Timely Writer during the early days of recovery, one would leave thinking the colt was no longer invincible and doubtful he would ever race again.

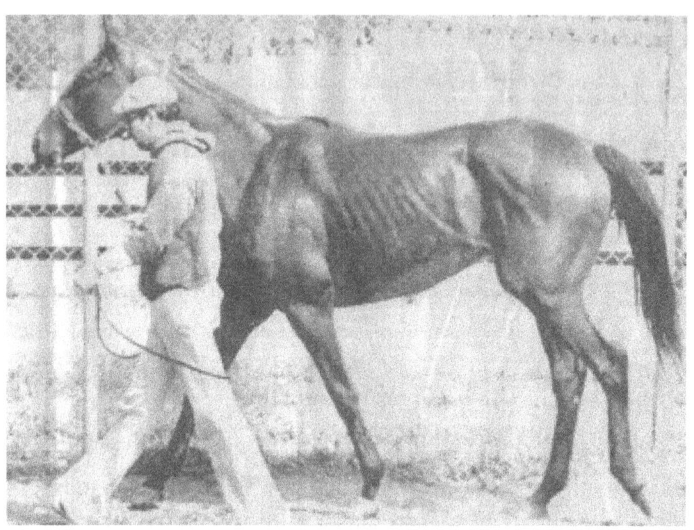

The 160-pound weight loss after surgery for Timely Writer

The week following Timely Writer's arrival at Mare Haven Farm brought an unexpected surprise. The colt was showing a remarkable level of energy and desire to move around. The manager at Mare Haven Farm, Lee Schlusemeyer, began hand-walking Timely Writer every day for weeks. Timely Writer had to walk before he could run, with the downtime allowing him to gain back the weight lost from surgery.

Peter Martin took the thousand-mile ride south from Dorchester to Kentucky to visit for a few days with Timely Writer and fellow owner Dr. Reed – the time spent assessing the health of Timely Writer. During one of his first mornings at the farm, Peter was making his way out to the barn, noticing Dr. Reed walking away from the horse stall where the upright Timely Writer was nibbling at his hay. As he approached Peter, Dr. Reed's eyes were welling up with tears. Peter exclaimed, "cut it out Doc, you've treated thousands of horses and lost a lot, why are you giving me the business about this one?"[132] Dr. Reed, slowly wiping away the droplets of tears, stared Peter in his eyes, explaining, "[t]his one is really special, Peter. You look at a lot of them and they're flesh and bones, but this one has a will, he wants to live."[133] As with Frannie, years of experience told Dr. Reed that

Timely Writer was a once-in-a-generation horse – the one horse that had the will to mount a racing comeback that had never been witnessed before.

Once the hand walking served its purpose at Mare Haven Farm, Timely Writer was re-introduced to the tools of racing and turned out in the paddock area. Timely Writer, a stubborn horse as a one-year-old, needed to get comfortable and confident once again with his athletic equipment - the saddle, bit, and reins. Most importantly, at some point, Timely Writer would need to acquiesce to a jockey on his back, directing and controlling his movements. To the amazement of everyone involved in the process, less than six weeks removed from invasive stomach surgery, Timely Writer showed he was ready to start jogging again with an exercise rider in the saddle. Time would be needed, though, for Timely Writer to increase his muscularity and endurance level. Concerns expressed by the doctors to Timely Writer's team were that muscle atrophy may have set in and weakened his physical condition.

At the end of May, after tremendous progress by Timely Writer, Jeffrey Fell was flown into Kentucky for some time in the mount on Timely Writer. Bringing Fell to Timely Writer was designed to reacquaint the two sooner rather than later. It also allowed Fell to push the colt's racing limits to see what the colt had left in him after the surgery. Once Fell finished training sessions with Timely Writer, a group decision would be made regarding whether a comeback for the champion was in his best interests. If not, the Martins and Dr. Reed would sit Timely Writer out for the remainder of the racing season, awaiting the day he could begin the next phase of his career as a stallion. With Timely Writer turning the age of 4 on the 1st of January in 1983, he would make his way over to the breeding barn for years to come.

Fell started the training sessions easy with his favorite colt, though Timely Writer would have none of it – physically pushing back at Fell when he was not pleased. An elite jockey sitting on the mount of a thoroughbred, with control of the reins, has the ability to direct the horse to do as much or as little as the jockey wants. The independent and intelligent Timely Writer, in combination with his sheer athleticism and raw strength, weighing in at nearly 1100 pounds, however, knew how to convey his ideas about his training regimen. Timely Writer's communications with his jockeys required a very experienced rider to understand the champion colt, or the pairing would not end well. As one spouse knows another spouse, Fell knew the stubborn side of Timely Writer. At Timely Writer's core, he possessed the instincts and determination of an elite athlete. When not pleased with Fell's leadership in the saddle, Timely Writer would collectively throw his head in a manner inconsistent with the jockey's path. It was a fight Timely Writer knew how to pick - and not one Jeffrey Fell could win. Timely Writer knew how to get his way while pushing the limits of Fell's comfort level in the saddle. Though the big colt could not speak, there was no doubt he knew how to communicate.

As Dr. Reed previously remarked about Timely Writer's brilliance, which aided the colt in surviving a life-threatening event, Fell also knew the beautiful mind of Timely Writer. Fell repeatedly witnessed it during the training sessions at Dr. Reed's farm. With Timely Writer repeatedly conveying his unhappiness with the slow pace of the training sessions, Fell was forced to speed up the plan and worked his running mate much harder. Fell tested Writer's quickness, fitness, responsiveness, and endurance throughout the training track over various distances. Pushing the limits of Timely Writer, the jock and his racing team wanted to ensure that Timely Writer was completely healthy and fit enough to return to elite racing.

Fell went on to survive the combative training sessions with his partner and came to the only logical conclusion. Timely Writer was stronger than ever, as fit as any horse could be, and was ready for competitive racing. Fell also spoke about Timely Writer's prickly personality, "I know he's meaner, for sure."[134] Timely Writer let his people know he was ready for a comeback, one where he was bigger, faster, and, as Fell found out, meaner than ever.

In May of '82, the *New York Times* had sources telling them a decision was made to send Timely Writer to Belmont Park as the last phase of their training plan. With what once seemed to be an improbable return, the *Times* began printing articles for its readers about the progress of Timely Writer.

The newspaper lets its readers know, "the overwhelming favorite to win the Kentucky Derby …… will take another step on his road to recovery when he arrives at Belmont Park by van from Kentucky."[135] Although the newspaper was a few weeks ahead of Timely Writer's return, the information was accurate as to the next stop. An equine van transport left Dr. Reed's Mare Haven Farm on June 9, 1982. As Timely Writer's van methodically made its way northeast towards the other side of Manhattan, Dominic was scheduling workouts for Timely Writer at Belmont Park, planning to increase their volume and duration with each passing week.

Shortly after settling into his stall at Belmont, Timely Writer appeared in an unannounced public appearance before the crowd. The rehabilitation plan included an early afternoon visit to the main track for Timely Writer to gallop in front of the crowd attending the day's races. The training session was scheduled just before the day's first race to get Timely Writer comfortable again in front of a large crowd. It did not take long, though, for the plan to take an unexpected turn. The workout for the reigning champion of the Champagne Stakes turned into an unexpected parade and celebration. Neither Timely Writer's crew nor the fans in attendance could have predicted the events over the following thirty minutes.

The afternoon event was designed for Timely Writer to go from the barn on the backside of the track towards the paddock area for saddling. Once saddled with a jockey atop the colt, Timely Writer would head to the track at Belmont, where he would pass through the tunnel leading onto the race track. It was to be an uneventful walk, which Timely Writer knew well, having made it many times during the prior fall racing season at Belmont Park. As Timely Writer began his walk from the barn for the workout, approximately 150 grooms and "hotwalkers" from the barns of other trainers began following the colt from behind and at his sides. Timely Writer's newly found entourage clapped in unison during the entire walk to the paddock area- showing their respect to the returning champion after his remarkable victory and return from the near-death event. The love, affection, and respect from the everyday race track workers towards a horse not trained by any of the supporters reminded on-lookers why Timely Writer was called the "people's champion." The noise of the walk-over was spreading throughout the surrounding areas within the grounds of Belmont Park, including the grandstand, where people began asking about the commotion.

Once Timely Writer arrived at the paddock area, he was dressed with his blinkers hood and saddled. Jeffrey Fell, who was scheduled to ride in races during the day's program, rushed to the paddock area for the saddling of a colt who would never know another jockey on his back. With the addition of Fell, Timely Writer made his way along the path leading towards the tunnel entrance onto the dirt track. At Belmont Park, horses and jockeys must go through a tunnel under the owners' boxes in the grandstands as they enter the dirt track for racing. As this was not a standard parade of horses heading towards the starting gate for a race, Timely Writer entered the tunnel as the lone horse. With horseshoes quietly clapping and echoing throughout the tunnel, a silhouette appeared in the dimly lit tunnel of the champion with Jeffrey Fell sitting upright in the saddle, the glint of an orange and black blinkered hood covering Timely Writer's head. The return of the Champagne Stakes winner was a vision the unsuspecting crowd was about to fall in love with once again as the pair made their way through the tunnel onto the dirt track.

Standing in daylight on the dirt track at the other end of the tunnel, one could see the silhouette of a thoroughbred slowly exiting through the tunnel in a near-gladiator-like fashion. Timely Writer was stepping back onto a dirt track where he last appeared in October of 1981 when the predominant crowd of New Yorkers gave a rousing send-off to the purported two-year-old colt of the year from Boston.

Training sessions at a racetrack are typically scheduled with multiple horses in the early morning hours on either the main track or at a training track some distance away. As Timely Writer took his first steps onto the sand of the track, the crowd remained curious about what was happening and who was disturbing the day's routine. As Timely Writer exited the tunnel onto the track, Jeffrey Fell gave his ride a tug of the reins, nudging Timely Writer further down the track. With a click of the heels from the jockey, Timely Writer began galloping in front of the main grandstand. Many of the crowd were looking towards the track, curious and confused about why one colt was starting a solo training session so close to the day's first race. Track announcer Marshall Cassidy, located up in his perch at the top of the grandstand, was preparing to call the day's races and noticed the colt and the commotion. Cassidy knew Timely Writer had been sent to Belmont for workouts at the track and immediately recognized the champion. Hitting the switch to turn on his microphone, Cassidy let the crowd in on the secret of the horse appearing before them. With his silky-smooth voice, Cassidy leaned into his microphone, "Yes, that's Timely Writer parading in front of the grandstand." [136]

Upon hearing Cassidy's words, the New York crowd, like the entourage from the horse barns who escorted Timely Writer to the paddock, knew the magnitude of the moment. The crowd rose to their feet, smiles spreading across their faces, hands clapping as Timely Writer paraded before them. In one of the most unique and unscripted moments in sports, the New York crowd stood as one giving the champion horse from Boston an ovation – for which they would not relent. Through the ovation, patrons shouted words of encouragement from the grandstand to Timely Writer during a simple galloping session. As the colt continued his session around the oval track, the crowd remained on their feet, with the applause never stopping and the decibels increasing as Timely Writer continued. The crowd did not stop until Timely Writer left the track through for the barn from which he first came. The training session and welcome back ovation lasted for over ten minutes. Without saying many words, the crowd conveyed their message, letting Timely Writer know he was their two-year-old champion - the people's champion – and letting the rest of the country know which horse they would be cheering on for the remainder of the racing season.

Regarding the workout, the galloping session went exceptionally well, as Frannie jokingly told people that the jockey had to put a wrestling move around Timely Writer to slow him down. As the New York crowd showed, a new and different level of admiration was engulfing Timely Writer. Upon Timely Writer's return to the public spotlight, perhaps out of sympathy, perhaps out of respect for the way Timely Writer and the Martins handled the tragedy, or the public's desire to see another chapter in the improbable fairy tale story, the colt, and the Martins would return more popular.

In the generations before the internet, with instant access to information and news, the print media narrated the public's perception of Timely Writer's comeback. With the press laying the groundwork for the fairly-tale script of Timely Writer's underdog owners taking on the racing establishment the previous year, the stories of the colt's rehabilitation progress and his return to racing continued the year-long center-piece stories in horse racing journals, newspapers, and on radio stations throughout the country. Tales about Timely Writer's rehabilitation were constant - as was the debate about where and when he would return. All of the continued love and support from around the country shown to Timely Writer and his family left Frannie in awe, commenting "you just can't believe how this horse captured the hearts of the people."[137]

The whispers of a healthy Timely Writer and an earlier-than-expected return to competitive racing were making their way out of the barns of Suffolk Downs and onto the streets of Boston - and straight up the stairs to the Office of the Mayor. Kevin White served as the Mayor of Boston from 1968 to 1984. One does not survive the politics of Boston for nearly two decades without understanding the city's people. White became the Mayor of Boston at the age of 38. The family he was born into and the family he married into were involved with the city's politics for decades. White's resume included a law school degree from Boston College and a graduate degree from Harvard University's John F. Kennedy School of Government. The mayor led the city through the Boston school desegregation busing crisis of the 1960s and 70s. White was a seasoned, effective, and flamboyant politician who transformed Boston into a first-class city. In the summer of 1982, White knew the city's pulse and people.

Mayor White saw the impact of Timely Writer's transformational sports story up close. White witnessed the story's birth in his city, then watched from a distance as it spread across the country. White spoke for all when he penned a column in the Boston newspapers during the summer of '82.

Mayor White shared his thoughts with readers as the first half of 1982 finished. White wanted the public to appreciate that the leading sports and human-interest story of the year was playing out in front of their eyes. Ironically, the Martins' story was not considered the most impactful due to the owners winning the "big one" at Churchill Downs. As Mayor White astutely observed, it was an honor earned because the brothers from Dorchester faced tragedy "by accepting misfortune with grace. Together they captured the imagination of every sports fan across the country, and they did this by sharing a dream .... and not giving up on that dream when things went wrong....... and looking ahead to tomorrow. [Timely Writer] was a symbol of men who followed a dream, worked hard, and despite setbacks, they never said quit."[138] The colt symbolized the blue-collar work ethic of the Martins and the city. It was a real-life story that brought sports and non-sports fans along for the ride, through good times and bad, teaching real-life lessons about faith and decency in men while tugging at every emotional cord.

The Mayor had the ability to take a step back from the story he knew up close and recognize why the family's journey was about more than horse racing. The Martin family and Timely Writer were a sports story unlike any other seen before. People were identifying with Timely Writer's journey, not because it was about winning or losing, but because of how the participants, underdogs many times over, played the game. Mayor White's instincts, political or otherwise, were spot on. He knew this was the leading story of 1982 because it involved sports intertwined with real-life, hard-working participants who were winning and losing at times while carrying themselves with dignity and grace.

Long-time *Boston Globe* journalist Michael Blowen concurred with Mayor White. By the nature of his profession, Blowen knew the city's people – and the patrons at Suffolk Downs thanks to his love of thoroughbreds. Blowen witnessed Timely Writer and the Martins' impact on the people of New England and Boston. "Having Timely Writer in Boston was like Elvis coming to town – an energy and excitement in horse racing never seen in the city. Their story made horse racing fans of people who had never followed the sport."

To fully understand the depths of Timely Writer and his owners' impact on the public and to which the mayor and journalist spoke, one must realize that the story shared sports headlines and the hearts of Bostonians with the Boston Celtics and the National Basketball Association (NBA) super-star Larry Bird in 1981 and 1982. Boston is well-known as a rabid sports city, and in the early 1980s, it was starving for a champion. In 1981, the last team in the city to win a championship was the Boston Celtics in 1976. The people of Boston look towards at least one of its teams to compete for a championship annually. With the Boston Red Sox not having seen a World Series trophy since 1918, the Boston Bruins last Stanley Cup trophy coming in 1972, and the New England Patriots having zero championships to show for their efforts since their inaugural season in 1960, the city was all too dependent upon the Boston Celtics for championships throughout the 1960s and '70s.

Larry Bird was feeding the appetites of sports fans in Boston as the Celtics began the next phase of the team's dynasty in 1980. Bird's rookie season in 1980 saw him lead the team to the single most significant increase in win totals from one season to the next. The Celtics of 1979 won a meager 29 games - and there wasn't much hope for the future. Bird's presence in the line-up in 1980 catapulted the team to 61 wins, earning him Rookie of the Year honors from the NBA. The following year, Bird led the Celtics to the 1981 NBA championship, finishing off the Houston Rockets on May 14, 1981. Though the Celtics would have the best record in the NBA during the 1981-1982 season, finishing at 63-19, they would come up short of winning back-to-back championships with a game-seven loss to "Dr. J" and the Philadelphia 76ers at the Boston Garden on May 23, 1982. Bird would go on to earn the nickname "Larry Legend," winning two more NBA championships in 1984 and 1986, the league's most valuable player three consecutive years from 1983-1986, and a gold medal as part of the 1992 basketball "Dream Team" at the Olympics in Barcelona, Spain. Bird's career culminated with his election to the NBA Hall of Fame in 1998. For a moment in time, though, the hearts of Boston and others throughout the country turned their affection towards a thoroughbred and his owners from Boston.

After being declared fit to return to training by his doctors in June of 1982, people were speculating where Timely Writer would make his comeback race. Fans and families, such as the Tobey family from Hingham, Massachusetts, looked forward to the news articles and the radio broadcasts for information on where Timely Writer would make his triumphant return. The colt could have raced at any number of racing tracks throughout the country. Dominic received numerous calls about securing Timely Writer's return to their venue for his comeback race. As June came to a close, and with the dramatic public appearance of Timely Writer at Belmont Park reported in the newspapers, the public and the racing industry would increase their questioning of where Timely Writer would make his remarkable comeback. Though the questions of where and when the comeback would remain unanswered, the Martin brothers privately knew the answer. The brothers were guys from Dorchester - loyal to their core. These were men who grew up in neighbors where the obituary of one of their own includes a cryptic acronym paying allegiance to their place of birth. The brothers genuinely felt sorrow for the loss of fellow Bostonians when Timely Writer could not race in the Kentucky Derby.

Despite Dominic answering countless telephone requests for the return of Timely Writer, the answer as to where the colt would begin his comeback was simple. The decision had nothing to do with where the brothers could make the most money. Frannie and Peter were negotiating privately with the President of Suffolk Downs about the Timely Writer's return to his home in Boston. The officials at Suffolk Downs went out of their way to secure Timely Writer's comeback race. Suffolk Downs moved their annual Yankee Handicap from the fall racing calendar to their summer schedule to accommodate Timely Writer's return to racing at the place he called home. Though Timely Writer's last competitive race was for a then-record purse of $250,000.00 in Florida, the brothers insisted his return would begin at Suffolk Downs in the $75,000 Yankee Handicap on August 14th in a one-mile race.

Many believed Timely Writer's return to Suffolk Downs would be the return of magic. Gone was the sickly-looking thoroughbred from May, where photos of a malnourished Timely Writer circulated in the media. Returning was a champion bigger and stronger than ever. Timely Writer had gained back more than the 160 pounds he lost from stomach surgery. He was older, more muscular, meaner, as jockey Jeffrey Fell found out, and perhaps faster - as his times during workouts showed. As Dominic met with media members at Suffolk Downs two days before the colt's triumphant return, he noted how Timely Writer "sure has become a favorite of the people. I do believe we're receiving more attention now that he's making a comeback than when he was heading for the Derby as the probable choice."[139]

One of the many young kids and teenagers following the improbable story of Timely Writer was Elizabeth Tobey from nearby Hingham. "Lizzy" as she was known, had been tracking the newspaper articles about the return of Timely Writer. It was after Timely Writer's near-death experience when Lizzy penned a note of support to the Martins, with Frannie returning a note and a picture of Timely Writer in appreciation. On Saturday, August 14th, Liz, a friend from school, and her family made the short drive to Suffolk Downs for Timely Writer's return to racing, broadcast on television screens nationwide. Liz and her family excitedly staked out their positions along the track rail for the opportunity to view the returning champion walk by them on the way to the starting gate. In hand, Liz was holding a hand-made pennant proclaiming Timely Writer as the top horse in the country. Timely Writer was given a hero's welcome upon his return to Suffolk Downs. The colt received standing ovations as soon as his legs hit the track. As Timely Writer made his way onto the track and along the rail towards Lizzy, the Martins and friends were in their usual seats at Suffolk Downs, looking down at Timely Writer with admiration and awe as the people's horse began his trot in front of the grandstands. As the Martins looked from above, a young girl's pennant supporting Timely Writer could be seen waving from her hand. Lizzy cheered and watched in amazement as Timely Writer and Jeffrey Fell trotted past her - the colt more magnificent in person than she ever imagined.

Lizzy's experience on that 14th day in August was later put into writing once the school year began. The young student's story, chosen for publication in her school newspaper, is an eyewitness account of a local champion's triumphant return on a warm summer day in Boston. Lizzy was a member of her elementary school newspaper in Hingham, the *Foster Free Press*, and published her first-hand account of Timely Writer's comeback. A two-part story from Lizzy, entitled "*Timely Writer: The People's Horse*," spoke of the popularity, beauty, and courage of a horse everyone viewed as their own. Through the eyes of an eleven-year-old, the sport of thoroughbred racing and its local champion was brought to life at an elementary school in Hingham, Massachusetts.

Lizzy first recounted in her article for her readers about the days after Timely Writer escaped his near-death experience - and the hundreds of letters the Martins received in support. The young girl remembering how "some said he would never race again." Lizzy never gave up hope in the aftermath of Timely Writer's sickness that one of the toughest thoroughbreds to ever race would return. She proudly told the readers that "on August 14th, 25,000 people filled the grandstand at Suffolk Downs, and I was one of them. When Timely Writer walked onto the track, he was given a standing ovation. He walked to the starting gate majestically .... with about fifty yards to go, he passed the leaders to win gloriously!"

In the second of the two-part series from the author, Lizzy shared author C.W. Anderson's words in describing Timely Writer's impact upon people. Lizzy let Anderson's words describe the greatness of Timely Writer. "Only rarely do they grudgingly call a horse great. He is the one who can do things with dash, finish, and assurance that pulls you to your feet." Despite not having raced competitively in nearly five months and coming off an invasive surgery, Timely Writer showed his greatness and sheer grit, coming within 1.2 seconds of the track record for the one-mile and seventy-yard race. The remarkable part was Timely Writer nearly broke the track record while not running a great race for him. As he was coming off the last turn, the race had been a struggle, and it was not certain he would win. Until the 1/8 pole, pure courage and heart placed Timely Writer within striking distance. Though difficult, it was the beginning of a return for which most people thought impossible.

Timely Writer's impressive race at Suffolk Downs on August 14th led to a group decision by his owners and trainer to return to one last race at Saratoga Race Course. Timely Writer's next race in his comeback was a return to the friendly confines of Saratoga Springs, New York. Timely Writer's last visit to the Spa wowed the crowds during his win at the Hopeful Stakes twelve months prior – the win was the start of discussions about his candidacy for the best two-year-old horse of 1981.

Timely Writer was joining his stablemates in Saratoga for August, 2-year-old Timely Hitter, purchased the prior year by Nitram Stables, and Soldier Boy, owned by Sandy Cooperstein. All three horses would be under the tutelage of trainer Dominic Imprescia. With an ambitious schedule of races for Timely Hitter and Soldier Boy, with three races in three weeks for each, Dominic took on a twenty-year-old assistant groom from Malden, Massachusetts, Michael Palmer. Palmer, with four years of experience from Suffolk Downs, came with a recommendation from "Oldsmobile Charlie" from Duxbury, Massachusetts. Charlie Tufankjian owned the largest Oldsmobile car dealership in Massachusetts, with a nice stable of horses at the Boston track where Palmer learned the craft. Palmer left Charlie and Boston in his 1969 Plymouth Belvedere, riding on four bald tires, for the roar of the crowd at Saratoga. -Palmer worked long hours in Saratoga, sleeping in the barn's equipment room for the horses.

Ten days after the Yankee Handicap, Timely Writer would enter the 8th race of the day as an entry in the Saratoga Hospital Allowance race. In the week leading up to the Saratoga Hospital, Imprescia noticed how Timely Writer was getting bigger and faster by the day. "He's even stronger than he was before the operation . . . . and he's getting tougher and sharper."[140] Evidence of this was on display for all to see at the training track in Saratoga Springs. In what was to be a gallop twice around the one-mile oval, Timely Writer's exercise rider Luke Dufresne, better known in racing circles now as "Cool hand Luke," thanks to Tony Everard, was having difficulties keeping Timely Writer in check. The rumors and stories from trackside about the greatness of Timely Writer, which had been told, re-told, and spread throughout the thoroughbred racing circuit during Writer's two-year-old and early three-year-old campaign, were once again on full display in the summer of 1982.

The clockers at the training track in Saratoga knew of the rumors and had witnessed what Timely Writer had done after crossing the finish line upon winning the Flaming Stakes and the Florida Derby. Unbeknownst to Dufresne, clockers at the track had the stopwatches going as Luke visibly pulled the reins back on Timely Writer to slow him down. Despite Luke's efforts, Timely Writer rolled through the last quarter mile of a workout in 25 seconds, then galloping out 3/8 of a mile in 36 seconds. As Timely Writer "galloped out" the final 3/8 of a mile, the clockers were left in awe at the sensational times for the workout. Afterward, Cool Hand Luke was giving interviews to the inquiring press about the colt's remarkable comeback, telling them, "I had all I could do to keep him from running off. The farther he gallops, the tougher he gets, and I'm not lightweight at 135 pounds."[141] Nearby, Dominic yelled to the gathered media, "the way he's been going, I think he could carry me."[142] Stories and observations from trackside for the past two years were indeed true. Timely Writer was a once-in-a-lifetime athlete, blessed with God-given speed, and as evidenced by his triumphant return to racing, he possessed the will and heart of a champion.

Going into his return race at the Spa, and based on how Timely Writer was training the week prior, the Martin crew knew there wasn't a horse in the Saratoga Hospital who would beat their prized colt. What they did not account for, though, was the continued growing fascination and support in upstate New York for their horse. Before the 8th race at Saratoga, Imprescia was saddling Timely Writer by the elm tree near the horse stalls, getting the colt ready for jockey Jeffrey Fell. The layout of the Saratoga race course is unique as it allows the crowd to watch the horses nearby as the competitors are dressed for the race. On average, it is about a five to ten-minute process to place the blinker hood on Timely Writer, along with his riding cloth, saddle, leather belts on each side of the saddle, and the buckling of the metal belts to secure the saddle.

As Imprescia brought Timely Writer out to the area by the tree, patrons started gathering nearby. As with any other race day at Saratoga, there are always curious on-lookers who want to get near the saddling process to see the beauty and strength of a thoroughbred. Though a simplistic saddling ritual, one cannot walk by without pausing to watch a thoroughbred standing at attention while his equipment is added for race day. This particular day under the elm by the paddock, though, was different as Timely Writer was saddled. The crowd increased around Timely Writer as the minutes passed while Dominic outfitted the colt. These were more than just curious on-lookers gathering. As Dominic was coming to the end of his routine, he looked around and saw the crowd, which was now six to seven people deep around the horse. People in the crowd asked if they could touch Timely Writer. Towards the end of the saddling, similar to what happened at Belmont Park, the crowd began talking to Timely Writer, which later grew to screams of encouragement as he was ready to leave the paddock arca. Grown men yelling to Timely Writer, "Go get em, Timely - go get em, babe."[143] To the people in the paddock area, Timely Writer was their champion - their fairly-tale story - and now the people's champion had returned.

As the fans of Timely Writer left the paddock area to find their spots trackside for the race, it would be jockey Jeffrey Fell's third day in a row at Saratoga directing a champion to victory. On Friday, Fell won the day's feature race with Winter's Tale, setting a record at Saratoga for the mile and 3/16ths. On Saturday, Fell won the main event for the entire Saratoga summer racing season onboard Runaway Groom in the Travers Stakes. As the Martins had chosen not to rush Timely Writer back for the demanding and challenging Travers Stakes, Jerry Fell was available for the race. The Travers Stakes is the most significant race of the year at Saratoga, tracing its history back to before the start of the Kentucky Derby. The Travers Stakes of 1982 included the winners of the three Triple Crown races from earlier in the spring competing against one another in a race known as the "Mid-Summer Derby."

At Fell's direction, underdog Runaway Groom stormed from last place, fifteen lengths back, crossing the finish line first in the most shocking upset in the history of the Travers. Jeffrey Fell became the first jockey ever to take down the reigning Kentucky Derby winner (Gato Del Sol), the Preakness champion (Aloma's Ruler), and the Belmont Stakes winner (Conquistador Cielo) in the same race. In a finish filled with great irony and classic Timely Writer style, Canadian Jeffrey Fell directed the Canadian-born Runaway Groom pass the American favorites from the outside of the pack, surging down the backstretch for the historic upset. After the Travers win, Fell was asked by the media about his mounts and the competition he had gone up against over the weekend. Though the questioner had not mentioned Timely Writer's name, Fell responded by letting the journalist know "[Writer's] an outstanding colt. If he can come back all the way, he's the horse to beat in the big races of the fall."[144]

On Sunday, Fell was back on the mount of his old friend. The Saratoga Hospital was 7 furlongs long - not the ideal distance for Timely Writer. As one local journalist noticed, trackside found a "crowd of 20,075 [which] included a large number of fans from the Boston area, where Timely Writer is regarded by racing fans as the biggest star since Ted Williams."[145] Four horses older than Timely Writer, whose experience and specialties were as short-distance speed horses, were aiming to end the champion's comeback. The competition included Castle Knight with future Hall of Fame jockey Jorge Velasquez, Lord Darnley with jockey Mary Russ, and Contare with future Hall of Fame jockey Eddie Maple. Fell and Writer would be taking on excellent competition with two Hall of Fame jockeys in the race and a third, Mary Russ, who made history earlier in the year aboard Lord Darnley in the Widener Handicap at Gulfstream Park - becoming the first female in North American thoroughbred racing to win a Grade 1 stakes race. A journalist observed that another well-known racing entry never made the starting gate. "Top sprinter Distinctive Pro was entered, but his ankle started hurting when trainer Jimmy Croll read that Timely Writer was in the race."[146]

The race began in typical Timely Writer fashion, the colt the last of the five throughout the first half. The quarterly times reported on the infield board indicated the group was blazing along. At the ¾ mile marker, all five horses were stretched across the track with Timely Writer on the outside of the pack. Four horses had their jockeys applying the horsewhip consistently to get more out of each horse. On the far outside was Timely Writer, "under the most confident hand ride you will ever see."[147] In an instant, when the colt felt the need, Timely Writer "swept by the leaders as if they were nailed to the track."[148] Writer surged down the stretch towards the finish line, 3 ½ lengths ahead of the second-place finisher as he crossed the finish line.

As Timely Writer was crossing the finish line, the remainder of the crowd who were sitting joined those who were standing, all showing their respect and amazement with a thunderous standing ovation. Timely Writer had given the crowd a show, traveling from last to first. The entertainment from the race included jockey Jeffrey Fell "literally standing up nearly 3/16ths of a mile from the finish line" as he tried to save Timely Writer's energy down the homestretch– and maybe save Timely Writer from himself. Despite Fell slowing Timely Writer down over the final $3/16^{th}$ of a mile, standing up in the irons hanging from the saddle, the pair came within one second of the track record for a seven furlongs race - clocking in at 1:21 and 3/5 of a second. It was a result unimaginable less than four months ago on that first Saturday of May in Kentucky. As Timely Writer crossed the finish line to a booming standing ovation, the cheers would not relent until his arrival at the winner's circle minutes later.

As the Martin crew waited for the colt's appearance in the winner's circle, words of superlatives were coupled with looks of amazement and disbelief on their faces. Frannie spoke of how he thought the horse was doing things as if he were "Superman." A horse racing fan since his youth and with over 40 years of experience at horse tracks, Frannie was bewildered at what he had just witnessed, thinking out loud, "The way he won it is beyond my comprehension."[149] The renowned Dr. Reed marveled, stating, "he's an incredible athlete."[150]

Timely Writer's overdue return to the winner's circle was met with euphoria, with supporters and critics alike sharing their amazement. Timely Writer had "made believers out of many cynics who never thought he'd ever make it back at all." With the media gathered, Dominic explained that horses never return to racing at this level of competition after such an invasive surgery. Dominic observed that not only was Timely Writer back, but he was better than ever. He remarked on how easy the seven-furlong race was for Timely Writer, belly-laughing when he saw jockey Jefferey Fell at the winner's circle, appearing more tired than the horse. Fell, as he was wiping the sweat from his face, agreed. "He did it all on his own…I wanted him to relax and settle down for me. Once he gets rolling, he gets strong on you. I couldn't pull him up until the half-mile pole."[151] Though Fell did not know it, race officials with stopwatches hit their re-set buttons after the pair crossed the finish line. Upon Timely Writer crossing the finish line, others watched and timed the distance the colt traveled. Unable to slow Timely Writer's top speed down for another 1/8 mile after the finish line, Fell would eventually return him to the winner's circle. Timely Writer was timed "coasting" around the track in an unheard-of one minute and 35 seconds.

As the literary representatives of the more than 20,000 people in attendance who witnessed the Sunday race, journalists in the days after would attempt to tell the tale of Timely Writer's return in his comeback at Saratoga Springs. All agreed that no matter what words were printed about the race, "between the lines is something you had to be there to see." "What was so awesome about Timely Writer's fifth performance of 1982 was how he ran seven furlongs so easily in 1:21 3/5. It was an exhibition on how to win a horse race without really trying."[152]

Fell was asked to compare the three champions he led to victory over the last three days. The jockey, who mounted hundreds of horses a year for countless owners, spoke honestly. Given the choice among Winter's Tale, who set the track record on Friday, Runaway Groom, who beat the three winners of the Triple Crown races on Saturday at the Travers Stake, or Timely Writer, his choice was Timely Writer. Fell assured people, "Timely Writer would make the others look as if they had been tied to a pole."[153]

Missing from the Saratoga summer races, as well as the Triple Crown races earlier in the year, was Timely Writer's 2 -2-year-old-racing nemesis Deputy

Minister. It seems the Eclipse Award winner had become injury-prone and was not fit to race after the challenging racing schedule put together by his owners at the end of 1981 and into the start of 1982. 1982 started with the Deputy Minister entering the Bahamas Stakes at Gulfstream Park in February. Expecting a Triple Crown champion, the Canadian Broadcasting Company began filming a documentary on Deputy Minister, starting with the Bahamas Stakes race. The day before the Bahamas Stakes, the trainer for Deputy Minister, John Tammaro, had worked him out and stated, "he'll handle all race tracks."[154] Deputy Minister, the favorite to win the Bahamas Stakes, finished in a disappointing 5th place. The following morning, it was announced that Deputy Minister suffered from an ankle injury. Any chance for Deputy Minister to prove the loss to Timely Writer at the Champagne was a fluke would never materialize as Deputy Minister was not fit to race for either the Flamingo or the Florida Derby, with the remainder of the year not getting any better for the Canadian champion.

As the summer racing calendar ended at Saratoga, the fall classics at Belmont Park would begin. Conquistador Cielo, the Belmont Stakes winner, retired to stud the day after his dismal performance at the Travers in Saratoga. Although Conquistador Cielo had won seven straight races entering the Travers, his owners at Claiborne Farm were more interested in preserving their breeding syndication agreement totaling $36.4 million.

With Deputy Minister's non-existent racing season, Conquistador's retirement from racing, and the Triple Crown races divided between three horses, the spotlight was shining directly on Timely Writer. The collective thought was that good showings at Belmont Park during his final three races would result in Timely Writer winning the Eclipse Award as the three-year-old horse of the year. The award was his for the taking.

Following along in Timely Writer's footsteps from Suffolk Downs to Saratoga Race Course and back to Belmont Park, Dr. Reed would also return to Belmont for the fall racing season. Dr. Reed looked forward to watching over his breeding investment while making himself available at his equine clinic near Belmont Park. Belmont's fall 1982 racing calendar included the annual end-of-the-year racing finale with the Champagne Stakes and Jockey Gold Cup scheduled on the same racing card. The races were set for Saturday the 10th of October- exactly one year after Timely Writer's win at the 1981 Champagne Stakes. Timely Writer would return to the scene of his greatest triumph in 1981, where he beat the best two-year-old thoroughbreds in the country.

The Martin team had finalized the last three races of Timely Writer's three-year-old racing season. The prestigious Jerome Handicap and the Marlboro Cup were the first two races, with the Jockey Club Gold Cup serving as Timely Writer's 15th and final race before retirement. As Timely Writer was a year older, he would compete in the prestigious $500,000 Jockey Gold Cup for entries three years old and over. After the Jockey Gold Cup, the remainder of Timely Writer's life would be spent as a stallion standing at Dr. William Reed's Mare Haven Farm in Kentucky. The return trip to Kentucky in the equine van was already booked for the Wednesday after the Jockey Gold Cup. The van would transport Timely Writer south into retirement while earning millions of dollars in stud fees as a stallion.

Chapter 11
Tragedy: Part II

Events through the years at Belmont Park exposed the cruel dichotomy of thoroughbred horse racing. Nationally televised broadcasts of the sport and its participants, depicting the agony of defeat and even death, were brought into sports fans' homes nationwide. Scenes of heartbreak splashed across the television screens for all to see, shedding light on the darkness of an otherwise vibrant sport. Dr. Reed, a breeder, expert equine doctor, and a racing fan, knew first-hand that grief is the price individuals pay for the love and loss of an animal.

Ruffian was the finest filly ever known to thoroughbred racing. She was foaled on April 17, 1972, at the historic Clairborne Farms in Paris, Kentucky. As her grandfather was a Native Dancer, Timely Writer's bloodlines made the colt a distant cousin to the Queen of Thoroughbred racing. Ruffian saw her most significant accomplishments and tragic ending at Belmont Park. Dr. Reed saved the lives of many thoroughbreds during his career, including 1967 Kentucky Derby winner Stymie, but he would forever be attached to the final chapter of Ruffian's short life. As Dr. Reed looked forward to Belmont Park's 1982 fall racing season, Ruffian's tragic death in 1975 was a lingering memory that he nor the sport could erase.

Often, the first stop for Dr. Reed upon his arrival at Belmont Park was the equine hospital he founded across the street from the horse barns located at 111 Plainfield Avenue. Reed had been a veterinarian at Belmont since 1947, operating on over 7,500 horses. For years, injured horses were transported to Cornell Veterinarian School in Ithaca, New York – some 300 miles away. The duration of the trip alone often proves fatal for an injured animal. To fix the flaw, Dr. Reed purchased a one-story red brick building across from the horse barns in 1961. He proceeded to design an operating room with metal ringlets attached to the side walls and a hoist hanging from the ceiling.

It was a system Dr. Reed created to better move around his equine patients. An enormous operating table was centered in the middle of the room, lined with gymnastic-style floor mats surrounding it. The table, similar to a car lift at an auto-mechanic shop, moved up and down from the floor with the added ability to tilt sideways so the horse was easier to place on top of it. Once the surgery was complete, the hydraulic system moved the operating table towards the exit door, where the horse, while still under anesthesia, was slid into the recovery room. The hospital's proximity to Belmont Park saved countless horses' lives. On July 6, 1975, at Dr. Reed's personally designed equine emergency room, Ruffian became a patient of the veterinarian.

Ruffian began her racing career in the spring of 1974 at Belmont Park, where she broke her maiden race at a distance of 5 ½ furlongs. Jacinto Vasquez, the filly's jockey, would later comment that when Ruffian walked into the starting gate during her first race, she changed before his eyes - becoming warrior-like. Ruffian stunned her competitors and the crowd, finishing 15 lengths ahead of the rest of the pack while tying the track record. The next race at Belmont Park was the Fashion Stakes, reserved for fillies-only entrants. Ruffian again made short work of her competition, winning by 6 ½ lengths and breaking the track record. Ruffian spent the remainder of the year winning every race entered while tying or breaking track records in each. She finished her two-year-old season undefeated in five races, winning the Eclipse Award as the Two-Year-Old Filly of the Year. She also received the highest compliment ever imagined in the racing industry – a comparison to the greatest thoroughbred ever to race. Upon watching her, Secretariat's trainer, Lucien Larien, told people, "as God as my judge, she might be better than Secretariat."[155]

Ruffian's three-year-old season was much like the previous - but only better. The filly had grown bigger and more muscular than the average colt. She also had a personality to match her beauty and strength - the lady had charisma. Ruffian let everyone know who was the best and who looked the best. After winning each race, she could be found at the winner's circle parading around with her head held high and ears pinned forward, commanding the attention of all. Ruffian was the modern-day Black Beauty. The spring and summer of

1975 saw Ruffian win the "Filly Triple Crown," with the last of the three races at Belmont Park. Ruffian's winning time over the one mile and ½ mile race at the American Oaks was 2/5 of a second *faster* than the time posted by the winning colt at the Belmont Stakes at the same distance two weeks prior. The unprecedented success of a filly made Ruffian a media darling throughout the country. She was the definition of a perfect 10 – having won all ten races in her career – never trailing at any mark during her races.

1975 also brought a talented colt and near Triple Crown winner named Foolish Pleasure, who was also attracting the public's attention. Leroy Jolley, who nearly became the trainer of Timely Writer, had the Martins sold to Peter Brant in 1982, was the trainer for Foolish Pleasure. Foolish Pleasure's resume also included an undefeated two-year-old season, followed by a win at the Flamingo Stakes to begin his three-year-old racing season in March of 1975. The colt would win the Kentucky Derby, then finish second in the Preakness and Belmont Stakes – two places shy of immortality. Foolish Pleasure's success from 1974 through 1975 placed him in the middle of a national debate.

As gender equality was at the forefront of the country in the early 1970s, significant pressure from all corners of society was placed on the owners of Ruffian and Foolish Pleasure for a potential match in a "battle of the sexes." The public and the media were clamoring for the unprecedented dual to determine which gender was the best. Negotiations for the match race set the distance at 1 and 1/4 miles with a total purse of $400,000 - $225,000 to the winner. The match race was marketed as the featured event on the day's racing card at Belmont Park on Saturday, July 6, 1975. The constant media hype leading up to the event made the Kentucky Derby look like another day at the races. A live television audience estimated at 20 million people tuned in to see whether it would be the colt or the filly wearing the crown as the best racehorse in the country. A record-setting crowd of over 50,000 people at Belmont Park included Dr. Reed and his wife Audrey, watching from their box seats.

The race itself, number 9 of the 10-race card, was scheduled for a 6:00 p.m. post time for the Saturday night prime-time national television audience.

Jacinto Vasquez, the regular jockey for Foolish Pleasure and Ruffian shocked many by choosing the filly as his partner for the race. Ruffian and Vasquez would be the gamblers' favorite, with post-time approaching and dark storm clouds forming over the area.

The two competitors were paraded before a standing-room-only crowd, with Ruffian in her red and white silks wearing number 1. She was placed into starting gate number 2, with Foolish Pleasure wearing number 2, and loaded into gate number 3, with gate number 1 on the inside rail left empty. Once the two were settled, the racing official hit the buzzer, springing the gates open. Ruffian appeared startled coming out of the gate, leaving her gate slower. Ruffian gathered herself quickly from the bad start, surging past Foolish Pleasure, leading the colt after the first quarter of a mile. The next quarter of a mile saw both horses running smoothly and effortlessly. As the competitors neared the first half-mile marker and over the thunderous noise of one-thousand-pound animals sprinting nearly forty miles per hour, both jockeys suddenly heard a crack – as if a large branch snapped from a tree. The sound was Ruffian's right leg collapsing beneath her. Hearing the noise and feeling the misstep of the right front leg, Vasquez reacted immediately by pulling up on Ruffian's reins to slow her down. With all his strength, Vasquez was trying to stop the hard-charging filly so he could get her to the ground. Ruffian would not relent, her competitive spirit and adrenaline pushing her another 50 yards on three good legs. The track announcer could be heard yelling into the microphone, "Ruffian has broken down, Ruffian has broken down!"

The once delirious crowd from the beginning of the race was now watching events transpire in collective silence, with many gasping from the sight of Ruffian running on the stump of her right leg - the hoof hanging limp and flapping, only attached by a few tendons. Vasquez, tears running down his face, was finally able to slow Ruffian down enough that he could dismount from his saddle. As Vasquez hit the ground, he held onto the reins of Ruffian, walking with the filly as she was pacing non-stop in a circular fashion. The first to arrive at the scene were the New York Racing Association (NYRA) veterinarians. The doctors immediately noticing the sesamoid in Ruffian's right front leg had exploded. A closer observation of Ruffian revealed dirt from the track's surface was scattered within the blood and bone fragments of her injured right leg.

With the help of Vasquez, one of the doctors immediately applied an air cast to Ruffian's leg. Vasquez's shirt, typically spotted with dirt kicked up during a horse race, was now covered with Ruffian's blood. The equine ambulance arrived shortly afterward, with Ruffian's veterinarian, Dr. Alex Harthill, and Ruffian's trainer, Frank Whitely, jumping from the ambulance doors. After some time spent calming Ruffian, the men got the anxious and frightened horse into the van and back to her stall for a medical assessment. While Ruffian was being examined, winning trainer Leroy Jolley could be seen pacing back and forth at the other end of the barn. A growing and concerned crowd was collecting outside Ruffian's stall, including Barbara Janney – the owner looking with her hand to her mouth, tears streaming down her face. As Ruffian was examined, the chaos within the barn area was increasing due to the volume of media and track employees filtering into the stall's location. Ruffian was cleaned at her stall, x-rays taken by the doctors, and a new air cast was placed on the right leg for support. As Ruffian was losing fluids, she appeared to be going into shock, which expedited the decision of the doctors to bring Ruffian across the street to Dr. Reed's hospital.

Upon seeing Ruffian's fall from his seat in the stands, Dr. Reed immediately headed to his operating room across the street. He gathered his surgical team, including Dr. Alex Harthill, and waited for Ruffian to be transported to his care. As Ruffian was being transferred, Stuart Janney brought his wife home to take her away from the events. Once his wife was home, Janney returned to the hospital, holding a vigil throughout the night. As the medical team received Ruffian, everyone inside the red brick building knew Ruffian would never race again. Their job was simple – save the life of the finest filly ever to run.

Ruffian was brought into the operating room, provided the required anesthesia, and loaded onto the table for surgery. The surgery lasted hours - with Ruffian fighting off death throughout. Ruffian's heart flatlined twice - requiring surgeons to resuscitate her each time. When not managing

Ruffian's heart failures, the team of surgeons spent hours placing a puzzle of shattered bones back together.

Dr. Reed and his team emerged from the surgical room after performing a medical miracle. Ruffian's shattered leg was pieced back together – supported by screws throughout to stabilize the sesamoid bones. Dr. Reed informed the gathered crowd outside his hospital that the operation was successful, though warning them that Ruffian's condition was still critical and her prognosis guarded. Dr. Reed knew of Ruffian's temperament, telling the family and media, "I suspect she'll not be the greatest patient in the world."[156] Dr. Reed and his colleagues were some of the best surgeons in the country, if not the world, but it is in the recovery room where difficulties present themselves, and doctors lose control of their patients.

After surgery, Ruffian was moved into a specially constructed recovery room with padded walls and hay placed on the floor for bedding. Coming out of anesthesia for elite racing horses is often problematic. They do not understand what is happening or where they are. As Dr. Reed explained, "you take a cheap, inexpensive horse that doesn't have the desire and they just lay there."[157] Elite horses such as Ruffian are often victimized by their greatest asset – their will to compete. As Ruffian lay on the floor under anesthesia, with a cast affixed to her right leg, men were positioned at her legs, ready for her to awake. Upon waking, it was as if Ruffian believed she was still sprinting on the dirt of Belmont Park, heading to the finish line. Shortly after opening her eyes, Ruffian's legs began churning, with none of the men able to stop the motion of her forceful limbs. Ruffian was tossing around grown men stationed at her legs as if they were stuffed toys. As this continued, Ruffian's legs struck the padded walls as she thrashed about. The cast placed on Ruffian's right leg eventually came off, causing further injury to the leg, with her other legs suffering additional fractures. The injuries, pain, and septic shock were increasing as the minutes dragged on. Frank Whitely, the only trainer Ruffian ever knew, was one of the men present in the recovery room. Doctors conferred with Whitely, who then left to speak with Mr. Janney about the recent events and prognosis.

Stuart Janney's request to his trainer was practical, "please don't let her suffer anymore."[158] Some of the best equine doctors in the world could not save Ruffian from herself. With permission from her owner, relayed by Whitely, a lethal injection of anesthesia was then administered to her neck of Ruffian. Five seconds went by, and Ruffian was gone. A grim Dr. Harthill, who would go on to save the life of the 1982 Kentucky Derby favorite Timely Writer from colic, emerged from Dr. Reed's hospital into the dark of night. As Ruffian's veterinarian, Dr. Harthill made the tragic announcement of her death at 2:00 a.m. The following days, weeks, and months left the horse racing industry and country in a collective state of depression over the tragic event. It is believed by many that the tragic race and death of Ruffian in July of 1975 forever left a dark cloud over a generation of horse racing fans and its participants. As later explained by Dr. Reed, the sobering reality of the sport of horse racing is that the body and muscles of its participants are supported by "fragile, delicate bones, bones nature intended to support nothing bigger than a pony."[159]

With Ruffian's passing, the immediate question was how to honor the grand dame of thoroughbred racing. Belmont Park opened its gates in 1905, and in the 70 years of the park's existence, no horse had ever been buried on its grounds. The NYRA requested that Ruffian be the first. Belmont was where she started and finished. She may have been foaled in Kentucky, but she belonged to Belmont Park and the people. Trainer Frank Whitely and the Janneys agreed. A gravestone with bushes organized in a horseshoe fashion was designed for the final resting spot of Ruffian. She was laid to rest, along with her red and white blankets, with a white shroud placed around her, and lowered into the grass infield of the track – her body facing towards the finish line.

As Dr. Reed stood at the rail of the track in October of 1982, watching over the early morning workouts of Timely Writer in preparation for the 113th running of the Jerome Handicap, the grave marking of Ruffian was across the way in the grass infield. Under the careful watch of Dr. Reed, Timely Writer was training in the fall weather at Belmont Park as if it were the spring racing season in Florida from earlier in the year. Timely Writer's times in the workouts were so impressive that bettors were prepared to make him the favorite for the race. Dr. Reed spent the week watching over the colt he became so fond of during the year while waiting for his friends and business partners from Boston to arrive in town.

A successful run at the three Belmont races scheduled for Timely Writer would finish off a year of racing like none other. Any success would continue a ground swell of support from the public and racing industry, allowing the wrong from the previous year to be righted and guaranteeing the colt an Eclipse Award from the same voters led down the wrong path the prior year.

As Dr. Reed tended to Timely Writer in his stall mid-week, he noticed the colt still suffered from a minor cough, which followed him after running in Saratoga. As a result, Dr. Reed, a former president of the Equine Practitioners of America and Timely Writer's veterinarian administered sulfadimethoxine, an antibacterial medication for respiratory discomfort.

Timely Writer's entry into the featured race of the day at Belmont Park, the one-mile Jerome Handicap on Labor Day, September 6th, saw over 31,000 people go through the turnstiles at Belmont Park on the Monday holiday to witness the second phase of Timely Writer's dramatic comeback story. The betting public made Timely Writer the heavy favorite for the race, with CBS television bringing it to a national audience. As Frannie, Mary, Peter, Mr. and Mrs. Dr. Reed, along with family and friends, were having lunch at the dining room during the early races, officials began paging Dominic. Knowing Dominic was resting in his hotel room, Frannie quickly got up from the table and headed to the stall of Timely Writer, with Dr. Reed heading to the office of the racing officials. Frannie encountered anger and bitterness at the barn as the groom and assistant trainer for Timely Writer let Frannie know the racing steward had telephoned, stating Timely Writer was ordered scratched from the Jerome Handicap. A stunned Frannie stood motionless, the shock of it all not permitting him to process what was said.

Meanwhile, at the office of the racing stewards, Dr. Reed found himself in a full-fledged argument upon arriving as the officials informed the veterinarian that Timely Writer was ordered scratched from the Jerome due to a positive blood test for an impermissible drug screen. Earlier in the year, the NYRA updated its drug policy to get better control of what trainers were administering to horses before races. In pre-racing blood testing, every entry from each race had blood drawn and tested at an on-site laboratory. When told of the order by the stewards, Dr. Reed began exchanging angry words with Jack Curran – a NYRA investigator. Further infuriating Dr. Reed was the stewards ordered the scratch of the colt without knowing which drug produced the positive result in the blood sample, nor did the NYRA provide an opportunity for Dr. Reed to be heard or appeal the disqualification. As Dr. Reed continued to argue, an announcement was made over the loudspeakers that Timely Writer had been scratched from the Jerome. Patrons throughout the track were stunned when the scratch was announced over the intercom system. Loud boos and moans permeated throughout the track as the patrons let the racing officials know their level of discontent.

Dr. Reed, not one to lose his temper, was livid. With a copy of the New York State Racing and Wagering Board Rules in hand, the doctor was pointing to the relevant section of the rules, which indicated that the only drug he administered to Timely Writer was permissible up to 48 hours before the race – and his colt was given it more than 72 hours ahead of time. Reed, one of the most respected equine practitioners in the country and one with impeccable credentials was looking to swear on a stack of Bibles, take a lie detector test, or do anything else requested to prove the stewards wrong. Reed threatened to file a lawsuit against the NYRA, blasting the stewards, "This is an outrage, we have been stabbed in the back by the association, and if there was ever a miscarriage of justice, this is it."[160] Dr. Reed explained that regardless of any "positive" blood test in pre-race screening, "horses have different metabolisms, and some hold the medications in their systems longer than others. It is a permissive medication anyway."[161] As one veteran trainer offered, "if Dr. Reed doesn't know how to medicate a horse properly and within the rules, then nobody knows. The stewards really blew this one and blew it big."[162]

After continued arguments with the stewards became pointless, the Martins and the Reeds ultimately returned to the dining room, choosing to remain at Belmont Park for the day of races. The owners looked on as Fit to Fight with 25-year-old Jerry Bailey in the mount recorded a 6-length victory in the Jerome Handicap. Frannie, sharing his thoughts of the Jerome afterward, opined, "The way the race was run, Timely would have buried them."[163] A local horse racing journalist agreed with Frannie's assessment, commenting, "The Jerome took on the quality of a $169,800 allowance race for second-string 3-year-olds." [164] Always one to find humor during times of despair, though, Frannie told one journalist on his way out of the racetrack, "We are driving back to Boston tonight, but we're not going over any bridges."[165] He also advised Mary as they approached the parking lot, "Maybe we better start looking for low-flying planes."[166]

The controversy at the Jerome would linger in the newspapers for the remainder of the week, with Dominic spending his days re-adjusting his plans to get his colt ready for the Marlboro Cup. Frustrated after the scratch, Dominic acknowledged, "this race would have set him up perfectly for the Marlboro."[167] When questioned how Timely Writer would prepare for the Marlboro Cup, Dominic responded, "I'll just have to drill him harder."[168]

With less than two weeks until the running of the Marlboro Cup, Dominic worked around Jeffrey Fell's schedule to get him atop Timely Writer. On September 11, 1982, in between the 2nd and 3rd races, Fell and Writer took to the track for a time-recorded 1 mile. Stablemate Timely Hitter was alongside Timely Writer, pushing the champion over the course of the one mile. Timely Writer covered the 1 mile in 1:37 4/5, with Fell telling the media afterward, "[t]his was the fastest he's gone in his comeback."[169] Five days later, and two days before the Marlboro Cup, Dominic sent Timely Writer out with an exercise rider for a gallop covering 2 ½ miles. If Dominic believed his strategy was what Timely Writer needed going into the Marlboro Cup, the results of the race proved him terribly wrong.

Timely Writer's entry into the featured race of the day at Belmont Park, the 1 ¼ mile Marlboro Cup, on September 18, 1982, required him to carry a weight of 121 pounds. The invitation-only $400,00 purse for three-year-olds and upwards provided $240,000 to the winner. As the race contained a mix of three-year-olds with older horses, the race required a handicapping system for the field of entries. The primary goal of this type of race is to create a competitive race by leveling the playing field between the horses regardless of age or gender. The science behind the approach is based upon several factors, though primarily race record and age of the horses – with three-year-olds getting a weight allowance. After weighing in each jockey and their racing equipment, racing officials add extra led weights into the pockets of the saddle of certain horses before the race begins. The additional weight in the saddle can impact the speed and stamina of the better horses throughout the race. The Marlboro Cup had a range of weight assignments, which included the weight of jockeys and equipment, ranging from Lemhi Gold at 115 pounds, Winter Tale at 116 pounds, Timely Writer at 121 pounds, and 5-year-old Perrault, at 128 pounds, who was a multiple grade 1 stakes winner on dirt and turf, including the Budweiser Million earlier in the year, now known as the Arlington Million.

The Marlboro Cup brought 27,000 fans to the venue, many of them converted Timely Writer fans. The patrons made Timely Writer the 2-1 pre-race favorite over his competitors, including Silver Buck, who Cornelius Vanderbilt Whitney owned. In a race named after a member of the owner's family from years past, Silver Buck was coming off a first-place finish at the prestigious Whitney Handicap at Saratoga Race Track. Also amongst the racing entries for the Marlboro Cup were future Hall of Fame jockeys Bill Shoemaker on Muttering, Jerry Bailey on Winter's Tale, Jacinto Vasquez on Lemhi Gold, and Laffit Pincay on Perrault – a grade 1 stakes winner on both the dirt and grass tracks in 1982. The $400,000.00 purse, with just under one-quarter of a million dollars to the winner, and nationally broadcast on CBS, brought in the best jockeys nationwide as owners chased glory and money. The start of the race predictably began with Timely Writer starting slowly, and with the Martins watching on in disbelief from the owner's box, the colt finished slowly. Timely Writer finished 7th in an eight-horse field, losing by 25 lengths to winner Lemhi Gold – with the 8th-place horse pulling up from injury. The champion colt was never in the hunt, leaving jockey

Jeffrey Fell stunned, "he had no life at all in him. He just didn't run when I asked him. He never grabbed the bit."[170] Fell added, "midway down the backside I know we weren't going to get anything." "I'm disillusioned, that's the first time he's ever failed to try hard for me. He just wasn't himself; he had no life in him at all."[171] In an interview after the race, Dominic commented that Timely Writer "never picked up his feet."[172]

The first two races mapped out for Timely Writer at Belmont Park ended in unexpected disappointment with a forced scratch by the stewards at the Jerome and a 7th place finish at the Marlboro – coupled with a head-scratching training strategy crafted by the colt's trainer in between the two races. What started as perhaps the most remarkable comeback in horse racing history had gone awry. Hope was not entirely lost, though, as Timely Writer had proven earlier in the year with a poor performance in his first outing of 1982, that he was more than capable of bouncing back with a dominating win. After the awful performance in the Marlboro, Dominic went looking for a race where the colt could rebound once again.

Rather than rest Timely Writer before the final race of his career, Dominic entered Timely Writer in the $35,000.00 Avatar Handicap on Saturday, October 2, 1982 – two weeks removed from the Marlboro Cup. The race, at a distance of 1 and 5/8 miles, was chosen to prepare the colt for the Jockey Gold Cup at 1 ½ miles. Timely Writer went off at 3-5 odds for the Avatar and, as predicted by the oddsmakers, won without much competition, finishing ahead of his nearest competitor by 7 ½ lengths. The challenge for Timely Writer going forward was that he would need to rebound for the Jockey Gold Cup in one week.

With Timely Writer's winning performance at the Avatar Handicap, balance in the three-year-old division appeared to be restored. The Jockey Gold Cup, a Grade 1 stakes race for three-year-olds and up, saw the purse increase to a staggering $565,000.00 - the winner receiving $340,000.00 and a chance at securing the three-year-old horse of the year honors. The race scheduled for October 9, 1982, marked one year to the day of Timely Writer's triumph at the Champagne. Cool Hand Luke Dufresne, the regular exercise rider for Timely Writer since the comeback began, worked the colt the Thursday before the Jockey Gold Cup. After the workout, similar to his spot-on glowing reviews of Timely Writer in Saratoga, Luke was telling people it was the best he had ever seen the colt run. "If today were racing day, nothing would beat him, it's the best he's ever been. I think he will win it, and I don't talk like that."[173]

Back in the stall of the barn, Timely Writer was at it again, though, showing his prickly personality to others. The newest member of the Timely Writer team, assistant groom Michael Palmer, had some of the more tedious duties grooming Timely Writer – such as picking the dirt out of the colt's hooves after a workout. After the workout, Palmer brought Timely Writer into his stall, looping a rope tie from his halter to a metal beam running along the back of the wall. Palmer began his work by taking the left foreleg of Timely Writer in his hands. Timely Writer wasn't in the mood for his feet to be worked on and communicate that to Palmer. As Timely Writer balanced himself on his right foreleg and hind leg, the colt swung his left hindleg forward towards Palmer's chest area, just missing the assistant groom. While Timely Writer's left hind leg cleared the area of Palmer's chest without striking him and still balanced on only two legs while tied to the back wall, the colt used his teeth to bite at Palmer's left shoulder area – with another miss. Palmer regained himself, acted like nothing happened, and finished his work with a moment in time cemented in his memory for a lifetime.

The 1 ½ mile race was ideally suited for Timely Writer, and the New York crowd of 27,311 again made the Boston horse their pre-race favorite. Due to the length of the race, Dominic advised jockey Jeffrey Fell to keep Timely Writer in 3rd or 4th place heading into the last turn before making his patented move. Everyone, including the New York bettors, expected to give Timely Writer a winning send-off into retirement with a lengthy career in the breeding shed to follow. Family and friends of the Martins and the Reeds gathered for lunch in the dining room before making their way down to the owner's seats for the Jockey Gold Cup. Off to the side and away from the male-dominated group, Audrey Reed and Mary Martin were deep in conversation, sharing private thoughts.

The Jockey Club Gold Cup racing entries totaled 10, including a horse entered by Boston's nemesis - trainer Johnny Campo. The rotund trainer was last seen by the Martins at Suffolk Downs with his then 3-year-old colt Johnny Dance on July 4, 1981, the pair winning the John Macomber Memorial Handicap raced on the grass turf. Campo had switched his turf runner to the dirt track as he chased the winner's purse for the Jockey Gold Cup. A young trainer named D. Wayne Lukas entered Island Whirl, the winner of the prestigious Woodward Stakes raced just before the Kentucky Derby, with Laffet Pincay as the jockey. With jockey Jerry Bailey switching back to the mount of Winter's Tale, Chris McCarron was flown in from California to ride Lemhi Gold. Other notable jockeys for the race were Jacinto Vasquez on Christmas Party and Angel Cordero on Silver Supreme.

The premier race of the year for three-year-olds and up was the marquee event for the Saturday afternoon racing card, with a national television audience watching the live event. Other than storm clouds gathering at post-time, the early part of the race went as many predicted, with Lemhi Gold and Irish Whirl in the lead and Timely Writer laying 3rd with the final turn approaching. As the Martins anxiously watched Timely Writer's last race from their owner's box, overflowing with family and friends, their colt was following in the shadows of the two leaders at about the one-mile mark. Jeffrey Fell had Timely Writer in his normal stalking mode and believed the two leaders were tiring. Fell, who had not yet asked Timely Writer to run, began moving to the front, letting the colt know it was time to take the lead.

Suddenly, in the blink of an eye, with Fell urging Timely Writer towards the lead, chaos exploded on the last turn. As Fell looked for the lead with the stretch run approaching, Timely Writer collapsed face-first into the dirt. Due to the speed at which Timely Writer was traveling, Fell was propelled over the head of Timely Writer. Other horses were coming up from behind a defenseless Fell as he tumbled over himself in the track's dirt. Fell was barely visible to his approaching competitors and dangerously exposed to injury. With Fell still tumbling and Timely Writer attempting to upright himself from the dirt floor of the track, a domino effect began with other horses and jockeys. Lesser-known horses, such as Sing Sing, quickly maneuvered past

Timely Writer by hurdling over him - just missing striking Jeffrey Fell in the process. As Sing Sing avoided both Timely Writer and Jeffrey Fell, he threw his jockey from his mount. Sing Sing was able to keep his footing and stay upright, thereafter sprinting without a jockey towards the grandstand and the finish line.

With Sing Sing hurdling over Timely Writer on one side, Johnny Dance fell over Timely Writer on the other side near the inner rail of the track. Upon hitting the ground, Johnny Dance struck the wooden vertical fencing of the track's inside rail – immediately fracturing his left radius above the knee. Khantango, bringing up the back of the pack, quickly swerved to the right side of Timely Writer as Sing Song had done. Due to the sudden change of direction, Khantango fell to the ground, immediately gathering himself and rising to his feet. While swerving, falling, and rising quickly, Khantango's jockey was also thrown from the saddle. As a live television audience watched, four jockeys were on the track's dirt, two horses lay injured nearby, and another two were riderless sprinting towards the finish line.

As the chaos continued, and in the generation before large screen television monitors were strategically placed in the infield of horse tracks, fans, owners, and trainers couldn't be sure which horses were still on the ground and which horses were upright. The scene was shocking. The crowd was stunned. Television cameras were uncertain where to turn their lenses as Lemhi Gold, Silver Supreme, and Christmas Party were racing towards the finish line, fighting for the coveted winner's purse – each stride leaving their injured competitors further behind. Removed from the view of the cameras, race track groundskeepers were sprinting onto the track, trying to corral the riderless Sing Sing and Khatango in the home stretch.

All available ambulances were dispatched to the scene, with medical personnel ready to tend to the needs of the jockeys and horses. As emergency personnel and vehicles were traveling to the scene, the now 27-year-old jockey from Dorchester crossed the finish line in first place aboard Lemhi Gold. The win for Chris McCarron was bittersweet from the moment he crossed the finish line. In post-race television highlights, the broadcast ignored the winner's stretch run, instead choosing to replay the tragedy at the far turn.

James Belden, the chief veterinarian for NYRA, arrived at the scene in the first ambulance with his assistants. Shortly after Dr. Belden's arrival, additional vehicles quickly brought large green privacy screens to the scene. Screens were set up to provide privacy to the participants while shielding the public and television cameras from the gruesome scene. The screens, though, left the crowd and owners further uncertain about the severity of the incident.

Upon Timely Writer falling, Dr. Reed and Audrey left the owner's box, heading towards an area of the track where the doctor could get to a motor vehicle ride out to the scene. Peter, knowing he would not be able to get transported to the scene of the accident, followed on the heels of the Reeds, where he would wait at the trackside for their return from the scene to get first-hand answers to the questions darting through his mind. At the same time, Frannie, Mary, and their two teenage daughters, Maryellen and Janice, left the owner's box for the stall of Timely Writer.

Dr. Reed's car ride, which included Audrey as a passenger, Dominic Imprescia, Jr. as the assistant trainer, and a journalist by the name of Kay Coyte, brought them to the scene shortly after track veterinarian Dr. Belden. Upon exiting, Audrey chose to remain in the vehicle, and Dr. Reed described what he observed upon arriving as "a sickening scene."[174] He first noticed Johnny Dancer lying on the dirt track in between the broken fencing of the rail – already dead. Dr. Belden had euthanized the horse upon arriving and viewing the injuries. Dr. Reed continued to look around, noticing all the jockeys upright, with none suffering from significant injuries, though all questioning what just happened.

Dr. Reed's attention was directed past the final turn where Timely Writer lay on the ground. A trail of blood could be seen mixed into the dirt, lying between the fallen Johnny Dance and Timely Writer. Due to his repeated attempts to continue racing, the injured colt was some distance from Johnny Dance. Dr. Belden could be seen kneeling next to Timely Writer, looking over the colt's injuries. Timely Writer's left leg revealed the radius of his foreleg snapped in half below the kneecap. A fracture, which left indecipherable pieces of his leg in the dirt of the track, was fatal for the colt. As Dr. Belden finished reviewing Timely Writer's condition, the veterinarian knew the champion could not be saved from his injuries.

Dr. Reed began walking away from the area where Johnny Dance lay lifeless towards Dr. Belden and the fallen Timely Writer. As Dr. Reed started the walk, Dr. Belden was taking a long needle from his veterinarian bag nearby, preparing the needle with a lethal injection, and inserting it into the neck area of Timely Writer as he lay on the dirt of the track. Unlike Ruffian's tragedy, Timely Writer would not suffer, nor would surgeons attempt to save his life. As with Ruffian's ending, five seconds passed, and Timely Writer was gone. The colt's last breath was taken as Dr. Reed walked towards one of his favorite champions with the grave of Ruffian in sight a short distance away - a moment hidden from the public by the privacy screens.

Dr. Belden continued with his duties by the side of Timely Writer while noticing Dr. Reed was approaching from the final turn. Dr. Belden stopped Dr. Reed in his footsteps on the dirt track, yelling that Timely Writer was gone. The information forced Dr. Reed to close his eyes after what he had just heard, his shoulders slumping downward for some time before gathering himself to finish the remainder of the walk. Upon arriving at the side of Timely Writer, Dr. Reed immediately noticed the left leg of Timely Writer, describing it as "a hunk of broken ice."[175] From the knee down, Timely Writer's leg looked as if a giant icicle had fallen from the roof of a building onto the cement below. Numerous indecipherable pieces of the broken leg were scattered about the dirt track. The doctor had seen enough, walking back to Audrey in the transport vehicle where she had remained upon arriving at the scene.

Running onto the scene was Timely Writer's assistant groom, Michael Palmer. Palmer had been watching the race by the winner's circle along the fence, eyeing the fall at the far turn about ¼ of a mile away. Like everyone else, Palmer wondered whether Timely Writer could be saved as he jumped the fence along the track, sprinting toward the tragedy. Like Drs. Belden and Reed, Palmer quickly concluded nothing could be done as he looked at the leg of Timely Writer. The twenty-year-old from just outside of Boston, with less than four months with the Timely Writer crew, was tasked with taking some of the equipment from the lifeless body of Timely Writer before he was loaded into the equine van and removed from the horse track.

Dominic Sr., in his capacity as the colt's trainer, was also rushed to the scene, arriving sometime after Dr. Reed. Looking around at the carnage, viewing blood in the dirt near Johnie Dance's lifeless body, with Timely Writer lying lifeless some distance away, Dominic could not bring himself to remain at the scene. The trainer began walking towards the barn and the empty stall of Timely Writer. Upon his arrival at the stall, Dominic put his back up to the wall, forever staring down at the empty white feed bucket with prominent black markings of "TW" scrawled on it.

Dominic would have to deliver the news to his wife, Ethel, Frannie, Mary, and their children. Frannie had been finishing the walk to Timely Writer's stall while listening to words of hope from Ethel, Mary, and his two daughters. Frannie's years of experience, though, taught him differently. Along the walk, Frannie noticed the sizeable green privacy screens going up at the far turn. The entire track corner was shut down, with ambulances behind the green screens. Upon seeing the green screens, "for a moment, [Frannie] thought the whole world had come to an end."[176] He had been in the business for over thirty years, and Frannie knew the answer to the question he, too, did not want to ask. Mary walked with her family, also staring out at the green screens while heading to the barn, unable to stop thinking about her dream from Tuesday night.

Meanwhile, Dr. Reed returned with Audrey to where Peter awaited their arrival. Along the motor vehicle ride back, Dr. Reed was sharing the details of the tragic news with Audrey - the couple both tearing up in grief. Upon parking the motor vehicle, Dr. Reed, with Peter in his eyesight some distance away, asked Audrey to speak with Peter as the doctor would speak with the media to provide an update on the jockeys and horses. As Audrey parted ways with her husband, she walked slowly towards Peter, her head looking down at the track's dirt. While Audrey made her way to Peter, journalist and photographer Kay Coyte from *The Horsemen's Journal*, who had walked back from the carnage at the corner of the final turn, was nearby writing notes from her interviews at the winner's circle. Six years after graduating from the University of Kentucky as a journalism major and a former journalist for *The Saratogian*, Kay worked the day's events for the monthly magazine. In the chaos surrounding the race and its finish, Kay was wrapping up her duties at the unusually somber winner's circle.

Upon noticing Audrey walking towards Peter, Kay reached for the camera hanging from her neck. Kay's instincts and experience taught her that a moment in time, however tragic it might be, was imminent in the still-developing saga. With the shutter of her camera clicking, Kay captured Peter Martin looking for signs of hope where none could be found. Audrey, her voice unable to say the tragic words, eyes unable to look into those of Peter's eyes, answered Peter's questions without speaking - the two embracing with Peter sobbing in her arms.

Peter Martin looks for hope while Audrey Reed searches for words.

As Audrey consoled Peter at one end of the track, Frannie, with his family just a few steps behind him, arrived at Timely Writer's stall to see Dominic leaning up against the side wall, staring downward. Snapping Dominic from his catatonic stare was Frannie calling the trainer's name. Upon noticing Frannie's presence, Dominic raised his head toward Frannie, telling the owner "he's gone Francis."[177] With those three words, Frannie could hear his wife and daughters crying – the husband and father helplessly unable to soften their grief.

Leroy Jolley, who befriended Peter and Frannie over the past two years and was the long-time trainer of Foolish Pleasure, made his way over to the barn to check on the status of the Martin family and Timely Writer. Jolley, who paced the same barn area at Belmont while doctors examined Ruffian, approached Frannie looking for hope. Frannie, like Dominic, was short with his words, telling his friend, "he's gone, Leroy."[178] Jolley broke down in tears upon hearing the news. Friends and colleagues continued gathering at the barn as each minute passed. The tragic news of Timely Writer's fall was whispered from one person to another. People were stunned. Even grown, experienced men in the horse racing business, like Leroy Jolley, could be seen sobbing in the barn area.

President Ogden Phipps of the NYRA drove to the barn to speak with the Martin family, offering his condolences and letting them know privately that Timely Writer would be honored in death by being laid to rest in the grass infield at Belmont Park. Phipps' statement to the media that night reflected the day's emotion, "my heart goes out to these fine people, I realize the trauma they are going through."[179]

In the event's immediate aftermath, many questioned how an elite racehorse such as Timely Writer could have fallen. Was the fall of Timely Writer, as Dr. Reed described in the immediate aftermath of the Ruffian tragedy, due to the inherently delicate frame of a thoroughbred? Was it simply a wrong step by Timely Writer? Was the fall a result of the poor condition of the Belmont Park surface?

An improperly raked or skimmed race track can leave dips or holes along the dirt surface, resulting in deadly conditions– especially in the turns where horses are angling their bodies and legs around the track's corners. Jockeys and trainers were quick to say the fault of the fall was the poor grooming at Belmont Park. Jockey Jean Cruguet attacked the condition of the infield surface, stating, "[t]he track is dead. It's in bad condition. It's a joke." Other trainers spoke off the record, saying the track was "deep and dull, not in the best condition."[180] Trainer Leroy Jolley went on the record, indicating, "The track is not being well cared for."[181]

In the early morning hours of Sunday, October 10th, Ogden Phipps let the public know the extent of the impact the Martins and Timely Writer had upon the racing industry and the country with his announcement that Timely Writer would be buried in the grass infield at Belmont Park. The colt would be laid to rest near the great Ruffian. Ironically, just six months before Phipps's announcement, Peter Martin observed how the public had adopted Timely Writer as the "people's champion." Fans fell in love with the story about a colt and his owners, partly because the Bostonians were not the same pedigree as the Phipps family, nor were they part of the establishment crowd. Now, during the hours and days of the family's grief, it was the establishment crowd who were wrapping their arms around the Martins.

As with everything in the tale of Timely Writer and the Martins, a somber ride home to Boston turned eventful the Sunday afternoon following the race. On Sunday, October 11th, the Martins made the four-hour drive home north, crossing through Hartford, Connecticut, and eventually making their way east towards Boston on the Massachusetts Turnpike (Mass Pike). As John and his friends made their way home with his friends from Belmont sometime after Frannie left, they were approaching the Fenway Park area on the Mass Pike when a car similar to his father's was pulled off to the side of the highway. A shorter, stout man was standing alongside the car. As John's vehicle approached the broken-down car, he and his friends noticed his father, the barrel-chested man, leaning against the car with his arms folded, with his mother and two sisters sitting inside the vehicle. John's vehicle parked behind Frannie to find out what happened. As they exited their car, John saw Frannie shaking his head in bewilderment. Laughing aloud as John came closer, Frannie shouted to the group, "the bridges in New York didn't get us, the low-flying planes didn't get us, but the dam roads in Massachusetts got us."

After the Martins made their way home, journalists were authoring poignant tributes in memory of Timely Writer. One journalist reflected on the prior two years, acknowledging how the story about a colt and his owners had captivated a country. "Maybe because the script read like a fairy-tale, or because of the hardships incurred along the way, everyone seemed to ride with Timely Writer."[182] With Timely Writer's burial imminent, the cold reality was "the magic, the bad luck, the fairy-tale – it all ended in one cruel twist of fate."[183] On the Tuesday following Timely Writer's fall, during the dark of night and without fanfare, Belmont Park workers, with the lights of the infield illuminating the area, lowered Timely Writer into his grave by the flagpole in the grass infield – he, too facing the finish line. Timely Writer and Ruffian forever immortalized together in death.

In the days after the tragedy, the Martins home was deluged with telephone calls and condolence cards. The phone calls and well-wishers were endless at Kyes Supply, which the brothers and their aunt sold just months prior for some well-earned rest and retirement. The new owners of Kyes Supply telephoned Peter and Frannie, offering their sympathies and letting them know the business was receiving hundreds of phone calls per day from clients and fans expressing the same. There were so many telephone calls for the brothers on the outdated telephone system that the new owners had to set up their own switchboard with the telephone company to handle the incoming calls.

In the aftermath of the Jockey Club Gold Cup, a startled Mary Martin revealed to a journalist a dream she had five days before the race - one confirmed by Audrey Reed and reported in *The New York Times*. As Mary was having her private luncheon with Audrey Reed in the dining room at Belmont Park some six hours before the running of the Jockey Gold Cup, she found comfort in conversation with her trusted friend. As the two ladies shared a table removed from their husbands, family, and friends, Mary spoke of a vision that came to her during her sleep on Tuesday night - and one she dared not share with Frannie before Timely Writer's final race. Mary explained to Audrey how she awoke Tuesday night from a fear that had overcome her body during the middle of the night. A vision so strong that it left her scared and feverish for nearly ten minutes. As she recounted to Audrey, Mary was sitting in the stands alone watching Timely Writer's last race when their colt suddenly broke down in front of her on the track. Audrey listened to the story of Mary's nightmarish vision over lunch, making light of the dream while trying to settle her friend's emotions. As fate would have it, six hours later, Audrey was the conduit to a grief-stricken Peter Martin, communicating the nightmarish conclusion to the life of Timely Writer.

Chapter 12

Legends & Legacies: News is the first line of history - legends take longer

Despite the sad ending to the 1982 racing season, Eclipse Award voters attended to their annual responsibilities - with the voters recognizing the impact Timely Writer and the Martins had on the racing community. Tom Whelan of the *Journal News* in White Plains, New York, let his readers know who he cast his Eclipse Award vote for in the category of Outstanding Owners, proudly proclaiming that it went to "Francis and Peter Martin, the brothers from Boston who burst upon the scene of the major tracks with their ill-fated Timely Writer."[184] Though the owners would not win the award, and Timely Writer would finish in 3rd place for the 1982 Horse of The Year honors, the colt's impact would forever live on in the 1982 Eclipse Award category for Photography.

As the crowd and employees exited the gates of Belmont Park on October 9th, journalist and photographer Kay Coyte made her way to LaGuardia Airport for her flight home. After a long and action-packed work day, Kay knew there would be time in the week ahead to gather photographs of the day from her reel of film, as well as reviewing her handwritten notes, in preparation for her monthly story in the November edition of *The Horsemen's Journal*. The long racing day was nearly complete for Kay with her flight's arrival at Baltimore Airport. Upon making her way to the long-term parking lot to retrieve her car, Kay sat in the driver's seat, pausing for a moment with car keys still in her hand, her mind reflecting on the day's events. Events from the day at the races not previously reflected upon were now flooding into Kay's thoughts. Thoughts racing into her memory of the walk to the horse barns after photographing Peter and Audrey.

As she sat in the driver's seat, Kay could see and hear the sights and sounds of grown men, women, and teenagers sobbing from the tragedy on the track. After viewing and hearing the audible emotions engulfing the horse barns, Kay could see herself walking away from the grief, stopping a short distance away at a quiet, fenced-off area by the racetrack. For some unknown reason, the day's events piqued her curiosity about what lay behind the fencing. Taking the time to approach and squint between the vertical privacy strappings of the metal fencing, Kay caught a glimpse of two lifeless horses sprawled out across the dirt without a blanket or burial cloth covering their bodies. The bodies of Johnny Dance and Timely Writer were placed in an area hidden from public viewing – a memory forever embedded in her mind. As Kay stood paralyzed for a moment in time, she could not comprehend the lack of respect shown towards two thoroughbreds who lost their lives for the sport.

Emotions from the day began taking over Kay's body as she sat in the car, her tear-filled eyes resting in the cup of her hands – her palms wet from the falling tears. As the memories of the day continued to rush through her mind, Kay began sobbing – her breathing difficult to control. Some minutes would pass before Kay would gather herself, sitting upright while questioning how all of this happened, why it happened, and what a cruel twist of fate to the ending of what was a fairy tale story. Kay's travel from the airport to her home ended without remembering the route traveled. Like Kay, a great many people went to bed that night crying for a horse they had never met and a family they did not know while trying to reconcile the tragic event throughout the following day.

The work week ahead brought light to the photographers from Kay's film reel. As Kay and her editors from *The Horsemen's Journal* stood reviewing the photographs at their offices in Rockville, Maryland, the raw emotions from the day appeared. Scenes of the elegant Audrey Reed conveying the horrific ending of Mary Martin's nightmare to an inconsolable Peter Martin. Peter's love for Timely Writer is evident through the outpouring of his emotions in Kay's photographs. Believing the photographs were unlike any other captured at a horse track, the magazine nominated Kay's work for the 1982

Eclipse Award for Excellence in Photography. The pictures accompanying Kay's article "*Tragedy on the Turn*" in the magazine's November issue. In late December of 1982, with the announcement of their annual awards, the voters of the Eclipse Awards agreed with the editors from the Horsemen's Journal - with Kay accepting the Eclipse Award with her proud parents and husband joining her at the banquet in San Francisco the following February. During the month Kay was named the Eclipse Award winner, The New England Turf Writers Association expressed their appreciation for the accomplishments of the Martin brothers at their 42nd Annual Awards dinner for Outstanding Contributions to New England Racing,

The spring season in New York brought the opening of the racing season at Belmont Park on May 1, 1983. Marking the grave site of Timely Writer was one of the first tasks for racing officials. Before the day's first race, Belmont track announcer Marshall Cassidy called the crowd's attention to the grass infield, where officials unveiled the gravestone honoring Timely Writer, followed by a respectful moment of silence. Four weeks later, Frannie and Peter made an emotional pilgrimage to Belmont Park for a more formal ceremony. Sentiments surrounding the Memorial Day ceremony of Monday, May 30th, were shared by *New York Times* journalist Stephen Crist as he expressed his thoughts in the morning newspaper. Timely Writer "never had the chance to prove he was worthy of joining Ruffian as one of only two horses to be honored by burial at Belmont. But the Belmont crowd always bet him and cheered him as if he were and was willing to accept as faith what circumstances prevented from being realized. The memorial to him is as decent a gesture as has ever been done by a racetrack."[185]

The big event for the racing card on Memorial Day was the $200,000 purse of the Metropolitan Handicap – and the race when the great Timely Writer and his owners would be honored. Before the parade of horses in front of the grandstand for the Metropolitan Handicap, track announcer Myles Cassidy took to his microphone, directing the crowd's attention to the grass infield area just inside the homestretch near the finish line. The announcer requested a moment of silence from the patrons and employees for the memorial service in honor of Timely Writer. As the quiet crowd stood looking past the finish line, Peter could be seen holding one side of the floral wreath arrangement, Frannie holding the other side, and the two brothers, with tears in their eyes, slowly walking across the infield grass toward their destination. Upon arriving at the gravestone of Timely Writer, the two brothers released their hold on the wreath, laying it on the grass before the stone while quietly saying prayers learned at St. Mark's in Dorchester.

After saying a final goodbye, the brothers left the infield to the sound of respectful clapping. The history of Thoroughbred racing and the irony of life's events was not lost on the brothers as they walked away. A colt owned by meat distributors from Boston, who never won a Triple Crown race nor an Eclipse Award, was bestowed with the greatest honor of all in death. As Timely Writer was quietly laid to rest during the dark of night six months earlier, the honor was historic. The NYRA had only once before granted permission for a burial in the grass infield at Belmont Park. Though Timely Writer could not match the racing record of the undefeated Ruffian, his career and fairy-tale story matched the passion and respect shown by a country to the greatest filly the country has ever known. Timely Writer's next to last chapter ended with the colt joining Ruffian as the only Thoroughbred laid to rest in the infield on the sacred grounds of Belmont Park – the colt's life and story forever immortalized.

Similar to individuals who pass away too young, the memories of Timely Writer are frozen in time while he is in the prime of his life. The elegant and stunning three-year-old surging past his competition with a combination of grace and power through the last turn of the racetrack. The vision of Timely Writer and his jockey wearing their orange and black silk markings pulling away from their competitors down the home stretch, the colt showing off for the crowd as he continues past the finish line - seemingly able to run forever. Timely Writer's running style and humble beginnings brought crowds to their feet as they waited anxiously for his patented move going into that last turn. He and his owners living a real-life fairy tale story in front of an entire country. All along the way, the colt and his crew challenging the racing establishment while bringing a country along for the ride.

It was easy to root for Timely Writer's owners as the gracious and fun-loving "little guys" from Boston. The Martins were also easy to empathize with. Their road to fame and fortune was filled with speedbumps, detours, and roadblocks right through that final fateful October day. The brothers taught people how to handle life's moments with dignity and grace throughout the good and bad times. Though the brothers never saw their ultimate dream of winning the Kentucky Derby come true, they experienced a life only dreamed about as young men.

Frannie and Peter's perception as blue-collar workers, who were good-natured and likable, was not a façade created for the media. The good guys from Dorchester were raised to show respect, kindness, and generosity to others – traits built and cemented into their foundation through their family and the neighborhoods of Boston. Principles that guided them before, during, and after their story with Timely Writer skyrocketed across the country. After Timely Writer's passing, with the cameras and media moving on to other stories, a young girl from Hingham, Massachusetts, penned her second letter in less than one year to Fran and Mary, sending condolences upon the passing of Timely Writer. Mary and Frannie exchanged letters with Liz Tobey throughout 1982, reassuring the young girl that their family was doing as well as expected and assuring the teenager that hope and faith should never be lost.

Frannie and Mary took a liking to Lizzy's letters and wanted to comfort her over the passing of Timely Writer as the holiday season approached. In reviewing the return address from the envelope of the condolence card, Mary found Elizabeth's home telephone number in the telephone book. Frannie telephoned Elizabeth's home one week before Christmas, speaking with her mom and then requesting to speak with Elizabeth. Frannie talked with the young girl, learning that Lizzy and her family were present at Timely Writer's return to racing at Suffolk Downs earlier that summer. Liz was the young girl who could be seen waving the pennant along the fence as the Martins watched from above. Frannie was thankful to Lizzy for her cards and support, also asking if he and Mary could meet with Lizzy and her family.

Frannie and Mary arranged to meet with the Tobey family two days before Christmas of 1982. The Martins arrived at the home bearing gifts for the heartbroken young girl. As they sat together talking about Timely Writer and horses, and to the great surprise of Liz, Frannie let her know that he and Peter were naming a filly after her, calling her "Liz T." Next, Frannie gave Liz a photo of a different filly. The photograph was of a one-year-old gray filly stabled at Tony Everard's training facility in Ocala. The filly needed a name, and Frannie asked Liz to help them in the coming weeks. One final surprise Mary brought was a Christmas gift for Liz. Liz excitedly opened the gift, and to her disbelief, she held a large framed photograph of the gorgeous Timely Writer standing upright on the horse track of Suffolk Downs. Forever thankful, Liz hung the framed photo in her bedroom that evening.

After the new year, and with time to think, Liz reported back to Frannie a name for the grey filly. In honor of the passing of Timely Writer, Liz came up with the heavenly name of Raise the Clouds for the beautiful gray filly. Over the next year, Mary sent notes with photographs to Liz from Tony Everard's training farm, documenting the beauty and strength of the still-growing filly. The pictures, with notes and cards from Mary to Liz, also updated the young girl about events in their lives.

As Mary relayed to Liz within one of her handwritten cards, Raise the Clouds was ready for her maiden race and was getting shipped north by Tony Everard in the spring of 1984 to the barns at Suffolk Downs. A short time after Raise the Clouds settled into her new stall, Liz and her mom received a telephone call from Frannie asking if they would be their guests for lunch and sit with them in their owner's box for the maiden race of Raise the Clouds. To Liz's delight, the afternoon produced winning results for her filly - the day complete with a photograph in the winner's circle of the Martin family, Liz, her brother, and her mom.

Liz Tobey (white summer hat) in the winner's circle with Fran and Mary Martin

In the years ahead, Liz continued with her education at various colleges, earning a Bachelor's Degree, a Master's degree, and a Doctorate in Art History. Liz's schooling and work opportunities allowed her to live in various places over the next forty years, including Washington D.C. and Florence, Italy. A constant keepsake in her life, brought to every place Liz called home along the way, was the gift the Martins presented to her at Christmas in 1982. To this day, the ageless Timely Writer is on full display in the home office of Elizabeth Tobey.

The friendship and story of Elizabeth Tobey, along with the compassion and generosity of the Martins, was never told to others by Frannie and Mary. A story only stumbled upon by the Martins' son John in 2022, as he viewed a thoroughbred posting on social media from an "Elizabeth Tobey" – who noted she came from Hingham, Massachusetts. The post referencing the great Timely Writer in conjunction with the recent passing of Boston sportscaster Bob Neumeier in October of 2021. The posting reminded John about a young girl from Hingham who would write his mother and father letters and that his father named a filly called Liz T. John and his sisters never knowing the young girl had come up with the name of Raise the Clouds, nor that his parents gifted her a framed photograph of Timely Writer.

Fran and Mary, as with Peter Martin, were not people who brought attention to their generosity. They gave as they chose because generosity helped others. When public sympathy arrived at the doorsteps of the Martins after Timely Writer's life-saving surgery, where individuals came to console the family, only to leave their presence having been the one consoled, the same was true when Lizzy T sent her condolences to the Martins. Rather than place the sympathy note to the side, never to be addressed, or a simple note of thank you in return, the Martins took it upon themselves to comfort Liz. An unexpected act of kindness and generosity by the Martins forever affected the life of Elizabeth Tobey.

As the Martins retreated from the newspaper headlines with Timely Writer's passing in the fall of 1982, focusing on family, friends, work, and quiet generosity, conflicting emotions stirred within trainer Dominic Imprescia. During November and December of 1982, the trainer was making his case to the Martin brothers that he was owed 20% of their insurance proceeds from the passing of Timely Writer – which had been publicly reported as up to four million dollars. Dominic had been the brothers' trainer for Nitram Stables for ten years, with the stable growing to 12 horses by the end of 1982. Still, he would leave bitter over the brothers' refusal to share money received from their equine insurance policy.

Before the start of the three-year-old racing season, with Timely Writer near certain to qualify for the 1982 Kentucky Derby and arguably the best two-year-old horse from the previous racing season, the brothers decided to purchase a colic and fatality insurance policy for 50% of the colt's value. The brothers, estimating Writer's value at the time was approximately six to eight million dollars, knew they would sell half of the colt's value to a potential buyer in the coming months. The brothers were also pretty good gamblers, with Peter as an accountant, and they also knew the value of "hedging" the asset in their possession. In the Martins ' case, the costs for a one-year fatality policy for a three-year-old thoroughbred in competition can be up to 10% of the insured value – or three to four hundred thousand dollars. Though others may have taken the risk and not paid the insurance premium, the brothers came up with the money to protect their future in a worst-case scenario.

Frannie, raising a family of five on his income from the meat business, took out a personal loan to pay his portion of the equine insurance premium.

Upon Dr. Reed purchasing 50% of Timely Writer's breeding rights from the brothers in March of 1982, the Martins set up a breeding syndication agreement. Though there was no obligation to do so, the Martins one-half of the breeding syndication agreement provided that 10% of their breeding income was to be distributed to Tony Everard, with 20% of it distributed to Dominic and the remaining 70% of the brothers' half split between them. When Timely Writer died before the start of retirement and breeding, so did the syndication agreement. Media reports indicated that Timely Writer's syndication agreement was valued at $24 million. Dominic was insistent with the brothers that he was entitled to 20% of everything - including any insurance proceeds - though he never paid any of the policy premiums nor was a signatory to the insurance contract. Frannie explained numerous times to Dominic that the insurance contract had nothing to do with the breeding syndication, telling him to read the agreement closely. Dominic would not relent in his position. The week before Christmas, he sought out a friendly journalist at the *Miami Herald*, blasting the Martin brothers publicly for not paying the money he believed was owed. The story from the *Miami Herald* made its way into other newspapers, including the *Boston Globe,* three days before Christmas – as the Martins were preparing to deliver Christmas gifts to Elizabeth Tobey.

In a phone call from a journalist from a Boston newspaper on a topic that Frannie always thought should have remained a private matter, Frannie agreed to explain his position regarding the distribution of Timely Writer's insurance proceeds. Choosing not to criticize Dominic, Frannie commented, "Peter and I like Dom and respect the great job he did with Timely Writer.....

Dom and I have been friends for years. I don't want hard feelings."[186] Choosing to go public and chasing money over friendship forever cost Dominic his relationships and business with the Martins and Nitram Stables. Frannie pulled all of the horses from Nitram Stables from the trainer and sent them elsewhere after the holiday season. In less than 90 days, the brothers had lost their champion horse and full-time trainer.

As the Martin family continued to recover from the loss of Timely Writer in 1983, the brothers' stable had grown to 12 horses, including a colt named Timely Hitter, some mares for breeding, and one share in the breeding rights of Perrault. Perrault was the 1982 Eclipse Award winner for Outstanding Male Turf who stood at stud at their friend and business partner Dr. Reed's farm in Louisville, Kentucky.

In the weeks, months, and years following Timely Writer's passing, journalists in all forms of the print media paid homage to the champion colt and his story while telling of a tragedy only Shakespeare could write. Countless people in the years following found time to approach and pay their respects to the Martin family for their loss, always sharing a personal story about one of Timely Writer's great moments, with some recounting where they were while watching one of the colt's great races.

Teenagers and young adults who lived through the tragic and magical tales of Timely Writer in the early 1980s moved forward in life - with some becoming journalists and writers. Youths forever affected by the story of Timely Writer during the early 1980s, sharing their personal experiences during their adult years about the love, admiration, and memories of a once-in-a-lifetime horse. Author Kimberly Gatto was one of those young teenagers who fell in love with Timely Writer. Kimberly once again brought to life the story about the people's horse and the Martin family for the next generation in an article entitled, *"Remembering Timely Writer 25 years after his death."* Gatto shared her views and those of others, writing, "Timely Writer was one of the greatest talents of his era."[187] She wasn't alone in her view, as Tony Everard, who went on to become a legend of his own while successfully schooling champions of the Kentucky Derby, Preakness, and Belmont Stakes, told Kimberly twenty-five years after Timely Writer's passing, "[h]e was the best horse that I've ever known – no question about it."[188]

Timely Writer, though, was more than just a great horse. Timely Writer was brilliant and courageous; his intelligence, mannerisms, and the nuances of his personality were nearly human-like. The colt left an impression with all he encountered that he had a mind of his own while also having the ability to make his independent personality part of the family unit. A champion colt who flaunted his charisma before small and large crowds. The great majority of thoroughbreds do not care to be approached while in the confines of the barn after a grueling race. A horse barn and stall to a thoroughbred is equivalent to his house and bedroom. It is where the horse resides, seeking comfort for quiet time to settle down after a race. Timely Writer was different, though. He was comfortable in any space, commanding attention wherever he may be while seeking out interactions with others. Timely Writer loved a camera and looked to be photographed. Following one of his wins, Timely Writer was approached by several photographers in the barn area. Rather than becoming spooked by the commotion, the horse seemed to relish the extra attention. Mary Martin laughingly remarked twenty-five years later, "every time he saw someone with a camera, [he] stopped and posed. They never had to make him stand or put his ears forward He had really become quite the ham." As he thought back a generation earlier, Frannie shared his wife's opinion, laughingly recounting, "[h]e really was quite a character."[189]

Fran and Mary Martin, some 25 years after Timely Writer passed, still remembered how their colt brought out the good in people. As the Martins spoke with Kimberly Gatto in 2007, they could still hear the deafening roar of the New York crowd supporting them that day in Saratoga when the Boston champion made his triumphant return to the Spa during the summer of 1982. "The memories of Timely Writer remind[ed] the Martins of the good of the sport, and the kindness of humanity in general."[190] With emotion in his voice, Frannie wanted people to know, "I could go on and on about the many wonderful folks who were there for us.... some truly outstanding people."[191] As depicted by the crowds in New York, Massachusetts, and Florida from the Spring of 1981 through the summer and fall of '82, Timely Writer brought people together from differing economic backgrounds. Timely Writer, as with the greatest of athletes, made his sport and the people in it better from having met him.

Timely Writer impacted people in a manner different from that of other legendary horses. Certainly, Secretariat, Affirmed, and the other legends of the sport impacted countless people. However, the affection for Timely Writer differed from the typical emotional attachment shown to other horse racing legends. Timely Writer and the Martin family personified old-fashioned hard work. The colt, a low-budget purchase by regular folks, skyrocketed to the ranks of an elite champion. The very nature of their rags-to-riches tale left others feeling as if they were part of the story. The colt's impact on others was apparent and tangible. Journalists recognized it, spoke of it, and forever preserved its effect in their writings. It was this unique connection that author Kimberly Gatto experienced first-hand, sharing it with her readers 25 years after Timely Writer's last race. A connection so strong that the author used only one other horse to compare – the great Seabiscuit.

As Carmelita Stafford of Nicholasville, Kentucky, depicted in her letter to Timely Writer in April of 1982, as he recovered from surgery, the colt impacted countless people – even people from Kentucky. Siobhan Delancey was another young teenager in 1982 who was so affected that years later, she named her horse after Timely Writer. In her remembrance article, Kimberly Gatto shared the story of Siobhann, a rider and trainer of show horses in Maryland in 2007. Siobhann grew up in Massachusetts and followed the career and story of Timely Writer and his owners. As an adult in Maryland, Siobhann showed her lingering affection and admiration for Timely Writer by naming her filly Timely Miss. Though Kimberly Gatto did not write of her admiration for Timely Writer in the anniversary article, she knew of the love and affection others shared for the colt. Three years before the remembrance article, Kimberly penned her story in a book, *"Beyond the Rainbow Bridge."*

Beyond the Rainbow Bridge chronicles the emotional and psychological fallout upon a horse owner from the loss of a horse, including the traumatic loss and subsequent recovery stages. Kimberly paid homage to her very first love in the prologue to her book, *"Timely Writer – the Horse Who Started it All."* The fateful Saturday afternoon in October of 1982 at Belmont Park carries vivid memories for the author. As she and her teenage friend flipped through her Timely Writer scrapbook before the national television broadcast of the Jockey Gold Cup, Kimberly thought, "[t]his horse is everyone's hero."[192]

Reflecting on those earlier years, Kimberly penned, "[t]o my youthful eyes, this horse was nobility."[193] In a beautifully touching, first-person prose, Kimberly Gatto summed up what many people felt about the impact of Timely Writer:

> I never met Timely Writer. I never saw him in person. But I knew everything about him and in a sense, he was "my" horse. I was as proud of him as I if I owned him. The memory of "my" Timely Writer and his all too brief life would impact me forever. Never before had I seen such heart and generosity of spirit from an animal that had unselfishly done what was asked of him, and lost his life in the process. . . Timely Writer's legacy remains in my heart ... when I look into the eyes of a thoroughbred, I always see the great heart of Timely Writer.[194]

One young teenage boy who grew up in New Jersey was able to see Timely Writer race in person. The boy and his father sharing time at Belmont Park by watching the legendary horses who made their way through the racetrack during the 1970s and into the 1980s. As an adult, the young boy from New Jersey couldn't help but reminisce about the golden years at Belmont without mentioning one particular horse – Timely Writer. The boy saw Timely Writer in person at the Champagne Stakes at Belmont Park in the fall of '81, remembering how all of the attention at Belmont that day was on the undefeated Before Dawn and the lighting-fast Deputy Minister. Patrons at Belmont that day talked about how they were there to see the undefeated filly take on the field of colts. The improbable horse from Boston, though, stole the headlines. Watching the homestretch running power of Timely Writer at the Champagne forever impressed the young boy from New Jersey, as the two undefeated horses could not handle the strength and endurance of Timely Writer.

The boy followed the roller-coaster racing season of Timely Writer in 1982, looking forward to the colt's improbable comeback during the fall racing schedule at Belmont Park. At the Jockey Gold Cup in October of 1982, the boy and his father were in attendance talking about how it was one year to the day when they last saw Timely Writer in person. As events developed on the last turn at Belmont that day, the 13-year-old could barely keep his eyes on the horrific scene. The boy from New Jersey would grow into a talented journalist and media executive, often remembering and writing about the legends of horse racing. In his heart, Timely Writer was a part of the legends from years ago.

Brian Zipse was the young boy from New Jersey during those racing days at Belmont Park in the autumn of '81 and '82. Zipse became the editor of *Horse Racing Nation* from 2010-2017 and its senior writer beginning in 2018. Nearly three decades after Timely Writer left racing, the colt's impact was still a part of the writer who became a well-respected voice in the horse racing industry. In an article in September of 2011 for Horse Racing Nation, Zipse paid tribute to the people's champion in *"Remembering...... Timely Writer."* Zipse spoke of the fallen colt, echoing the feeling of those who rode along with Timely Writer and his family a generation ago. "The Eclipse Awards may have never said so, but he was more than the people's champion, he was a true champion. Now each fall as I watch the great racing from Belmont Park, I can't help but to think of him with great fondness. I remember you Timely Writer."[195]

As evident from the youthful memories of Kimberly Gatto, Siobhann Delancey, Elizabeth Tobey, and Brian Zipse, Timely Writer captured the affection of an entire country. However, the affection for Timely Writer had nothing to do with the colt winning the Kentucky Derby, the Triple Crown, or Horse of the Year awards. The love and affection from the public towards Timely Writer were genuine and palpable. The legion of fans supporting Timely Writer was more significant in volume than other horses who had success at the elite level – and the average person knew why. Most thoroughbreds are owned and controlled by men and horse farms of unfathomable wealth. Men with an unlimited monetary budget, who board the most expensive horses at the best farms in the country, and who use the best trainers available, are not stories easy to identify with by the average person. Timely Writer and his owners were the exception to the norm. The relationship between Timely Writer and the Martin family was a team people could identify with and support. The colt was a championship horse on center stage with owners who wore the shoes of the common man.

In the years and generations following the passing of Timely Writer, the champion colt would be honored by many for his heart and courage. Within the year of Timely Writer's passing, General Manager and Vice President of Suffolk Downs, Robert M. O'Malley, on August 29, 1983, penned a letter to Frannie informing him that Suffolk Downs was retiring the annual Yankee Handicap. A race run at Suffolk Downs every year since 1935 - and the one which Timely Writer won in his return from the life-threatening illness the previous summer. Within the letter, O'Malley announced Suffolk Downs would run the Timely Writer Handicap every year on Labor Day weekend. Peter and Frannie were present as honorary guests for the inaugural Timely Writer Handicap on September 5, 1983, with the brothers presenting the trophy in the winner's circle.

Gulfstream Park in Hallandale, Florida, was also gracious enough to host a memorial race in Timely Writer's honor. As Suffolk Downs did in 1983, Gulfstream Park honored the colt with the Timely Writer Stakes in March of 2011. Though the Martins and Dominic could never mend their fractured relationship over the years, Frannie never doubted his trainer's abilities and affection for Timely Writer. Trainer Dominic Imprescia, 91 years old at the time of the stakes race, was given the spot-lite one last time at Gulfstream Park.

The colt from Boston who became a legend

Uncle Mo, the two-year-old horse of the year in 2010, finished his racing season with wins at the Breeder's Cup Juvenile and the Champagne Stakes, covering the distance 2/5 of a second faster than Secretariat in 1972. The colt's trainer and owner, Mike Repole, began the three-year-old racing season by entering Uncle Mo in the Timely Writer's Stakes as a prep race for the Kentucky Derby. Uncle Mo won the race in Timely Writer style, going away down the stretch. Dominic represented the Timely Writer crew in the winner's circle, presenting the trophy to Repole.

In the following month, Uncle Mo went off as the 1-9 favorite at the Wood Memorial in New York on April 9th - coming in a disappointing 3rd place in an important Kentucky Derby prep race. Shortly after the race, it was revealed a gastrointestinal infection was affecting Uncle Mo. Owner Mike Repole sent his colt to Churchill Downs, hoping to recover and eventually race in the Kentucky Derby on the first Saturday in May. Uncle Mo, however, like Timely Writer before him, did not run in the Kentucky Derby due to the illness. He would retire that November after a 10th place finish at the Breeder's Cup Classic – having never come close to the horse he was before the infection. Beginning with the 2012 breeding season, Uncle Mo retired to Ashford Stud Farm, becoming the leading freshman sire in 2015 and the leading second-crop sire in 2016. The fee for Uncle Mo's service as a stallion in 2024 was $150,000.00.[196]

Shortly after the 25th anniversary of Timely Writer's passing, he was inducted into the New England Racing Hall of Fame. A few years later, Frannie and Peter's colleague and friend joined Timely Writer in the Hall of Fame with his introduction in 2012. Frank Bertolino was honored for his over forty years in the thoroughbred racing business, including being one of the nation's top ten owners nine times. As of 2024, at 90 years young, Frank was still sending his one-year-olds to the training center in Ocala, Florida, overseen by the forever youthful Tony Everard.

Timely Writer's full-time jockey Jeffrey Fell from Hamilton, Ontario, was 16 years old when he started riding horses professionally in 1972. He was Canada's leading apprentice jockey in 1974 and its leading rider from 1975 through 1977, leaving the following year for the more challenging racing circuits in the United States. In addition to his success aboard Timely Writer, Fell will forever be regarded as the jockey who directed one of the biggest upsets in thoroughbred racing history when he took the mount aboard Canadian-bred Runaway Groom at the Travers Stakes at Saratoga in August 1982—Fell, directing the colt to a win over the three champions from the 1982 Triple Crown races. Injuries and illness forced Fell to retire prematurely in 1990, but his success and talent did not go unnoticed with his induction into the Canadian Horse Racing Hall of Fame in 1993.

Similarly, Dorchester native Chris McCarron found professional success as a jockey – though at a level unmatched by few. After winning Timely Writer's last race at the Jockey Gold Cup in October of 1982, McCarron finished his career in 2002 after 28 years of racing and a record 7,141 wins. The wins included first-place finishes six times in the Kentucky Derby, the Preakness Stakes, and the Belmont Stakes. Before McCarron's retirement, at the age of 34, he was inducted into the United States Racing Hall of Fame in 1989. The year after his retirement, McCarron served as a technical advisor and actor in the movie *Seabiscuit*. Three years after his retirement, the Hall of Famer helped to found the first-ever riding academy in the United States, known as the North American Racing Academy in Louisville, Kentucky. The academy continues to serve as an accredited college, offering various degrees, including one in equine studies, which focuses on the schooling and production of jockeys, horsemen, and racing officials.

A true character of the sport, the "King of the Fairs," Carlos Figueroa eventually made his way to Saratoga Race Course in the mid-1990s, entering a few of his horses for his enjoyment. Figuera stood at the rail of the historic grounds, a smile spread across his face, and without a care in the world, watching each of his horses lose by large margins. It was in 1994 when the New England Turf Writers Association honored the larger-than-life personality with a lifetime achievement award for his contributions to the sport. In the following decade, Figueroa self-promoted a horse record he had set. As Carlos promised *ESPN*'s Bill Finley, his record as a trainer would never be broken – a historic losing streak of 146 consecutive races. Figueroa retired at the age of 81 from horse racing in 2010, later passing in 2017.

The annual Kentucky Derby parties for over a thousand guests hosted by Preston and Anita Madden at Hamburg Place will be forever remembered. Preston and Anita Madden's marriage lasted 62 years, and both lived a successful and colorful life. Two years after the 1982 Kentucky Derby, Preston bred a foal named Alysheba, who went on to win the 1987 Kentucky Derby and fulfill Preston's lifelong dream. Preston outlived Anita, passing away at his horse farm three days after running the 146th Kentucky Derby in May 2020. A sentence in Preston's obituary paid tribute to the entertainment skills of him and his wife, "their famous Derby parties will never be duplicated or forgotten."[197]

Former Suffolk Downs owner Bill Veeck sold his Chicago White Sox in 1981 for $20 million, after which he began rooting for his boyhood team, the Chicago Cubs. Veeck could often be found during the summer months sitting in the bleachers cheering on the Cubs and singing along to the lyrics of "Take Me Out to The Ballgame" with announcer Harry Caray during the seventh-inning stretch. Veeck passed away from cancer on January 2, 1986, survived by his wife and eight children – as thousands honored a veteran of

World War II and a life well led. Attending the funeral was his friend George Carney from Brockton. In 1991, even in death, Bill Veeck got the last laugh when Major League Baseball inducted him posthumously into the Baseball Hall of Fame in Cooperstown, New York.

After a decade of fortifying his legislative positions in Massachusetts and helping politicians see things his way, the *Boston Sunday Globe* proclaimed George Carney as the person who ran racing in Massachusetts in December of 1981. For over two generations, Carney was a central figure in racing in Massachusetts. George was the common denominator in Massachusetts as numerous politicians, lobbyists, businessmen, dog and horse owners, and various racing opposition groups made their way in and out of the political arena, looking to tailor racing and gambling legislation to fit their needs. Carney had a front-row seat to the theatre of the absurd, managing the politics of it all as well as anyone while challenging all comers who were a threat to his interests. As state leaders placed greed and their political agendas above the good of the racing industry, Carney witnessed the rise and fall of horse and dog racing in Massachusetts. By 2022, neither dog nor horse racing was legal in the state. In a state once too pious to legalize gambling, it took politicians less than 80 years to build up the industry and tear it down, replacing it with their state lotteries, gambling casinos, and sports gambling parlors.

Former horse owner Gerry Cheevers' hockey coaching career ended during the 1984-85 season. Cheevers would inherit the old job of Bob Neumeier, becoming the color commentator for the Hartford Whalers from 1986-1995, then later taking the same role with the Boston Bruins from 1999-2002. Cheevers also served as a scout for the Bruins for 11 years. Despite Cheever's youthful confidence that he would one day get to the Kentucky Derby, he was never lucky enough to find another horse with the same talent as Royal Ski.

Another horse owner, Peter Fuller, owner of Dancer's Image, predicted in his interview with the *Boston Globe* before the 1982 Kentucky Derby, "I promise

I'll be back at the Derby someday with my horse."[198] Peter Fuller died in 2006 – never returning to the Kentucky Derby.

Dr. William Reed lived a life of 83 years, passing in October of 2004. As *Bloodhorse* magazine acknowledged upon Dr. Reed's death, he was "internationally regarded as one of the finest equine practitioners of his time."[199] As Frannie and Peter would admit, only in the sport of horse racing could two blue-collar brothers from Dorchester become the best of friends and partners with a wealthy and internationally recognized equine veterinarian doctor.

George Steinbrenner went on to win 7 World Series championships as the owner of the New York Yankees over his 37 years. The Boss passed from Alzheimer's Disease during the morning of July 13, 2010, hours before Major League Baseball's All-Star game. Although a controversial figure in baseball, he was beloved in the thoroughbred business and throughout Ocala, Florida. When not running the Yankees, Steinbrenner was often at Kinsman Farm in Ocala, walking the barns and feeding sugar cubes to his horses. The tough-minded baseball owner constructed breeding and foal barns for the mares, installing windows so he and his family could watch the miracle of birth - the baby rising and walking within the hour. Steinbrenner and Tony Everard often saw each other around Ocala, sharing a laugh and talking horses, with Tony sometimes reminding the Boss how he fired him. Steinbrenner had seven entries in the Kentucky Derby over the years, with none finishing first.

The horse farm Steinbrenner and his wife bought in Ocala in 1969 is still run by his family. After becoming the first manager for Steinbrenner's farm, Everard watched horses from his training facility finish first in the Kentucky Derby, Preakness, and Belmont Stakes. Everard has never wavered on one opinion during his historic career - none of the champions he schooled were better than Timely Writer. Tony Everard and his family made Ocala their home - never moving from their adopted hometown for other pastures. As a resident spanning more than fifty years, Everard watched Ocala grow to become the largest thoroughbred town in the country. In 2023, over

1,200 registered horse farms were operating in Ocala, with one of the town's originals still having the time of his life buying and selling horses through his mid-80s.

Bob Neumeier, the multi-talented 30-year-old sports reporter from Weymouth, Massachusetts, spent his next 40 years following his human-interest story about Timely Writer and the Martins showcasing his talents and personality before television audiences regionally, nationally, and internationally. Neumie worked for WBZ-TV channel 4 in Boston until 2000, covering the New England Patriots pre-game television shows, handling play-by-play announcing for the Boston Bruins, and handicapping horse races for *ESPN* from 1989 through 2000. Neumie showed his gambling skills in horse racing in 1990 while defeating 350 of the world's top handicappers and winning the Caesar's Palace World Series of Handicapping. The championship thrust Neumie onto the television broadcast team for the Triple Crown races carried for NBC in 1990 and the Breeder's Cup, where he would remain for over twenty years. The kid from Weymouth also landed himself a spot on the network team for the 1992 Summer Olympics. In 2006, NBC added Neumie to its National Hockey League television coverage in addition to his horse racing and Olympic duties. Over the years, though, whether it be at Saratoga Race Track, Suffolk Downs, or Belmont Park, Neumie always remembered one of his first horse racing stories. Whenever the occasion presented itself, Neumie always found time to catch up trackside with his old friend Frannie. Neumie would pass away too young in October 2021 at the age of 70 from congestive heart failure, leaving thousands of friends and fans across the country better off having known him.

Deputy Minister and owner Robert Brennan separated at the end of 1983. The colt returned to racing as a four-year-old, winning three stakes races, two of which were at Gulfstream Park. Deputy Minister, a son of Northern Dancer, was every bit the stallion many believed he would become. He quickly produced quality foals, including future Hall of Famer Go for Wand in 1987. Go for Wand winning the Eclipse Awards in 1989 and 1990 as filly of the year. Due to the number of winners produced, Deputy Minister was the leading sire in North America in 1997 and 1998. The stud fee for Deputy Minister from 1999 through 2002 was $150,000.[200]

Time and a life of defrauding people finally caught up with Deputy Minister's owner Robert Brennan. In 1994, the Securities and Exchange Commission ordered Brennan to pay $75 million in restitution as part of a civil forfeiture. A court judgment from a civil suit in the same year found Brennan liable for damages of another $55 million. It was estimated that Robert Brennan, between 1988 and 1995, defrauded his clients of approximately $300 million[201] – more than $100 million swindled by Jordan Belfort of the *Wolf of Wall Street* fame in the late 1990s. Finally, in April 2001, a federal criminal trial found the swindler guilty of money laundering and bankruptcy fraud, with the judge sentencing Brennan to 110 months in federal prison with five years of supervised release.

Johnny Campo's career in thoroughbred racing was cut shorter for reasons far different than Robert Brennan's. Once a rising star many considered the best trainer in the country in 1981, Campo's career did not track his early success. Campo, the winning trainer of the 1981 Kentucky Derby and Preakness Stakes, would never again win a Triple Crown race. Tragedy at Belmont Park touched Campo at the 1982 Jockey Gold Cup with the death of Johnny Dancer and then again in 1986. In a far greater tragedy, a fire swept through Campos' horse barn, killing 36 of the 38 horses under his care. Ten years later, after suffering a stroke, Campo retired from racing, eventually passing away at the age of 67 in 2005 at his home in Long Island.

Dominic Imprescia lived a long life of 93 years, training tens of thousands of horses, though always remembering that special one. A little over 18 months after Timely Writer passed, Dominic shared his thoughts on the loss of his favorite during an interview about the sudden passing of Swale in 1984. Swale, who was the son of Triple Crown winner Seattle Slew, was trained by Dominic's friend Woody Stephens, and had unexpectedly passed away during his sleep. Dominic shared his experiences with the journalist about what his friend must be going through. As a trainer, Dominic was in the habit of not letting himself get emotionally attached to any one horse. For

Dominic, though, losing Timely Writer was "like losing a member of the family."[202] As a tribute, Dominic hung a framed portrait of Timely Writer in his living room, though "it's not the same as going out to the farm and visiting him."[203] The framed photo was a small way Dominic was reminded daily about the once-in-a-lifetime horse. Dominic explained how training and knowing Timely Writer was an honor and privilege. "[O]ne like him comes along just once in a lifetime. You could spend millions of dollars trying to replace him, and it would never happen again." "Timely Writer was the people's horse. . . he was an ordinary horse who made good, and that made me care for him even more."[204]

Two months after the Timely Writer Stakes at Gulfstream Park in March of 2011, and one week after he watched his last Kentucky Derby, Dominic Imprescia passed away in his sleep on May 8, 2011, in Hallandale, Florida, content to leave life after a distinguished career, loving family and friends, and having experienced a once in a lifetime horse he and others only dreamed about. Dominic, even in death, would not have his name mentioned without reminding others about the blessings given to him by an old friend. Dominic's obituary reflected upon his life and career in horse racing, letting people know he found "glory at the top of the sport in 1981 and 1982 with a horse named Timely Writer."[205] Whether it was from the confines of his stall, with Dr. Reed watching from a distance, the training track at Suffolk Downs with Dominic looking on, or from the pasture that first afternoon Tony Everard stood gazing at him, Timely Writer touched seasoned professionals in the same manner he impacted every other person he came across.

Though Frannie and Peter never repaired their fractured relationship with Dominic, they forever respected his ability and work with Timely Writer, never taking the opportunity to speak badly of the friend they had at one time. It was the quality of character that made Frannie and Peter easy to like – hard-working, family-oriented, quick-witted, and humorous. They were respectful, treated people well, knew who they were and where they came from. As they were living out their dreams, no matter how bumpy the journey became, and as the Mayor of Boston observed, the brothers exemplified grace while appreciating and enjoying the ride they found themselves on. They knew they were in the middle of a once-in-a-lifetime opportunity and were willing to share it with everyone who wanted to join them on the ride.

Just six months after sharing the winner's circle with his brothers and Elizabeth Tobey at Suffolk Downs, a sudden and deadly stroke took the life of Peter Martin - passing away far too early in life at the age of 66 on January 27, 1985. The bachelor for life was true to his character and upbringing in Dorchester - living a life of quiet charitable giving. Church services at St. Brendan's in Dorchester saw hundreds of people attend, including Elizabeth Tobey and her mom. After his brother's passing, Frannie agreed to an interview at the request of a Boston journalist for a news story about Peter's life. Frannie spoke of all the good Peter did for people throughout his lifetime – without anyone ever knowing who the anonymous donor was. Describing the man Frannie knew privately, the youngest brother spoke of how Peter went through life as a philanthropic individual, though never calling attention to his causes or himself.

Frannie's memories about his older brother were shared in a story authored by Sam McCracken in the *Boston Globe* entitled, *"In the sport of Kings, Peter Martin was a Prince."* As his business partner, brother, and friend, Frannie witnessed Peter's charitable work and anonymous monetary donations to countless people over the years. Sam McCracken, who had come to know the brothers over the years, described Peter "as a generous man, a philanthropic man, a man who gave because he wanted to, not because he thought he had to."[206] When given the opportunity to brag about the specifics of his brother's benevolent gifts during his lifetime, Frannie told the writer about the brothers' unspoken pact. "I wish I could tell you how many people he helped financially over the years, but he would not have wanted it that way." [207] As with his life, Peter's generosity in death extended to his family and numerous charitable programs. Peter left a portion of his money to every niece and nephew of his three brothers, with the remainder of his estate, well into seven figures, designated to various charities and educational scholarships.

In the year after following the obituary article about Peter Martin, Sam McCracken was presented with the Walter Haight Award for Excellence in Journalism at Churchill Downs during Kentucky Derby Week of 1986. Less than two years after writing the story about Peter Martin and a year after winning the Award for Excellence in Journalism, cancer took the life of Sam McCracken at 59 years young in November of 1986. Colleague, friend, and award-winning journalist Leigh Montville of The Boston Globe honored Sam's life and family with a two-page story entitled *"So Long Sam."*

Francis Martin outlived his brother by more than 25 years, passing away in October of 2009 - content with life and the ride it took him on. He retired from the horse business in 1997, spending his final years with Mary, with the two of them often hosting their three children and their six grandchildren at their home in Canton, Massachusetts – a home purchased in 1984 with their winnings from horse racing. Frannie's weekends at the horse track during the summers were gladly replaced in retirement with time spent around the pool at his home in Canton, entertaining his six grandchildren Brian, David, Miranda, Renee, Nicole, and Danielle. When not hosting family and friends, Frannie found time every month for luncheons with his lifelong friends from Dorchester. Though many in the OFD group had moved away from the town where they were raised some eighty years prior, nobody could ever take Dorchester away from them.

After Frannie's passing, Mary lived independently for over a decade in her home in Marshfield, Massachusetts, passing away in 2021 at 93. In the basement of her house, Mary left a collection of storage boxes tucked away in the corner for others to cherish. One piece from the memorabilia was an award the Governor of Kentucky bestowed upon Frannie. Enclosed within the glass-framed plaque was the highest civilian award the state of Kentucky can grant. Francis X. Martin, in 1986, was declared an Honorary Kentucky Colonel by the Governor in recognition of his philanthropy - an award and the reasons for it, which Frannie never shared with others.

As fate would have it, the final chapter of Timely Writer's story would end in the land of Kentucky more than 40 years after his death. Michael Blowen, the *Boston Globe* journalist who was so moved from his days working with thoroughbreds under the tutelage of trainer Carlos Figueroa at Suffolk Downs in the late 1990s, set out to change the horse racing industry upon his retirement. The pairing of Blowen and Figueroa began one day at Suffolk Downs when Michael started chatting with Carlos outside the grandstand area. Wanting to learn more about the inner workings of horse racing and thoroughbreds, primarily to improve his gambling skills, Blowen went to work for Figueroa for the next 18 months. Blowen reported daily at 5:30 a.m. to Figueroa's horse barn at Suffolk Downs. The writer's duties at the barn included mucking stalls, feeding and walking the horses, and tending to the day-to-day needs of the animals. Michael learned to listen to thoroughbreds by watching and learning at the side of Carlos.

Michael and his wife, Diane White, both *Boston Globe* journalists in 2001, were amongst the many writers offered early retirement buyout packages from the company. With their son living in Australia, the couple followed Michael's passion to improve aftercare for thoroughbred horses once their racing careers were finished. Michael's love for the animal and the sport led them to the state of Kentucky. In 2003, the couple started *Old Friends* in Georgetown, Kentucky. Blowen believed Thoroughbred aftercare programs were an immediate need within the industry, which he first identified while working with Carlos at Suffolk Downs. Blowen's vision for the program began with one leased paddock, one horse, and a golf cart. Over the next twenty years, Blowen transformed the racing industry, creating multiple aftercare retirement farms for thoroughbreds. As of 2024, the charitable organization includes a 230-acre farm in Georgetown, Kentucky, with another three satellite farms providing support. The farms offer a home and medical services to more than 250 horses. Big Brown, the 2008 Kentucky Derby and Preakness Stakes champion, is the Georgetown farm's most recent resident. Fittingly, Michael's efforts earned him and *Old Friends* the 2014 Eclipse Award for Extraordinary Service to the Sport of Thoroughbred Racing.

In 2023, with Blowen approaching retirement as the Director of Old Friends, Belmont Park in New York was in the middle of a $1 billion redevelopment program, which required the reinterment of both Ruffian and Timely Writer. The logical choice for Ruffian was to return her remains to the historic Claiborne Farms, where she was foaled and raised – a farm that had existed since 1910. Timely Writer, though, was a thoroughbred from humble beginnings with no family farm for his return. The writer from Boston, though, knew where Timely Writer belonged.

Michael Blowen at Old Friends. Winner circle photos from the 1981 Hopeful Stakes in Saratoga and Mayflower Stakes in Boston.

In November 2023, more than forty years after his tragic fall, Belmont Park delivered Timely Writer's remains to a former Bostonian and admirer from decades past. The colt who conjured up images of Seabiscuit was reinterred in the cemetery on the grounds of *Old Friends*. Timely Writer's final resting place may list an address in Kentucky, but it feels like Boston as the former

Boston Globe writer watches over the colt's grave from the farm he first thought to create while at the stalls of Suffolk Downs.

As was his story during life, the journey to Timely Writer's final resting place reads like a work of fiction. In 1982, the *Daily Racing Form* published an article commenting, "the story of Timely Writer reads like a Hollywood script."[208] Whether in life or death, the colt's story, though, was neither fictional nor scripted. It was a real-life tale covering more than five decades and one preserved through the guiding hand of a wise woman.

During the Martins' years together, along with hundreds of thousands of other fans, they traveled through the gates of horse tracks across the country annually. It was a sport that carried a country through the difficult times of the Great Depression and the turbulent times of the 1970s. It was once the most popular sport in the country, with millions cheering on the best of the races every weekend from the comforts of their homes. An era when people spent their leisure time reading stories about the sport and its characters - as authored by the most talented journalists of the generation.

It was a sport and a time that gave birth to the story of two blue-collar butchers from Dorchester pursuing their love and passion for horses and horse racing at non-descript racetracks throughout New England. It was a sport that allowed the brothers to chase a dream with no promise of an outcome – but a sport that gave them reason to hope and the ability to chase those dreams. These were the times in which the Martins lived not so long ago. It is a sport that has survived in our country for over 150 years, though drastically changed from just two generations ago - the foundation of it consumed by an ever-changing country.

Mary Martin passed in November 2021 at the age of 93, leaving behind a significant collection of news articles, magazines, trophies, racing programs, photographs, and videotapes of every Timely Writer race, which also included news interviews of the leading characters of the Timely Writer crew. All of the memorabilia organized and stored away in boxes – much of it untouched for over forty years. Mary's collection is a time capsule of a story and an era that may have been forgotten, though never lost. As Frannie tirelessly worked to provide for his family and three children, often gone for most of the work week, Mary was the foundation at home. Like many at the time, Mary put her professional career aside for the betterment of her family, managing the family home and raising their children, allowing Frannie and his brother to chase their dreams. Mary's literary mind penned the name for their young colt, which seemed to roll off the lips of everyone who repeated it. It was Mary's patience, quiet leadership, and enduring faith that allowed the dreams of the brothers to become a reality. When the dream came to its tragic ending, Mary, forever believing that individuals were only given what they could handle, did not permit the family to fall victim to thoughts of what was lost - instead, giving thanks for what had been gained.

Perhaps there was a more meaningful reason why Mary's nightmarish dream before Timely Writer's fifteenth and final race was proven prophetic. The memorabilia Mary left behind for others to marvel at does not catalog death and despair. Instead, the time capsule is filled with encouragement, showcasing the fulfillment of life's dreams. Peeling back the protective plastic coverings of Mary's memorabilia albums reveals a country and a sport that once was. Turning the pages makes one pause and wonder about the story Mary would tell of the champion colt and her family.

Mary's tale, for sure, would be similar to those she recounted at their home in Canton with a younger friend of the family. During private discussions later in life, Mary shared stories of her past with an inquiring Susan Lawlor (OFD). Susan gently nudging and persuading Mary to bring to life the tales she had heard from others. Mary, as those who knew her, would share the family's untold story while sitting in her office chair adjacent to the family's kitchen. On the shelving near her desk sat Mary's memorabilia albums. The albums' plastic pages preserve Mary's paper clippings from newspapers, magazine articles, and photographs. Straight ahead, unbeknownst to Mary's listeners, a small television with an outdated cassette player sits atop their office cabinet brought from the family's old Quincy home. Sliding the front plywood doors of the cabinet to the side reveals forty-year-old cassette tapes safely stored in their cardboard coverings. In remarkable condition, the tapes depict video and audio footage of national and local television stories about the family's improbable journey. Inserting the recordings into the cassette player reveals footage of a once-in-a-lifetime horse preserved for another generation.

Mary's introduction of the family's journey to her listeners begins with the birth of an unnamed colt on a small horse farm in Ocala, Florida. The first memorabilia album to be opened sits in Mary's lap, showcasing articles and newspaper clippings from Timely Writer's maiden race in Monmouth Park. A race where Frannie, Tony, and the rest of the Timely Writer crew perfected their plan to ensure the financing of their prized colt's two-year-old racing season. An unimaginable tale about a champion colt's maiden race only hinted at over the years, finally detailed more than forty years later.

The second and third unopened albums lay atop one other on the coffee table to Mary's right. Albums revealing the wonderful times with Timely Writer, the Martin family, and their friends at horse tracks in Massachusetts, New York, Kentucky, and Florida. Mary, with her proud smile, flips through the pages of each album as her audience is brought into the sport of horse racing – with the listeners occasionally asking questions about the fascinating tale. They listen to Mary's real-life account of a colt who went from a horse nobody wanted to a thoroughbred everyone needed to call their own. Throughout the tale, each listener feels a part of Mary's family as they hear about a colt from Boston who captured the country's affection, sympathies, and support. A colt who was here far shorter than he should have been, but while here, took Mary, her family, and the country on The Ride of Their Lives.

Epilogue

After sprinting to the scene of Timely Writer's tragic fall at Belmont Park on October 10, 1982, Michael Palmer, the assistant groom from the Boston area, stood near the soon-to-be lifeless body of Timely Writer. Shortly after Palmer's arrival, the colt was stripped of his equipment before being transferred into the equine ambulance for transport away from the scene. The saddle, reins, and blinkers' hood were handed to track personnel. The black saddle cloth, with the name Timely Writer in large gold lettering running across the bottom and a large white number "1" above his name, was handed to Palmer. In the chaos and surreal moments engulfing the area after Timely Writer was removed, Palmer walked across the track to the grandstand area from where he came, noticing a bar nearby. It seemed the perfect place to stop, calm his nerves, and drink away some of the day's events. The bartender told Palmer he was closed as he sat atop the bar stool. After announcing the bar was closed, the bartender noticed the saddlecloth Palmer was holding and immediately looked towards Palmer's eyes. In return, Palmer stared back at the bartender, nodding in the affirmative. With that, the bartender asked what Palmer needed. The bartender delivered Palmer a complimentary tall glass of Seagram 7 whiskey, which he sipped for about thirty minutes.

Upon finishing his whiskey, Palmer slowly walked over to the now nearly empty barn and stall of Timely Writer, eventually returning to his sleeping quarters with the saddlecloth in hand. The next day, the Martin family returned north to their homes while Dr. Reed and Dominic arranged for Timely Writer's burial. Michael Palmer searched for a moment to speak with Dominic and return the saddlecloth to his boss, which he had stored in the area of the tack room. With the Belmont fall racing meet winding down, Dominic readied Timely Hitter and Solder Boy for transport south to Florida for some winter rest. Dominic also headed to southern Florida, where he would remain working as a trainer for some years after the breakup with Nitram Stables.

The twenty-year-old Palmer returned to his parents' home in Malden, Massachusetts, putting Timely Writer's saddlecloth in a safe storage space. Palmer worked in thoroughbred racing for another five years before moving on with life and adulthood, though he never lost his passion for horse racing and the many memories of his three months with Timely Writer. Palmer would never see his former boss again after that last day of racing at Belmont Park in 1982.

In the aftermath of Timely Writer's passing, the Martin family, friends, colleagues, and fans grieved over Timely Writer's loss. Only time could help the healing process. Years and decades would pass with the memories of Timely Writer shared through newspapers, magazines, and books, along with personal stories recounting the tales of a legend. Over the next five decades, as with Mary Martin's memorabilia collection, Michael Palmer stored and safeguarded the saddlecloth from Timely Writer's last race, never knowing when and where it should be returned, though appreciating the significance of keeping it safe.

Less than two weeks after the publication of *The Ride of Their Lives*, Palmer was preparing to move into a new apartment in November 2024. One particular day, Palmer searched a storage unit for some items. Opening up a storage tub, he unexpectedly found where he last placed Timely Writer's saddlecloth. Evoking memories from over forty years ago and appreciating it was a piece of horse racing history, Palmer photographed the saddlecloth and the colt's broken halter, later posting it for others to see on a horse racing community web page. Almost immediately, Palmer began receiving hundreds of comments and likes – and an offer to purchase the saddlecloth.

Unbeknownst to Palmer, Timely Writer's remains had been relocated from the grass infield at Belmont Park one year prior and moved to the cemetery at Old Friends Retirement Farm in Georgetown, Kentucky. Nor did Palmer know that the authors of *The Ride of Their Lives* had published the untold story of Timely Writer. One observer of Palmer's saddlecloth posting was Lorita Lindemann – the contact at Belmont Park of Michael Blowen who helped relocate Timely Writer's remains to Old Friends. Lorita and Palmer arranged a telephone call and spoke for nearly one hour. Palmer then spoke separately with Michael Blowen and *The Ride of Their Lives* authors, with everyone sharing stories and memories of horse racing and Timely Writer. More than forty years after working with Timely Writer, Michael Palmer remarked that the colt was the best athlete he had ever seen in person. Timely Writer did things on the track and in his stall that no other horse could do. As Palmer could personally attest, remembering that day with Timely Writer in his stall at Belmont Park in the fall of 1982, the colt could balance himself on two legs just as easily as if he had all four on the ground.

As the calendar turned to 2025, Michael Palmer received a second phone call from the same individual asking if the saddlecloth was for sale. Palmer informed the caller that he would not sell the saddlecloth or put it up for auction. With the Martin family's blessing, Michael Palmer would deliver the saddlecloth to the only place it belonged – nearby Timely Writer's grave as part of the Old Friends Collection at the Josephine Abercrombie Visitor's Center in Georgetown, Kentucky.

Jeffrey Fell settles in above the saddlecloth of Timely Writer for their last race together.

Notes

____

As we researched the subjects and topics for this book, we had unlimited access to the private scrapbooks of Mary and Francis Martin. The memorabilia dates back over forty years, including numerous newspaper articles, magazines, photographs, letters, and cassettes. The keepsakes did not always include complete publishing information (e.g., the editorial of Mayor Kevin White, which appears as the prologue). In very few cases, the exact date of publication and/or the source of publication was unclear. In the following section, we have done our very best to give as much information as possible when crediting sources.

<u>Chapter 1</u>

[1]Gatto, K.. Saratoga Race Course: The August Place to Be. History Press, 2011.

[2]Madden, M. (1981) *Two butchers, a horse, a Dream*. The Boston Globe, October, 25.

[3]Madden, M. (1981) *Two butchers, a horse, a Dream*. The Boston Globe, October ,25.

[4]Reed, B. (1982). *Timely Writer a prospect? Bet your Flamingo Jacket.* Louisville Courier Journal, March, 7.

[5]Nuewer, H. (1982) *Two Men and a Horse*. Boston Magazine, June 1982.

[6]Nuewer, H. (1982) *Two Men and a Horse*. Boston Magazine, June 1982.

[7]McCracken, S. (1981) *$3m bid for share of Timely Writer*. Boston Globe, October, 16.

[8]McCracken, S. (1982) *Martins stuck with Imprescia*. The Boston Globe. March, 8.

[9]McCracken, S. (1982) *Martins stuck with Imprescia*. The Boston Globe. March, 8.

[10]McCracken, S. (1982) *Martins stuck with Imprescia*. The Boston Globe. March, 8.

[11]McCracken, S. (1982) *Two heavyweight horses, handlers spar*. The Boston Globe, April 1.

[12]Grace, A. (1982) *Timely Writer is a Triple Crown Threat*. The Miami News, April, 5.

[13]Crist, S. (1982). Timely Writer gest High Derby Rating. New York Times, April, 5.

[14]Hummer, S. (1982) *Timely Writer Turns in A Winning Script: Derby Winners' Tale Could Pass for Fiction*. The Palm Beach Post. April, 4.

[15]Phillips, W. (1982) *Timely Writer: Perfect Script*. The Daily Racing Form, April 5.

[16]Grace, A. (1982) *Timely Writer is a Triple Crown Threat*. The Miami News, April, 5.

[17]Phillips, W. (1982) *Timely Writer: Perfect Script*. The Daily Racing Form, April 5.

Chapter 2

[18]Hirsch, J. (1982) *Untimely Illness a Shock to Derby Favorites Connections*. Daily Racing Forum, April, 22.

[19]The story behind 'Originally from Dorchester' | Dorchester Reporter (dotnews.com)[1]

[20]Nuewer, Hank, "Two Men and a Horse," Boston Magazine, June 1982.

[21]McCracken, S. (1985) *A Man of the People*. The Boston Globe, January, 25.

[22]Madden, M. (1981) *Two butchers, a horse, a Dream*. The Boston Globe, October, 25.

[23]McCracken, S. (1976) *New Cheevers horses can accelerate like Orr*. The Boston Globe, July, 1.

Chapter 3

[24]Cowperthwaite, W. (2020). *Summer of Nostalgia: That time when horseracing was a sure bet at Marshfield Fair*. The Patriot Ledger August, 22.

[25]Miller, M. (1964) *Brockton Fair Invites Beatles*. The Boston Globe, March 7.

[26]Blowen, M. (1982). *Making a Run at the other Triple Crown*. The Boston Globe, October, 3.

[27]Thorton, T.D. (2017). *New England's Colorful King of the Fair's Dies at 88*. Thoroughbred Daily News, January, 13.

[28]Lucie, S. (2022). A Legend Behind the Lens. National Museum of Racing and Hall of Fame Magazine, Official Guide, 2022.

1. https://www.dotnews.com/2020/story-behind-originally-dorchester

[29]Hillebrand, Laura. *Seabiscuit: An American Legend,* (Ballantine Books, New York, 2001.) p. 33-34.

[30]Veek, Bill and Linn, Ed. *Thirty Tons a Day*, (The Viking Press, 1972.) p. 119.

[31]Veek, Bill and Linn, Ed. *Thirty Tons a Day*, (The Viking Press, 1972.) p. 99.

[32]Veek, Bill and Linn, Ed. *Thirty Tons a Day*, (The Viking Press, 1972.) p. 115.

[33]Veek, Bill and Linn, Ed. *Thirty Tons a Day*, (The Viking Press, 1972.) p. 120.

[34]Veek, Bill and Linn, Ed. *Thirty Tons a Day*, (The Viking Press, 1972.) p.122.

Chapter 4

[35]Madden, M. (1981) *Two butchers, a horse, a Dream.* The Boston Globe, October, 25.

[36] A Guide to the Charles James Apperley [Nimrod] Papers 1797-1851 Apperley, Charles James [Nimrod] Papers, 1797-1851 11080 (virginia.edu)[2]

[37]Jones, D. (2003) *Trainer revels in One that got Away.* Florida Today, May, 10.

[38]Jones, D. (2003) *Trainer revels in One that got Away.* Florida Today, May, 10.

[39]Indrisano, R. (2003) *Funny Cide's prior owner had eye for talent.* The Boston Globe, May, 14.

[40]Jones, D. (2003) Costly decision to neuter Funny Cide was logical. Florida Today, May, 10.

[41]Jones, D. (2003) Former owner will cheer from Florida. Florida Today, June, 7.

[42]Nuewer, H. (1982) *Two Men and a Horse.* Boston Magazine, June 1982.

[43]Nuewer, H. (1982) *Two Men and a Horse.* Boston Magazine, June 1982.

[44]Nuewer, H. (1982) *Two Men and a Horse.* Boston Magazine, June 1982.

[45]Nuewer, H. (1982) *Two Men and a Horse.* Boston Magazine, June 1982.

Chapter 5

[46]Hanna, Linda, "Barbaro, Smarty Jones & Ruffian," p. 3, Middle Atlantic Press, 2008.

2. https://ead.lib.virginia.edu/vivaxtf/view?docId=uva-sc/viu01434.xml#bioghist_1.1

[47]Christine, B. (1982). *Maybe They Should Have Named Him Untimely Writer*. New York Times, September, 7.

[48]Will, J. (1982). *I Plan to Duck a Lot of it*. The Horsemen's Journal. May 1982 issue.

[49]McCracken, S. (1981) *$3m bid for share of Timely Writer*. Boston Globe, October, 16.

[50]Wertheim, J. (2021) *Pleasant Colony and the Crown of Thorns*. Sports Illustrated," April,27.

[51]Goldstein, H. (1981) *Lejoli Heads 10 in Spa Special*. Daily Racing Form, August, 2.

[52]Grace, A. (1981). *Dominic Imprescia enjoys a summer of fateful success*. Miami News, August 25.

[53]Manning, L. (1981) *A Best-Seller for Timely Writer*. The Saratogian, August, 23.

[54]Manning, I.. (1981) *A Best-Seller for Timely Writer*. The Saratogian, August, 23.

[55]White, R. (1981) *Writer adds a final chapter to Spa's novel book of upsets*. Knickerbocker News, August, 24.

[56]White, R. (1981) *Writer adds a final chapter to Spa's novel book of upsets*. Knickerbocker News, August, 24.

Chapter 6

[57]Whelan, T. (1981). *Before Dawn Wins Matron*. The Journal News, September, 20.

[58]Leggett, W. (1981). *A day of wine and Roses*. Sports Illustrated, October, 15.

[59]Duckworth, Ed. (1981). *Timely Writer Wins*. Providence Sunday Journal, October, 11.

[60]Duckworth, Ed. (1981). *Timely Writer Wins*. Providence Sunday Journal, October, 11.

[61]Duckworth, Ed. (1981). *Timely Writer Wins*. Providence Sunday Journal, October, 11.

[62]Duckworth, Ed. (1981). *Timely Writer Wins*. Providence Sunday Journal, October, 11.

[63]Duckworth, Ed. (1981). *Timely Writer Wins*. Providence Sunday Journal, October, 11.

[64]McCracken, S. (1981). *Timely Writer easily wins Champagne Stakes*. The Boston Globe, May, 10.

Chapter 7

[65]Johnson, Keeler J. (2021). *'Eclipses' an Important Part of Racing History*. Bloodhorse Magazine, January, 27.

[66]Harding, B. (1983). *Minister caps Career in Big M Cup*. The Jersey Journal, November, 17.

[67]Christine, B. (2001). *Rise and Fall Saga Ends for Brennan*, The Los Angeles Times, June, 5.

[68]Christine, B. (2001). *Rise and Fall Saga Ends for Brennan*, The Los Angeles Times, June, 5.

[69]Christine, B. (2001). *Rise and Fall Saga Ends for Brennan*, The Los Angeles Times, June, 5.

[70]Grace, A. (1981) *The Vote here is still for Timely Writer*. The Miami News, November, 24.

[71]Grace, A. (1981) *The Vote here is still for Timely Writer*. The Miami News, November, 24.

[72]Austin, D. (1981). *Canada Colt wins Laurel Futurity*, The Baltimore Sun, October, 25.

[73]Evans, L. (1981) *John Henry is Horse of the Year*, Miami Herald, December, 23.

[74]Griffith, B. (1981) *Eclipse shuts out Writer*. The Boston Globe, December, 23.

[75]Griffith, B. (1981) *Eclipse shuts out Writer*. The Boston Globe, December, 23.

[76]Griffith, B. (1981) *Eclipse shuts out Writer*. The Boston Globe, December, 23.

[77]Griffith, B. (1981) *Eclipse shuts out Writer*. The Boston Globe, December, 23.

[78]Griffith, B. (1981) *Eclipse shuts out Writer*. The Boston Globe, December, 23.

[79]Pierson, J. (1982). *Timely Writer sizzles in Spa triumph*. New York Post, August, 25.

[80]Indrisano, R. (1982). Deputy Minister misses cue. The Boston Globe, February, 5.

[81]Indrisano, R. (1982). Deputy Minister misses cue. The Boston Globe, February, 5.

[82]Gaffer, W. (1976). *Royal Ski and Bold Forbes Among Best Bets in Eclipse*, Daily News, December, 5.

[83]*A first for Gerry?* (1976). The Report Dispatcher (White Plains, New York), November, 20. p. 31.

[84]Feldman, D. (1977). *From hockey to jockeys . . . Cheevers has a Derby shot*, Press and Sun Bulletin, January, 30.

[85]Hirsch, J. (1982). *Imprescia Took the Timely Course*. Daily Racing Form, January issue.

[86]Beyer, A. (1982) *Writer gets high Deby rating*, New York Times, April, 5.

Chapter 8

[87]Moran, P. (1982) *Heart of Timely Writer classier than connections*. Fort Lauderdale News and Sun Sentinel, March, 28.

[88]Crist, S. (1982). Timely Writer gest High Derby Rating. New York Times, April, 5.

[89]Joseph, D. (1982) *Martins' Kentucky Derby fairy tale comes to untimely end*. Patriot Ledger, April, 22.

[90]McLaughlin, L. (1982) *Common malady grew into a crisis*. Boston Globe, April, 22.

[91]Kitchener, N. (2014) *Shock: When the Body Shuts Down*. Horse Canada, October, 17.

[92]McCracken, S. (1982) *Timely Writer out of Derby*. Boston Globe, April 21, 1982.

[93]Best, A. (1982) *Derby Dreams Go Up in Smoke, Obscuring the Picture*. Washington Post, April, 22.

[94]Montville, L. (1982) *Work, no tears for Peter Martin*. Boston Globe, April, 22.

[95]McLaughlin, L. (1982) *Common malady grew into a crisis*. Boston Globe, April, 22.

[96]McCracken, S. (1982) *Timely Writer out of Derby*. Boston Globe, April, 21.

[97]Crist, S. (1982) *Timely Writer out of Danger*. The New York Times, April, 22.

[98]Crist, S. (1982) *Timely Writer out of Danger*. The New York Times, April, 22.

[99] Hirsch, J. (1982) *Untimely Illness a Shock to Derby Favorites Connections*. Daily Racing Forum, April, 22.

[100]Hirsch, J. (1982) *Untimely Illness a Shock to Derby Favorites Connections*. Daily Racing Forum, April, 22.

[101]Crist, S. (1982) *Timely Writer out of Danger*. The New York Times, April, 22.

[102]Crist, S. (1982) *Timely Writer out of Danger*. The New York Times, April, 22.

[103]Hirsch, J. (1982) *Untimely Illness a Shock to Derby Favorites Connections*. Daily Racing Forum, April, 22.

[104]Hirsch, J. (1982) *Untimely Illness a Shock to Derby Favorites Connections*. Daily Racing Forum, April, 22.

[105]Hirsch, J. (1982) *Untimely Illness a Shock to Derby Favorites Connections*. Daily Racing Forum, April, 22.

[106]Hirsch, J. (1982) *Untimely Illness a Shock to Derby Favorites Connections*. Daily Racing Forum, April, 22.

[107]Kirshenbaum, J. (1977) *He was a two-time Loser*. Sports Illustrated, May, 16.

[108]Kirshenbaum, J. (1977) *He was a two-time Loser*. Sports Illustrated, May, 16.

[109]Marantz, S. (1982) *The Boston Jinx*. The Boston Globe, May, 1.

[110]Joseph, D. (1982) *Martins' Kentucky Derby fairy tale comes to untimely end*. Patriot Ledger, April 22.

[111]Joseph, D. (1982) *Martins' Kentucky Derby fairy tale comes to untimely end*. Patriot Ledger, April 22.

Chapter 9

[112]Best, A. (1982) *Derby Dreams Go Up in Smoke, Obscuring the Picture*. Washington Post, April, 22.

[113]Madden, M. (1982) *The Boston Jinx*, The Boston Globe, May, 1.

[114]Madden, M. (1982). *The Boston Jinx*. The Boston Globe, May, 1.

[115]Eaton, Y. (1982). *Browns' theme isn't just Derby, it's 'Oh! Kentucky*. The Courier-Journal, May, 2.

[116] Eaton, Y. (1982). *Browns' theme isn't just Derby, it's 'Oh! Kentucky*. The Courier-Journal, May, 2.

[117]McCracken, S. (1982). *Martins on hand – as spectators. Boston Globe*. May,

[118]Lord, K. (1986) *Samuel McCracken, covered racing for the Globe for 39 years*. The Boston Globe, November, 5.

[119]Lord, K. (1986) *Samuel McCracken, covered racing for the Globe for 39 years*. The Boston Globe, November, 5.

[120]McCracken, S. (1982) *Martins on hand – as spectators. Boston Globe*, May, 2.

[121]McCracken, S. (1982) *Martins on hand – as spectators. Boston Globe*, May, 2.

[122]Moran, P. (1982). *Heart of Timely Writer classier than connections*. Fort Lauderdale News and Sun Sentinel, March, 28.

[123]McKracken, S. (1982) *Timely Writer out of Derby*. The Boston Globe, April, 21.

[124]Indrisano, R. (1983) *The un-Timely-est cut of all*. The Boston Globe, May, 6.

[125]Madden, M. (1982). *The Boston Jinx*. The Boston Globe, May, 1.

[126]Christine, B (1988) *The 1968 Kentucky Derby: The Victory that Wasn't, Dancer's Image, Who Finished First, Was Disqualified after Positive Test for Illegal Medications*, Los Angeles Times, May 1.

[127]Christine, B (1988) *The 1968 Kentucky Derby: The Victory that Wasn't, Dancer's Image, Who Finished First, Was Disqualified after Positive Test for Illegal Medications*, Los Angeles Times, May 1.

[128]Christine, B. (1988). *The 1968 Kentucky Derby: The Victory that Wasn't, Dancer's Image, Who Finished First, Was Disqualified after Positive Test for Illegal Medications*. Los Angeles Times, May, 1.

[129]Madden, M. (1982). *The Boston Jinx*. The Boston Globe, May, 1.

[130]Madden, M. (1982). *The Boston Jinx*. The Boston Globe, May, 1.

Chapter 10

[131]Welsch, M. (1982) *"Everyone is Prepared for a Hometown Hero,"* The Boston Globe, June,

[132]Crist, S. (1982) *Thoughts of Timely Writer's Courage Ease the Grief.* The New York Times, October, 11.

[133]Crist, S., (1982) *Thoughts of Timely Writer's Courage Ease the Grief.* The New York Times, October, 11.

[134]Joseph, D. (1982) *Timely Writer on the Mend: Excitement swelling as 'the people's horse' is readied,* The Patriot Ledger, August.

[135]Welsch, M. (1982) *Everyone is Prepared for a Hometown Hero,* Daily Racing Form, June,

[136]Joseph, D (1982) *Timely Writer on the Mend: Excitement swelling as 'the people's horse' is readied,* The Patriot Ledger, August.

[137]Welsch, M. (1982) *Everyone is Prepared for a Hometown Hero,* Daily Racing Form, August, 9.

[138]White, K. (August 1982). The Martins Show the Boston Spirit. The Boston American.

[139]Welsch, M. (1982) *Everyone is Prepared for a Hometown Hero,* Daily Racing Form, June,

[140]McCracken, S. (1982) *Timely tries short course at Saratoga.* Boston Globe, August 24.

[141]McCracken, S. (1982) *Timely tries short course at Saratoga.* Boston Globe, August 24.

[142]McCracken, S. (1982) *Timely tries short course at Saratoga.* Boston Globe, August 24.

[143]McCracken, Sam, *"Timely Writer Turns it On,",* Boston Globe, August 25, 1982.

[144]Leggett, W. (1982) *Another Body for the Graveyard: Favored Conquistador Cielo dug a deep hole for himself in the Travers,* Sports Illustrated, August, 30.

[145]Harris, R. (1982) *Timely Writer wins second straight,* The Daily News, August, 24.

[146]McCracken, S. (1982) *Timely tries short course at Saratoga*. Boston Globe, August 24.

[147]McCracken, S. (1982) *Timely Writer Turns it On*. Boston Globe, August, 25.

[148]McCracken, S. (1982) *Timely Writer Turns it On*. Boston Globe, August, 25.

[149]Harris, R. (1982) *Timely Writer wins second straight*, The Daily News, August, 24.

[150] Harris, R. (1982) *Timely Writer wins second straight*, The Daily News, August, 24.

[151]McCracken, S. (1982) *Timely Writer Turns it On*. Boston Globe, August, 25.

[152]Piesen, J. (1982) *Timely Writer sizzles in Spa Triumph,"* New York Post, August, 24.

[153]McCracken, S. (1982) *Timely Writer Turns it On*. Boston Globe, August, 25.

[154]Indrisano, R. (1982) *Deputy Minister misses Cue*, The Boston Globe, February, 5.

Chapter 11

[155]Hanna, Linda. *Barbaro, Smarty Jones & Ruffian*, (Middle Atlantic Press, 2008), p. 15.

[156]Gaffer, W. (1975) *Why Broken-Legged Horses must die*. New York Daily News, July, 8.

[157]Oreskes, M. (1975) *A Horse Surgeon Is Much in Demand*. New York Daily News, July, 13.

[158]Hanna, Linda. *Barbaro, Smarty Jones & Ruffian*, (Middle Atlantic Press, 2008), p. 15.

[159]Gaffer, W. (1975) *Why Broken-Legged Horses must die*. New York Daily News, July, 8.

[160]Crist, S. (1982) *Stewards Scratch Timely Writer*. The New York Times, September, 7.

[161]McCracken, S. (1982) *Stewards find drug, scratch Timely Writer*. Boston Globe, September, 7.

[162]McCracken, S. (1982) *Stewards find drug, scratch Timely Writer*. Boston Globe, September, 7.

[163]McCracken, S. (1982) *Stewards find drug, scratch Timely Writer*. Boston Globe, September, 7.

[164]McCracken, S. (1982) *Stewards find drug, scratch Timely Writer*. Boston Globe, September, 7.

[165]Christine, B. (1982). *Maybe They Should Have Named Him Untimely Writer*. New York Times, September, 7.

[166]Crist, S. (1982) *Thoughts of Timely Writer's Courage Ease the Grief*. The New York Times, October, 11.

[167]Christine, B. (1982). *Maybe They Should Have Named Him Untimely Writer*. New York Times, September, 7.

[168]McCracken, S. (1982) *Stewards find drug, scratch Timely Writer*. Boston Globe, September, 7.

[169]Whelan, T. (1982) *Paddock Patter*. The Reporter Dispatch, September, 12.

[170]Harris, R. (1982) *Lemhi Gold Stuns Marlboro field by 8 ¾*. Daily News, September, 19.

[171]Harris, R. (1982) *Lemhi Gold Stuns Marlboro field by 8 ¾*. Daily News, September, 19.

[172]Harris, R. (1982) *Lemhi Gold Stuns Marlboro field by 8 ¾*. Daily News, September, 19.

[173]McCracken, S. (1982) *Gold Cup's No. 1 post to Writer*. The Boston Globe, October, 8.

[174]Christine, B. (1982). *Maybe They Should Have Named Him Untimely Writer*. New York Times, September, 7.

[175]Christine, B. (1982). *Maybe They Should Have Named Him Untimely Writer*. New York Times, September, 7.

[176]McCracken, S. (1982) *Timely Writer is destroyed*. The Boston Globe, October, 11.

[177]Crist, S. (1982) *Thoughts of Timely Writer's Courage Ease the Grief*. The New York Times, October, 11.

[178]Crist, S. (1982) *Thoughts of Timely Writer's Courage Ease the Grief*. The New York Times, October, 11.

[179]McCracken, S. (1982). *'Writer' to be buried in N.Y.* The Boston Globe, October, 11.

[180]McCracken, S. (1982). *'Writer' to be buried in N.Y.* The Boston Globe, October, 11.

[181]McCracken, S. (1982). *'Writer' to be buried in N.Y.* The Boston Globe, October, 11.

[182]Joseph, D. (1982). *Two Jumps from end, fate deals last blow to Timely Writer*. The Patriot Ledger, October, 11.

[183]Joseph, D. (1982). *Two Jumps from end, fate deals last blow to Timely Writer*. The Patriot Ledger, October, 11.

[184]Whelan, T. (1983) *Here's Our Vote*. The Journal News, January, 4.

Chapter 12

[185]Crist, S. (1983) *It is happening at Belmont Park*. The New York Times. May, 30.

[186]Kinsley, B. (1982) *Martins, Imprescia have Falling Out*. The Boston Globe, December, 22.

[187]Gatto, K. (2007). *Remembering Timely Writer 25 years after his death*. Bloodhorse Magazine, September issue.

[188]Gatto, K. (2007). *Remembering Timely Writer 25 years after his death*. Bloodhorse Magazine, September issue.

[189]Gatto, K. (2007). *Remembering Timely Writer 25 years after his death*. Bloodhorse Magazine, September issue.

[190] Gatto, K. (2007). *Remembering Timely Writer 25 years after his death*. Bloodhorse Magazine, September issue.

[191]Gatto, K. (2007). *Remembering Timely Writer 25 years after his death*. Bloodhorse Magazine, September issue.

[192]Gatto, Kimberly. *Beyond the Rainbow Bridge, "Timely Writer – the Horse Who Started it All,"* (Half Halt Press, 2005) Introduction.

[193]Gatto, Kimberly. *Beyond the Rainbow Bridge, "Timely Writer – the Horse Who Started it All,"* (Half Halt Press, 2005) Introduction.

[194]Gatto, Kimberly. *Beyond the Rainbow Bridge, "Timely Writer – the Horse Who Started it All,"* (Half Halt Press, 2005) Introduction.

[195] Remembering ... Timely Writer (horseracingnation.com)[3]

---

3. https://www.horseracingnation.com/blogs/zatt/Remembering_Timely_Writer_123

[196]UNCLE MO | Thoroughbred Stallion Guide[4]

[197]www.legacy.com/us/obituaries/kentucky/name/preston-madden-[5]obituary

[198]Madden, M. (1982) *The Boston Jinx*. Boston Globe, May 1.

[199] Top Veterinarian William O. Reed Dies - BloodHorse[6]

[200]Tapp, I. (2010) *Deputy Minister: Champion Racehorse and Sire. Bloodhorse* Magazine, October, 22.

[201]Patridge, M., Dr. (2019). *Great frauds in history: Robert Brennan's boiler room.* Money Week Magazine, September, 10.

[202]Carson, J. (1984) *Timely Writer's trainer shares in the Sorrow*. The Miami Herald, June 21.

[203]Carson, J. (1984) *Timely Writer's trainer shares in the Sorrow*. The Miami Herald, June 21.

[204]Carson, J. (1984) *Timely Writer's trainer shares in the Sorrow*. The Miami Herald, June 21.

[205]Jicha, T. (2011) *Trainer Imprescia dies at 93.* Sun Sentinel, May 13.

[206]McCracken, S. (1985) *A Man of the People.* The Boston Globe, January, 25.

[207]McCracken, S. (1985) *A Man of the People.* The Boston Globe, January, 25.

[208]Welsch, M. (1982) *Everyone is Prepared for a Hometown Hero*, Daily Racing Form, August, 9.

---

4. https://www.stallionguide.com/stallions/uncle-mo/

5. http://www.legacy.com/us/obituaries/kentucky/name/preston-madden-

6. https://www.bloodhorse.com/horse-racing/articles/173405/top-veterinarian-william-o-reed-dies